Philadelphia Architecture
A Guide to the City

Second Edition

LIBRARY OF CONGRESS CATALOG CARD NUMBER: 94-072347

ISBN 0-9622908-1-5 (PBK.)

PRINTED AND BOUND IN THE UNITED STATES

DESIGN BY PARADIGM:DESIGN
PHOTOGRAPHS COPYRIGHT ©1994 BY PETER B. OLSON
TYPE BY DUKE & COMPANY
PRINTING BY STRINE PRINTING CO.

Philadelphia Architecture

A Guide to the City

Second Edition

Prepared for the Foundation for
Architecture, Philadelphia, Pennsylvania
by the Group for Environmental
Education, Inc.
John Andrew Gallery, General Editor

Published by the
Foundation for Architecture

Introduction to the Second Edition

This second edition of *Philadelphia Architecture* expands the catalog of buildings to include those completed between 1983, the end date of the first edition, and 1993. In keeping with the approach of the first edition, buildings have been selected to represent a range of building types and to illustrate the varied character of contemporary architectural design. Significant buildings by nationally-prominent architects were included automatically and a special effort was made to identify notable buildings by the generation of Philadelphia architects whose work came to prominence during the 1980s and early 1990s.

The final list is dominated by office buildings and institutional buildings with relatively few examples of residential design. This may suggest that Philadelphia's growth during the past ten years has been concentrated in Center City and rehabilitation of older buildings has been a more successful way of adding housing than new construction.

No buildings have been added to the catalog for the period prior to 1983, simply for ease of re-publication. However, many late 19th century and early 20th century buildings have been brought to my attention which deserve inclusion in a future edition. Many buildings included in the first edition were restored or renovated for other uses during the past ten years. Architects responsible for those changes have been identified and added to the building descriptions. Remarkably, only one building included in the first edition has been demolished—the White Tower hamburger store built in 1932—a testimony to Philadelphia's pride in its architectural heritage.

Acknowledgments

The selection of buildings to be added to this edition was aided by the willingness of Philadelphia architects to suggest examples of their own work and that of others. Further suggestions were made by a committee consisting of Barbara Kaplan, Dr. Richard Tyler, Craig Schelter, Karen Butler, Helen Pitcher and John Higgins, executive director of the Foundation for Architecture. John's thoughtful recommendations on building selection, text and photographic issues contributed greatly to the final form of the book. Many other individuals submitted comments or suggestions for corrections to the original text, for which I am most appreciative.

The visual form of the book is the result of the graphic design of Joel Katz and the photography of Peter Olson, both of whom were important participants in the first edition. Many architects generously contributed photographs of their recent buildings.

Because this second edition is based in large part on the first, it seems appropriate to acknowledge those individuals who made this publication possible in the first place. Leslie Gallery-Dilworth, founding director of the Foundation for Architecture, provided the initiative for the project and contributed greatly to the concept and design of the book. Nancy Williams, Christine Cavajal and Caroline Piven were responsible for much of the basic research, writing and editing. Peter Lapham and Joan Hepp prepared the final manuscript.

Many organizations contributed materials to the first edition and continued to make them available for this edition; the Philadelphia Historical Commission, Free Library, Pennsylvania Historical Society, the Library Company, Athenaeum and the Philadelphia Museum of Art deserve special recognition.

Lastly, this book continues to be indebted to its predecessors. *Man Made Philadelphia,* written with Richard Saul Wurman, gave me the first opportunity to think about the physical form of the city; *Architecture in Philadelphia: A Guide,* by Edward Teitelman and Richard Longstreth, though long out of print, is still a valuable resource and reference; and *Philadelphia Preserved,* by Richard Webster, continues to be the definitive source of detailed information about Philadelphia buildings in the Catalog of the Historic American Building Survey.

John Andrew Gallery

Contents

Introduction and How to Use the Book

Philadelphia, more than any other American city, represents the history of architecture in the United States. As the leading city of the colonies and the nation's first capital, Philadelphia was the center of cultural, scientific and civic leadership in the 18th century. It was a principal channel through which changing architectural tastes in England were introduced to the United States.

In the 19th century, Philadelphia's important scientific community placed the city in the forefront of industrial change. At one time, Philadelphia was the largest manufacturing center in the country. New building types and the thousands of houses built for the rapidly growing population made the 19th century one of the richest periods in the city's architectural history. In the 20th century, Philadelphia was one of the first to focus on problems of urban development and historic restoration. Major civic projects were begun in the early decades of the century, and after World War II, the city was an acknowledged leader in urban renewal, architectural design and education.

The architectural heritage of over 300 years is visible on every street in every section of the city: Philadelphia is quite literally a museum of American architecture. Its "collection" includes examples of every type of building and virtually every important style found throughout the United States. This collection includes outstanding work by such important architects as William Strickland, Thomas U. Walter, Frank Furness, McKim Mead and White, Daniel Burnham, George Howe, Louis Kahn, Robert Venturi, Romaldo Giurgola, I. M. Pei and Helmut Jahn. In addition, there are thousands of distinctive buildings by local architects and builders.

This book is a catalog to that collection. It contains a limited selection of buildings intended to illustrate the city's best architecture as well as a representative sampling of building types from different historic periods.

The book is divided into two parts. The first, the catalog of buildings, contains three sections roughly corresponding to the 18th, 19th and 20th centuries. Each section is preceded by an essay, which describes the development of the city during that period, and by an illustrated glossary of architectural terms. Brief biographies of important Philadelphia architects are also included.

The catalog has been organized deliberately to present a variety of building types ranging from houses and apartment buildings to offices, industrial, commercial, religious and institutional buildings. The chart, beginning on page 154, shows the distribution of buildings by type and general date. Entries in the catalog are listed chronologically, rather than by geographic area, so that it is possible to trace the history of the city through its buildings and to follow the evolution of architectural styles. Each building is cross-referenced to tour or location maps.

Sample Catalog
Entry

Each catalog entry has been assigned a three-digit number. The first digit corresponds to the catalog section in which the entry appears.

Letter codes refer to the map or maps on which the building can be located.

Italic letter codes:
OP—Open to the public
PR—Private residence

107 B,J *OP*
Christ Church, 1727–44
2nd and Market Sts.
Dr. John Kearsley, supervisor

Although Penn founded Philadelphia to provide a refuge for Quakers, he extended freedom of worship to all religions. One of the first groups to exercise this right was the Anglicans of the Church of England, whose interests had also been protected by Charles II in his charter to Penn.

The second part of the book contains nine walking and driving tours as well as information about other places of interest. The tours focus on areas that have significant concentrations of buildings listed in the catalog or that represent different historic periods. Each tour entry described in the book is cross-referenced to the catalog. Other buildings of interest in the area are also noted.

Sample Tour
Entry

1 **Second Street Subway Station**
2nd & Market Sts.
1976–79, Murphy Levy Wurman

2 **Christ Church**
22–26 N. 2nd St. **107** *OP*

3 **Girard Warehouses**
18–30 N. Front St. **143**

4 **Trotter Warehouses**
36–44 N. Front St. 1830s

5 **Smythe Building**
101–11 Arch St. **219**

6 **Elfreth's Alley**
Between Front & 2nd, Arch & Race Sts. **106** *PR*

The general reader or visitor will find it most useful to read the introductory essays to each section of the catalog and the introductions to the tours first. This will provide a quick overview of the development of the city and indicate areas where the most interesting buildings are located. After reviewing the catalog, tours can be selected that relate to individual interests or time available to see the city. Persons interested in specific buildings or the work of a particular architect can use the index, catalog and maps to create an individual tour. The tours and the buildings listed in the catalog should be viewed as an introduction to the many other fascinating buildings waiting to be discovered throughout the city.

Each tour entry described in the book is followed by its catalog number for cross-referencing.

All three building catalogs and the map section are tabbed to facilitate cross-referencing.

1

The
Founding of
the City
1682–1701

The
Colonial
City
1701–1835

The Founding of the City
1682–1701

The American colonies were founded in an era of intolerance and economic unrest. Throughout most of the 17th century, English history was marked by sharp differences between kings and people. Religious persecutions sent many groups into exile on the continent and provided the initial motivation for colonial settlements in Massachusetts and Virginia. But of all the colonial settlements, none was more deliberately planned to offer a contrast to the prevailing English ideas of religious and personal freedom as was Philadelphia.

The Colony of Pennsylvania and the City of Philadelphia were created by one man, William Penn. Penn was born into a wealthy English family. His father was an admiral. Penn was a country gentleman with large land holdings, but he had lived in London and in many cities in Ireland and on the continent. As a member of the Religious Society of Friends (Quakers), Penn was persecuted for his religious beliefs and spent several periods of time in jail. While in prison he conceived the idea of a colony in the new world that would offer freedom from religious oppression.

William Penn

In 1681, Penn obtained a charter for his colony from King Charles II in exchange for a debt the King owed his father. The King named the new colony Pennsylvania (Penn's Woods) and Penn chose the name Philadelphia for its principal city, from the Greek word meaning city of brotherly love.

Penn viewed his colony as a holy experiment, to be founded on principles of tolerance and justice. He offered religious and personal freedoms that were radical innovations in the 17th century. These included the freedom of worship for all people and the right to trial by jury in an open court. Penn combined his political philosophy with a liberal land policy. His concept of land development was directed toward the rural middle class, who were unable to afford sizable land holdings under prevailing conditions in England. Large tracts of land, 500 acres or more, at reasonable prices were a unique economic opportunity. This combination of political philosophy and liberal land policy attracted many colonists from England, Wales, Holland and Germany.

Penn had very specific ideas about the physical plan of his colony. This plan encompassed the entire region, not just the small city of Philadelphia. Penn expected most settlers to purchase 500 acres or more in the countryside combined with lots located in the city. He offered individuals of similar backgrounds the opportunity to purchase 5,000 acres as a group, to be subdivided as they saw fit. Through this means, he hoped to establish independent townships. The most successful of these was Germantown, settled by Daniel Pastorius and a group of Dutch and German Quakers. Similar grants to Welsh Quakers created the townships of Haverford, Mercer and Radnor. Penn also created eight manors outside the city, including his country seat at Pennsbury, each consisting of several thousand acres.

Central to Penn's plan was the establishment of a great town. Penn envisioned a town of 10,000 acres with each major landowner having 10 to 100 acres in the town in addition to his holdings in the countryside. Houses would be built in the center of the town lots, surrounded by gardens and orchards, forming what Penn referred to as a green country town.

After formulating these plans and offering land for sale in England, Penn dispatched his surveyor, Thomas Holme, to lay out the city. When Holme arrived in 1682 he found the site selected by Penn already occupied by Swedish farmers. Holme went up the river and purchased land at the narrowest place between the Schuylkill and Delaware rivers. Here he laid out a portion of the 600,000 acres, purchased by 470 prospective colonists, in lots along the Delaware River. When Penn arrived, he was dissatisfied with the plan and extended the city westward to cover the two-mile area between the two rivers. Holme's final plan established a grid of streets broken by four public squares of 8 acres each and a central square for civic buildings at the intersection of two major streets. The overall plan is reminiscent of military outposts such as Londonderry, Ireland, which is believed to have been a precedent for the plan of Philadelphia. Holme reduced the lots in the city to one acre for each 5,000 owned in the countryside. In exchange for this reduction, 10,000 acres north of the city were set aside as "Liberty Lands"—a rural area where property owners had access to additional holdings. Holme laid out the initial lots on both riverfronts, in the hope that development would move inward and increase the value of the land still owned by Penn.

Thomas Holme's plan of the City of Philadelphia, 1682

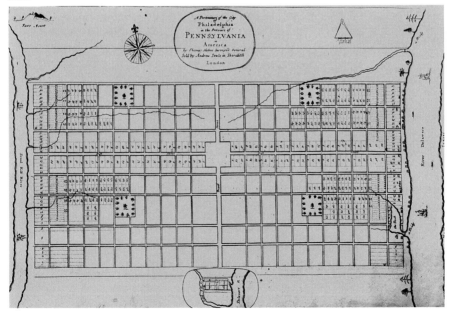

When settlers arrived, the land designated as the site of the city was covered with forest. The first homes were in caves along the Delaware River bank and then in log cabins copied from the Swedish settlers. When construction of houses began, most people remained along the Delaware River edge. No one wanted to settle inland on the Schuylkill riverfront, which was isolated from the port and other settlers by forest. At the time Philadelphia was founded, the English placed great emphasis on fireproof construction as a result of the Great Fire of London in 1666. Brick was the common building material. The ready availability of local clay in Philadelphia led to the establishment of the first brickyard in 1695. In contrast to the wood frame construction, common in New England and Virginia, colonial buildings in Philadelphia were brick almost from the start.

When Penn left the city for the last time in 1701, Philadelphia was established. There were about 2,000 people living in modest brick homes near the Delaware River. Most were Quakers of English, Dutch, Welsh and German backgrounds. But in testimony to Penn's philosophy, there were also Scots-Irish Presbyterians and Anglicans. The streets and lots of the city had been laid out according to an overall plan that would guide the city's growth for many years. The riverfront was covered with wharfs and there was sufficient activity in the port to support four shipbuilding yards. The first markets had been established on High Street (now Market Street) and the city was populated with merchants, shopkeepers and craftsmen. Though most people lived in the city, there was an established pattern of country estates and farms as well as a small independent settlement in Germantown. This expansion over a large geographic area was facilitated by the Quaker form of worship, in houses, rather than the more formal relationship to a single church building, which kept New England towns within close physical limits. Penn's plan was a social, religious and economic success; it had started the city well on its way.

Thomas Holme's plan of the Province of Pennsylvania, 1687

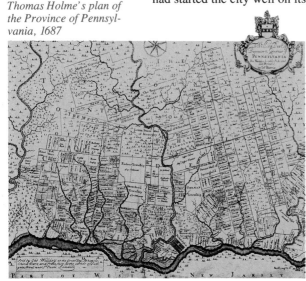

The Colonial City
1701–1835

Furnishings also reflect the changes in tastes and styles that influenced architectural design.

This silver tankard is representative of the fine craftsmanship of early Philadelphia silverwork. It was made by Johannis Nys in 1714 and was owned by James Logan, William Penn's secretary.

The slat-back chair was very popular in Philadelphia. It came in a variety of sizes, was made of maple and painted. The slats of this chair, from 1725–50, are arched and have a concave curve for greater comfort.

In the 75 years after William Penn left Philadelphia, the city grew from a modest village to the most important city in the colonies and the second largest in the English-speaking world. Throughout the 18th century, the port of Philadelphia was the primary entry point for immigrants to all the colonies. Many immigrants remained in the area because of the religious and personal freedoms established by Penn and because Philadelphia had the finest agricultural countryside of any colonial city. Land was cleared and farms created at such a rapid rate that the export of food was soon one of the major activities of the port. The growing population in the countryside increased the demand for other goods and services, which attracted craftsmen and merchants to the city.

The focus of life in the city was the port. The riverfront was covered with wharfs servicing ships that exported fur, lumber and food supplies and imported rum and sugar from the West Indies and manufactured goods from England. Shipbuilding was a major industry. The early residential sections of the city were located as close to the port as possible. Houses were built individually or in pairs on deep, narrow lots at the edge of the forest, not in complete rows as we now know them. Initially the city must have had the character of the green country town advocated by Penn, for there was ample room for barns and gardens around the houses.

The first houses were based on the country house of the English yeoman. They were modest in size and still medieval in style with steeply pitched roofs, prominent chimneys and small windows. Most were two stories high with one room per floor and a winding stair. Furnishings were simple, stressing functional requirements rather than decorative design. English building traditions were modified by the Quaker emphasis on simplicity and by the presence of craftsmen from Holland and Germany who introduced features such as glazed brick, Flemish bond brick patterns and the pent eave roof.

In the colonial city there were no large businesses or places of work. Most people were individual entrepreneurs who worked in their homes with their families or single partners. Even the shipyards were small, with eight or ten employees usually brought together for specific jobs. The only places set aside for purely commercial purposes were the city taverns and market sheds, and even these were of residential scale and character.

Philadelphia grew rapidly. In 1740, the city had a population of 10,000 and was second only to Boston in size and volume of trade. The developed area extended for a mile north and south along the river and as far west as 4th Street, with the greatest concentration between Market and Race streets. It was a dirty city, with unpaved streets often filled with garbage.

Dresses from the first half of the 18th century were as elaborate as Georgian design. This taffeta dress, from 1740–50, has a wide skirt supported by panniers, three-quarter-length sleeves and a low, laced bodice.

But by 1750, this began to change and, by 1765, the city had a population of 25,000, which substantially surpassed Boston. English and Welsh Quakers and Scots Presbyterians had been joined by Irish, Dutch, Swedish and German settlers of all religious backgrounds. The population expanded southward, necessitating the creation of a second city market and the construction of several new churches. By this time Philadelphia was the center of social and intellectual life in the colonies. It had several theaters and an active political climate centered around the many taverns. New institutions had been created, including almshouses for the poor, libraries, schools and colleges, and hospitals. Because nearly 80 percent of the housing was built as an investment to rent, the concern for property protection led to the creation of insurance and fire companies. There were several newspapers, and Benjamin Franklin had already inaugurated his postal service. Residents of the city were prominent artists; the finest doctors in the colonies; skilled craftsmen famous throughout the colonies; and prospering furniture makers, textile workers and printers. Some of the colonies' most creative individuals lived in the city, including such scientists with a worldwide reputation as John Bartram, the botanist; David Rittenhouse, an inventor; and of course Benjamin Franklin.

The transformation of the city was also reflected in its physical appearance. The low skyline of two-story houses was broken by the towers of Christ Church and the State House (now Independence Hall). New residential and civic buildings were built in the latest English architectural styles. In the early 18th century, English architecture was transformed by the rediscovery of the work of the 16th-century Italian Renaissance architect Andrea Palladio. By 1715, Palladio's adaptation of Roman classical design became the precedent for all serious English architects. The Palladian style is known as Georgian in the colonies. It was transferred through the travels of the merchants back and forth to London and through the publication of handbooks on Palladio's work.

The first Georgian building in the colonies was in Williamsburg. But after 1720, Georgian elements were applied over the basic brick shells of colonial architecture in every city. Some of the most elegant Georgian houses and public buildings were produced in Philadelphia. Exteriors often were toned down in deference to the continued dominance of Quaker attitudes, but interior rooms were large and sumptuous in paneling and details. These interiors demanded elegant furnishings usually produced by local craftsmen. The Georgian style remained popular in the city throughout the 18th century due to the conservative influence of the Carpenters' Company. The company, founded in 1724, was modeled after the builders' guilds in London. It disseminated information about building techniques, established

This 1755 compass-bottom chair may have come from the parlor of Samuel Powel's house on South 3rd Street. It has a handsome curved form, decorated with restrained ornament in the form of scrolls, leafage and shells.

construction prices and provided mutual aid among its members. Its Rule Book, produced in 1786, was based entirely on Georgian principles and reflected none of the later stylistic changes that became important in other cities. Most of Philadelphia's master builders belonged to the company, including Robert Smith, the greatest master builder of the times.

Massachusetts and Virginia were in the forefront when the colonies began to organize to express their differences with England. Pennsylvania had mixed allegiances; many conservative leaders were unwilling to make the break with English rule. Despite this, Philadelphia was the logical meeting place for the revolutionary cause. It was centrally located and was the most advanced city in the colonies. Delegates to the First and Second Continental Congresses were impressed with the city's cultural resources, fine houses and abundance of civic institutions. Because of its urban character, Philadelphia was the logical choice as the nation's first capital.

During the Revolutionary War, the city prospered economically. It was a chief supplier of military arms, blankets and uniforms and a major port of trade. But the city was attacked and occupied by the British for a time. Many civic buildings were converted to stables, barracks and hospitals. By the end of 1783, the city was in serious disrepair. The development of the city after the war was complicated when the Pennsylvania Assembly took over the ownership of all of Penn's holdings. The Assembly sold land rapidly to repay war debts, with little regard for Penn's plan. Lots were subdivided by numerous alleys and significant portions of the northern liberty lands were sold for housing.

By the time of the first U.S. Census in 1790, the population of the area had grown to 53,000. It was still concentrated north and south along the river but had expanded as far as 7th Street. The forest finally had been cleared to the Schuylkill River. Independent townships were established in Southwark and Frank-

Growth of the City

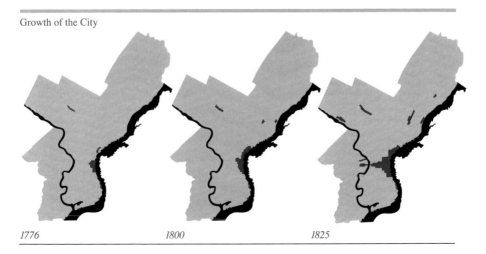

1776   1800   1825

Windsor chairs were produced in Philadelphia from 1748 into the early 1800s. They were used in houses and public buildings. This chair, produced between 1785 and 1807, was made of hardwood and was painted. Its simple lines and square back reflect the influence of the Hepplewhite and Sheraton styles.

This ensemble of sideboard, knife boxes and cellerate, made in 1825, is a rich example of the Philadelphia Empire style. It is mahogany with brass and ebony panels. Some of the details are similar to designs of Robert Adam.

ford. The city was still dirty from the war and had no system to handle garbage. Yellow fever epidemics in 1793 and 1796 hampered the city's return to normality and forced virtually all inhabitants to flee. Most went to Germantown, including George Washington, because it was on higher ground and thought to be safer. From then on, Germantown became a popular location for the summer homes of wealthy families.

As the city began to rebuild after the war, new construction was once again influenced by English architectural tastes. English architects interested in classical design based their work on Roman domestic architecture. One of the principal advocates of Roman design was Robert Adam. Adam's work was more graceful and delicate than the heavier and more robust Georgian style. In this country, it became known as the Federal style because it was most popular at the time of the formation of the federal government. The Federal style was not as important in Philadelphia as it was in other cities primarily because it was barely recognized by the Carpenters' Company. But many townhouses, country estates and civic buildings were designed in this refined manner and furnished with elegant furniture by Sheraton and Hepplewhite.

By the end of the 18th century, Philadelphia was once again an impressive city. Sumptuous Georgian and Federal houses lined paved streets. Country mansions had developed along the Delaware and Schuylkill rivers and in Germantown. Impressive civic and religious buildings had been built as well as many new houses, all of a uniform character, made of brick with stone or wood trim, which gave the city a strikingly modern appearance. Philadelphia was still a major port, the center of shipbuilding, and the financial center of the new nation.

In 1800, Philadelphia had a population of 80,000 in the city and surrounding countryside. It was the largest city in the country, but New York was growing at a faster pace and would surpass it by 1810. The city was concentrated in the area between 7th Street and the river, stretching north and south into Frankford and Southwark. Most of the residents still were merchants and craftsmen, working in their homes; the rich and poor were mixed together in no particular pattern. But the economic conditions of the city had already begun to change in a manner that would greatly influence future patterns of development. Although the city still had an active port, Philadelphia had begun to look inland for its economic growth. Coal and iron were brought to the city by newly created canals to be exported around the world. Local businesses prospered when embargoes on the importation of European goods encouraged factories to replace them with local products. Papermaking, printmaking, books, shoes and foundries were among the more prominent businesses.

This growth of manufacturing was facilitated by the presence of many inventors in the city and by the general availability of skilled labor. Philadelphia's craftsmen were recognized as the best in the colonies.

Much of the new manufacturing located along streams outside the city. This further encouraged construction of new houses in such areas as Kensington, Spring Garden and Moyamensing. This dispersed growth presented many problems, such as an inadequate water supply and police and fire protection outside the city proper. Within the city, the population growth led to the speculative development of complete blocks of row houses. Once again, changing English architectural tastes provided the inspiration for new building design.

By the end of the 18th century, architects began to draw directly on Greek and Roman forms. Classical Greek orders became available in England through architectural handbooks. They were introduced in America as early as 1798 by Benjamin Latrobe, an English architect who emigrated to Philadelphia. But the Greek Revival did not really flourish until after 1820; not only did Greek Revival architecture sweep the country, but cities and towns were named after Athens, Sparta and other Greek cities.

In Philadelphia the prominence of Greek Revival design was due to the influence of Nicholas Biddle, president of the Second Bank of the U.S., and to the appearance of the first professional architects. William Strickland, John Haviland and Thomas U. Walter designed prominent Greek Revival buildings in the city. The use of classical orders and temple forms made buildings much more impressive than their Georgian and Federal predecessors. But beyond decoration and detail, Greek Revival buildings in gleaming white marble stood in sharp contrast to the uniform red brick of previous periods.

By 1830, the Philadelphia area had a population of 188,000. The city had expanded to 10th Street. In the countryside around the city there were mills, manufacturing centers and semi-independent townships. Each township had its own name, businesses, shops, fire companies and taverns, all loosely connected to the city. The development of new methods of manufacturing had already begun to change the way people worked and where they lived. Philadelphia was a handsome and sophisticated city on the verge of becoming an industrial metropolis.

Quaker dress, like building design, was plain and simple but usually made of fine material. The 1766 silk wedding dress with simple silhouettte has no adornment, not even buttons.

Glossary of Architectural Terms

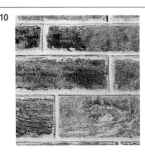

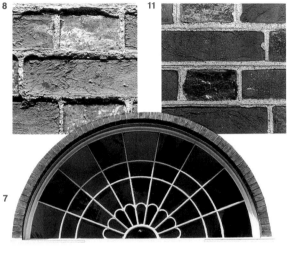

1 ashlar
stone that has been cut and squared, generally used on a building's facade

2 balustrade
a low wall formed by a series of short posts, shaped like a vase, with a rail on top; often found along the roofline of Georgian buildings

3 cornice
any molding or ornamentation that projects from the top of the building

4 cupola
a small, domed structure rising from the roof

5 dormer
a window in a small structure on the roof, allowing light to enter the attic

6 entablature
the horizontal member, above the column capitals, consisting of the architrave, frieze and cornice

7 fanlight
a semicircular window located above a door

8 Flemish bond
a brick pattern laid by alternating long and short ends; believed to have been acquired by exiled English builders living in Holland during the reign of Oliver Cromwell

9 gable
the triangular section of wall on the side of a building with a double-pitched roof; the roof is often called a gable roof

10 Germantown stone
local stone, known as Wissahickon schist, found near the surface of the earth; used in its rough condition as *rubble,* with heavy mortor joints, or cut and dressed for use on the main facade

13

16

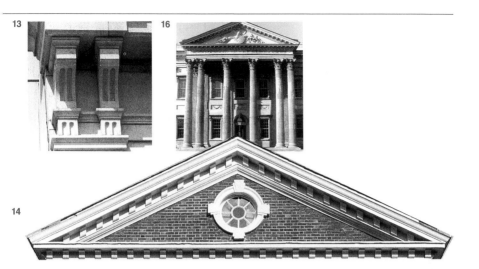

14

12

18

15

17

18

11 glazed header
the short end of a brick, with a darker glazing; used in a Flemish bond to produce a checkerboard pattern on the facade

12 Greek orders
the three forms of columns and entablatures from classical Greek architecture: Doric, with plain capitals; Ionic, with scroll capitals; Corinthian, with capitals decorated with acanthus leaves

13 modillion
an ornamental bracket used to support the cornice

14 pediment
the triangular surface formed by a gable roof and a cornice, generally used on a portico or over a doorway

15 pent eave
a small, wooden roof located between the first and second floors; originally used to protect wood and plaster facades from rain

16 portico
a roofed porch, supported by columns, found over the doorway

17 quoins
stones or bricks used to form the outside corner of a building

18 water table and belt course
elements of Georgian design in which the brick is projected slightly beyond the facade to deflect rain; the water table being the widened portion of the wall at the base, and the belt course being the projected lines of brick between the upper floors

1682
*Philadelphia founded by
William Penn*

1683
*Germantown settled by
Daniel Pastorius*

1685
*Bradford prints first book
in middle colonies*

102

103

101   K   *PR*
Wynnestay, 1689/1700/1904
5115 Woodbine Ave.
Thomas Wynne, builder

In 1681, Thomas Wynne, a Welsh physician, bought 5,000 acres of land from William Penn, on which he later built a one-room farmhouse, probably as a gift to his son. Wynne's house is typical of many Welsh farmhouses throughout the Philadelphia area. It is built of local stone found on or near the surface of the earth. The stone is set in wide mortar joints; the walls are two feet thick, with low and wide windows. Between the first and second floor of the original house is a pent eave, a common feature of early Philadelphia architecture. The pent eave was originally designed to protect plaster and wood outer walls from rain. It was incorporated into colonial designs even though the houses were built principally of stone or brick. The house was enlarged in 1904 by the addition of a rear wing in a compatible style.

102   G   *OP*
Wyck, from 1690
6026 Germantown Ave.
Hans Milan, builder

Hans Milan, a Dutch Quaker, also used readily available stone to construct a simple dwelling with thick walls, which kept his family warm in winter and cool in summer. His original house is the oldest building in Germantown. According to family tradition, Milan built a second house next door for his daughter. Sometime before the Revolutionary War, the two houses were joined at the second floor. A carriageway passed under the bridge between the two houses. The exterior was stuccoed in 1799.

In 1824, Milan's descendants hired the Greek Revival architect William Strickland to modernize the houses. In the carriageway between the houses, Strickland built a new room, which extends the depth of the house and looks out over the gardens at either end. In this new room he installed the novel feature of sliding glass doors.

103   K
Gloria Dei, 1698–1700
929 South Water St.

While the early Welsh and German settlers were building stone farmhouses, the Swedes, who had been in the Delaware Valley since the 1630s, were building their first permanent church. Gloria Dei is the oldest church in the city and the only remaining building by Swedish settlers. The Swedes brought log construction to the new world. But for their first church, they chose brick and hired English carpenters and masons to build it.

These craftsmen built in the tradition of English vernacular architecture, a mixture of medieval and gothic influences. These may be seen in the decorative shapes created with glazed brick headers next to the tower door and in the steep slope of the roof, the narrow tower windows and steep pedimented gable.

Three years after completion, the side walls began to bow under the stress of an inadequate roof truss. A vestry and entranceway were added to buttress these walls.

104   D   *OP*
Letitia House, 1713–15
Lansdowne Dr. near West Girard Ave.
Attributed to James Smart, house carpenter

William Penn expected early settlers to build modest houses in the center of garden lots. He described such a house in his pamphlet, *Information and Direction To Such People As Are Inclined to America.* Letitia, one of the earliest documented houses in Philadelphia, is an example of the house Penn suggested. The house was originally located near Front Street.

105

106

Like most early row houses, Letitia is made of brick laid in Flemish bond with gray glazed headers alternating with stretchers, giving the surface an intimately scaled checkerboard pattern. The paneled shutters and the small window sash also help create an orderly, tidy appearance. The center placement of the door is unusual for a town house, as is the hood supported by carved brackets over the entrance.

The house is two rooms deep; fireplaces placed back to back in one corner share a common chimney. A space-saving set of winding stairs, in a tight vertical box, rises from the cellar to the attic.

105 K

Bel Air, between 1714 and 1729
Southwest Corner 20th and Pattison Ave.

Ambitious colonial settlers followed the English pattern of creating country homes as well as maintaining a city house. Bel Air is one of the earliest surviving country seats. It was probably built for Samuel Preston, one of the city's first mayors.

Although an early Georgian home, Bel Air shows traces of the English medieval style as seen in the steep pitch of the roof, the narrow window proportions and the angular gables set over the dormers. The wide, symmetrical facade, the horizontal axis of the belt course and the water table that thickens the wall on the first floor reflect the classical influences of the Georgian tradition. The second floor balcony, with protective hood built into the cornice, is an unusual feature in colonial architecture.

Bel Air's interior has fine Queen Anne paneling and decoration. A large Tudor arch with a heart-shaped medieval pendant decorates the hallway and staircase.

106 B,J PR

Elfreth's Alley, Houses from 1720
Front and 2nd, Arch and Race Sts.

Elfreth's Alley, the oldest continuously inhabited street in the country, was created in 1703 when two property owners on Front Street made a cartway to the rear of their lots to subdivide their land. By the end of the 18th century, Elfreth's Alley had assumed its present character as a street of modest row homes. The oldest homes are simple two-and-a-half-story structures with parlors entered directly from the street. Some have pent eaves. Exterior woodwork is simple, as are doorways and transom lights. Most of the houses were built for rent and lived in by craftsmen. The Museum House at 126 is typical of these early homes. It was occupied by a dressmaker who had her shop on the first floor and living quarters above.

The three-and-a-half-story houses were built after the Revolutionary War and show the influence of the Federal style in the classically framed doorways with pilasters and pediments.

107

107   B,J   *OP*
Christ Church, 1727–44
2nd and Market Sts.
Dr. John Kearsley, supervisor

Although Penn founded Philadelphia to provide a refuge for Quakers, he extended freedom of worship to all religions. One of the first groups to exercise this right was the Anglicans of the Church of England, whose interests had also been protected by Charles II in his charter to Penn.

When the Anglicans outgrew the wooden church built in 1697, they modeled their new church on the work of Sir Christopher Wren, the English architect who rebuilt fifty-two churches in London after the Great Fire. Construction was supervised by John Kearsley, a physician, who probably was responsible for the design. He was the first of many gentlemen-architects who designed important civic buildings.

Christ Church is symmetrical in plan and elevation. The decoration on the facade is classical. Two-story brick pilasters alternate rhythmically with round arch windows. The cornice is decorated with modillions, and a balustrade hides the vertical slope of the roof. On the east end, a large Palladian window provides light for the chancel. The classical forms are made more dramatic by the strong curving lines of fat scrolls on the east pediment and by the robust curves of the roof urns, capped by carved flames.

Christ Church was the most sumptuous building in the colonies. It was the most sophisticated example of Georgian design in spite of a few awkward details. One of the most noticeable is the failure of the cornice on the side to match the cornice line of the projecting pavilion on the east end.

Robert Smith, the most prominent master carpenter of the time, worked on the steeple, which was added in 1751–54. It also was designed with classical details: round arch windows, pilasters and pediments over circular windows. The brick tower was finished quickly, but it took three lotteries, sponsored by Benjamin Franklin, to raise enough money to add the wooden part. The 196-foot steeple, probably the tallest in the colonies, was a prominent landmark on the early Philadelphia skyline.

1697
America's first stone
bridge at the "Pennepacka"
Creek

1709
First private mental
institution founded by
Quakers

1712
First ocean-going vessel
launched on Delaware

108

The Georgian Style

The rebuilding of London after the Great Fire of 1666 provided a unique opportunity to introduce new architectural ideas. Many of the new buildings were influenced by the recently discovered classical architecture of the 16th-century Italian Renaissance. The work of the Italian architect Andrea Palladio was the dominant influence in London after 1715. Publications such as Campbell's Vitruvius Britannicus *and Gibb's* Book of Architecture *made Palladio's work available throughout England and the colonies.*

The Palladian style incorporates classical columns, pilasters, cornices and other decorative elements over the traditional brick building shell. These elements may be seen in elaborate doorways, heavy cornice lines, window treatment and brick detailing. The most prominent exterior feature is the Palladian window, a large, three-part window with an arched central bay.

The Palladian style is known as Georgian in the colonies. It was the dominant style for homes of the well to do, churches and civic buildings prior to the Revolutionary War.

---

108 K *OP*
Stenton, 1728
Courtland and 18th Sts.

Stenton was built on a 500-acre estate by James Logan, William Penn's personal representative in the early years of the colony. Logan was a fur trader and iron merchant. He served as mayor of Philadelphia and chief justice of Pennsylvania.

Stenton is a magnificent example of an early Georgian country house. The facade is formal and symmetrically balanced. Simple brick pilasters mark the principal divisions and provide a strong accent at the corners. Modillions along the cornice provide ornament under the eaves of the hipped roof. Logan was a Quaker, and his manor house

reflects the influence of Quaker plainness on the Georgian style, particularly in the restrained use of ornament.

Inside, a generous staircase and fireplace fill the center hall, which was used as another room in the house. It is believed that the large front room on the second floor was Logan's library, which was the most distinguished in the colonies.

---

109 A,B,J *OP*
**State House
(Independence Hall),** 1732–48

See page 24.

---

110 K
Glen Fern, 1733–39
Livezey Lane, Fairmount Park

While Georgian houses were being built with classical ornament, the Shoemaker family of Germantown built a simple farmhouse with doors and windows spaced irregularly on a plain rubble facade. The house was later purchased by Thomas Livezey, who added a second story to the original one-and-a-half-story structure. In the 1850s, the kitchen and dining room were added laterally to the main block, resulting in a long, rambling structure typical of many country houses.

At its prime, the Livezey estate was self-sufficient. It included a grist mill, a forge, a shop for making barrels, a bridge across the Wissahickon Creek and a smokehouse. By the middle of the 19th century, steam-powered machines made water-powered mills obsolete. The mill was abandoned, and all that remains is the farmhouse and a dam with its mill race.

23

109

109 A,B,J *OP*
State House
(Independence Hall), 1732–48
Chestnut St. between 5th and 6th Sts.
Andrew Hamilton with Edmund Wooley

In 1729, Philadelphia lawmakers decided to move the government from the cramped quarters of the Town Hall at Second and Market streets. Andrew Hamilton, a well-known lawyer, proposed the block of Chestnut Street between Fifth and Sixth streets as the site of the new building, and the Provincial Assembly voted to buy the land even though it was on the outskirts of town.

Although not all scholars agree, it seems likely that Hamilton also drew the plans. He had traveled to England, had seen the recent work of English designers and also owned the requisite books on architecture. He worked on the State House complex until his death, in close collaboration with Edmund Wooley, a member of the Carpenters' Company and master carpenter.

The State House was conceived as a five-part plan based on the Palladian principle of two secondary buildings linked to a main block by arcades. The State House is an outstanding example of Georgian design. Although it was an important civic building, it is not as elaborate as Christ Church. In fact, except for its length, it is domestic in scale and detail. The main building is a self-contained rectangular block, visually framed by quoins or cornerstones. The cornice, balustrade, belt courses and water table emphasize the horizontal. The soapstone panels between the second and first floors, the marble keystones and the acanthus-carved modillions provide restrained decoration for the facade.

In 1750, the Assembly voted to commemorate the fifty years of Penn's Charter of Liberties by adding a tower to the rear of the State House. Wooley was in charge, and he made some awkward mistakes. For example, he placed the Palladian window almost directly on top of the door frame, omitting the proper classical spacing. At the same time, a large clock was built against the west end of the building. The long case, made of rusticated stone, hid the weights and lines necessary for an eight-day clock.

The high point in the history of the State House was the turbulent years before the Revolutionary War. The Assembly Room, the setting for the dramatic debates on independence, was the room in which the Declaration of Independence was signed. For ten years (1790–1800), the State House was the capital of the new nation before the government moved to Washington.

In 1830, John Haviland, the Greek revival architect, was hired by the city to restore the building to attract new tenants. His restoration marked the first of many. In 1950, the National Park Service undertook an archeological study of State House buildings, which provided the information necessary to restore it to its 1776 appearance.

● **1717**
First life insurance company: the Presbyterian Minister's Fund

● **1719**
City's first newspaper established

● **1723**
Benjamin Franklin, age 17, arrives from Boston

113

111 K *PR*
109–25 Kenilworth St., 1740–1800

Kenilworth Street, like Elfreth's Alley, is an example of the modest row house developments that predominated in the 18th century. The earliest houses were crowded close to the Delaware River in the city and adjacent townships, such as Southwark. Kenilworth Street, or Almond Street as it was then known, was created when Edward Shippen sold part of his Southwark estate. The new lots were long and narrow, measuring 18 or 20 feet by 60 feet. Simple, utilitarian houses were built on the lots over a period of 60 years as the influx of immigrants steadily increased. They were occupied by shipwrights, mast and sail makers, pilots, mariners and others whose work was tied to the port and the sea.

112 K *OP*
Grumblethorpe, 1744
5267 Germantown Ave.
John Wister, builder

John Wister emigrated from Germany in 1727. He became a successful wine merchant and built an unsophisticated summer home in Germantown, six miles from Philadelphia. During the next 50 years other well-to-do families followed Wister's example and built summer homes in Germantown to escape the heat, noise and smell of the city.

Wister's house was built of local stone, known as Wissahickon schist, as were other houses in the area. The Wissahickon schist, with flecks of mica, is dressed and coursed on the front but left as rubble on the side and rear. The pent eave has a balcony in the center, and a heavy, projecting cornice surrounds the gable end. Round windows, instead of the traditional dormers, provide light and ventilation to the attic.

113 A,J
Head House and Market Shed, 1745/1804
2nd St., Pine to Lombard Sts.

The original markets of the city were open sheds in the center of High Street (now Market Street). As the residential area expanded south, a second market was created at Lombard Street by Joseph Wharton, a wealthy merchant, and the then mayor, Edward Shippen. The market shed, with sixteen stalls, was constructed of paired brick piers supporting a gable roof over a vaulted plaster ceiling. Farmers set up their carts beneath and around the shed. By 1797, the market extended to South Street and was terminated by a firehouse, later demolished.

The market was also extended north to Pine Street, and the present Head House was built in 1804. It housed fire apparatus and served as a meeting place for volunteer fire companies. The building is late Georgian, with Federal-style fanlights flanking the arched passageway. It is topped by a cupola, which once contained a firebell. The Head House and sheds, restored in 1960, are the oldest of their kind in the country.

114 G
Green Tree Tavern, 1748
6023 Germantown Ave.

Green Tree Tavern is one of the best examples of Georgian architecture in Germantown. It was built by Daniel Pastorius, grandson of the founder of Germantown. The tavern is made of Wissahickon schist. The pent eave and heavy cornice across the front are typical of most Germantown buildings. Because the land rises uphill, the southern sides of buildings along Germantown Avenue were visible to people coming from Philadelphia. Consequently, the south walls usually were treated just like the fronts. On the tavern this wall also has a pent eave and gable cornice and is dressed with ashlar stonework. The remaining two sides are rubble.

1724
*Carpenters' Company
founded*

1728
*John Bartram establishes
first botanical garden*

1731
Library Company formed

116

118

In 1930, the tavern was moved to accommodate an addition to the First United Methodist Church of Germantown, which uses the tavern for its parish offices.

---

115 K *PR*
Workman Place, 1748/1812
742–46 South Front St.
George Mifflin, John Workman, builders

As more immigrants came into the city, many property owners built small houses or tenements for rent on the rear of their lots. Workman Place is typical and is one of the earliest rental housing complexes still in similar use. The first small tenements were built by George Mifflin, as evidenced by his initials and the date 1748 worked in brick. These houses originally had one room to a floor and two apartments in each building. He sold these houses and a large lot to John Workman. Workman added three elaborate houses on Front Street, which created the courtyard.

The Workman family owned these properties until 1906. By that time the houses had become slums as immigrants crowded the older housing near the Delaware River. The houses were bought by Lydia S. Clark, an early advocate of housing reform, and subsequently taken over by the Octavia Hill Association, which continues to operate them as rental properties.

---

116 A,J *OP*
St. Peter's Church, 1758–61
3rd and Pine Sts.
Robert Smith, carpenter-architect

By 1750, Christ Church could no longer accommodate the number of people who wanted to have seats there. It also was inconvenient for parishioners living south of Walnut Street. The Penn family donated land for a second Anglican church, the "chapel of ease," as St. Peter's was first called. Robert Smith designed and built the church. Dr. John Kearsley, who had directed work on Christ Church, was the supervisor.

St. Peter's is a subdued version of a Palladian church. It contains a grand Palladian window on the chancel wall, and the sides of the church are pierced by round arch windows, but there is an absence of elaborate detail. St. Peter's still retains its original high-backed pews, raised off the floor to keep out drafts. In an unusual arrangement, the altar and pulpit are at opposite ends of the main aisle.

The steeple was added in 1852 by William Strickland. The simple tower, six stories high, is in keeping with the church's restrained exterior.

---

117 A *PR*
Abercrombie House, 1759
268–70 South 2nd St.

Early 18th-century houses had small rooms and were only two or three stories high. Georgian houses were much larger, often with large libraries and ballrooms on the upper floors. This Georgian townhouse was built for a Scottish sea captain who settled in Philadelphia. The house is situated on high ground that must have once commanded a fine view of the port, possibly explaining the decked gable roof with balustrade, a feature not found in any other remaining house in the area. In spite of its height the house retains a horizontal emphasis, typical of Georgian design, through the use of belt courses, water table and a heavy cornice. The house, used as a warehouse early in this century, was restored in the 1960s and occupied by a toy museum for many years before returning to residential use.

●
1732
*Stage coach line to
New York inaugurated*

●
1736
*Franklin organizes world's
first volunteer fire company*

●
1740
*University of Pennsylvania
founded as "charity school"*

119

120

---

118   A   *OP*
Man Full of Trouble Tavern, 1760
127 Spruce St.

In colonial days, inns were places for
socializing. Over a meal and drink people
would exchange business and political information as well as gossip. Man Full of
Trouble Tavern is one of the many taverns
that served the colonial city. The tavern had
rooms for travelers on the second floor and
in the attic, whose gambrel roof gave more
head room than the more common pitched
roof. The first floor dining room and serving
bar have been restored.

In the colonial period, there was very
little difference in the design of residential
or commercial buildings. Only the sign in
front that graphically depicts the Man Full
of Trouble indicated that the structure was
more than a home.

---

119   D   *OP*
Mount Pleasant, 1761
Mount Pleasant Dr.

Of all the country estates around Philadelphia, Mount Pleasant was the most elegant.
It was built by Captain John MacPherson, a
Scottish privateer. He drew on Palladian
principles of design, building a main house
symmetrically flanked by two small buildings. The distinguishing feature of Mount
Pleasant is the projecting pavilion with its
pediment. Both the east and west sides of
the building have Palladian windows. Mac-
Pherson contrasted the texture and color of
brick in the belt courses and quoins with a
warm-colored stucco ruled to look like
stone. This provides a pleasing variation on
the usual solid brick or stone houses. The
interior is equally handsome, with finely
carved paneling.

MacPherson could not afford to live in
his expensive mansion. In 1779 he sold it to
Benedict Arnold, who planned to give it to
his wife as a wedding present. Before the
couple could move in, Arnold was charged
with treason.

120   G   *OP*
Cliveden, 1763–67
6401 Germantown Ave.
Benjamin Chew with Jacob Knor, master
carpenter

Cliveden was one of the most elegant Georgian estates in the colonies. Benjamin
Chew, an important lawyer, designed the
house himself, probably working closely
with Jacob Knor, a local master carpenter.
The house represents a compromise between
Palladian fashion and the local Germantown
building tradition.

The exterior is distinguished by a projecting pavilion, capped by a pediment, and an
entrance framed with classical details. The
facade is dressed with ashlar of Wissahickon
schist, while the rear wall is plain rubble.
On the sides, stucco over rubble is scored
to imitate stone.

The center hall, the largest room in the
house, was the most elaborate of its type in
the colonies. It is separated from the
stairhall by a screen of four finely carved,
fluted Doric columns.

The Chew family lived in the house until
1972, when they gave it to the National
Trust for Historic Preservation.

---

121   A
Shippen-Wistar House, 1765
238 South 4th St.

William Shippen, a leading colonial physician, built this house and gave it to his son,
probably as a wedding present. From Fourth
Street it looks like most other townhouses
in the area except that there is no front door.
Shippen took advantage of the corner lot to
place the door on the long side of the house,
allowing for a more interesting interior plan.
The first floor has two rooms on each side
of a central hall. The rooms are more easily
accessible and of better size than in a typical
plan, where the rooms are lined up behind
one another.

27

1741
America's first magazine published

1747
American Philosophical Society founded

1748
First exclusive dancing society, the Assembly, founded

122

125

122　A,J　OP
Powel House, 1765
244 South 3rd St.

The Powel House is the finest Georgian row house in the city. It was built by Charles Stedman. Before he could live in it, he sold it to Samuel Powel, the first mayor of Philadelphia after the Revolution.

Powel was a Quaker who later turned Anglican. This change can be seen in his house. The restrained exterior reflects the Quaker concern for simplicity. The brick facade is Flemish bond, with cheaper common bond on the side. The only decoration is the Doric frame surrounding the door. Inside, restraint gives way to luxurious rooms decorated with fine paneling, elaborate carving and delicate plaster work.

The plan of the house is quite sophisticated compared to the typical town house. The front door enters into a generous hall. The parlor and dining rooms are to one side, and at the rear, framed by a large arch, is an open mahogany staircase. A ballroom with elaborate woodwork and plaster ceiling is on the second floor.

Robert Smith, the prominent carpenter-architect, worked on this interior.

123　K
St. George's Methodist Church, 1769
4th and New Sts.

St. George's was the center of Methodism in the colonies and is the oldest Methodist church in continuous use in the United States.

Originally, Philadelphia Methodists met in private homes. But, in 1768, they purchased the shell of this church from a German congregation that had fallen on hard times. The church exterior is almost as plain as a Quaker meetinghouse. The only ornamentation on the facade is the barely noticeable corner pilasters, whose caps blend into the cornice line. Even the classical frame found around the door of most churches is absent. This plain exterior masks a delicately scaled, attractive interior, which was finished by the Methodists.

In 1921 the church was almost torn down to make way for the Benjamin Franklin Bridge. It was saved by moving the bridge 14 feet south and lowering Fourth Street. A flight of steps was added to reach the ground floor of the church.

124　K　OP
Bartram Hall, 1730/1770
54th St. between Elmwood and Gibson Aves.
John Bartram, builder; Renovated 1990, Dagit/Saylor Architects

John Bartram was an eccentric Quaker farmer and a respected, self-taught botanist. He traveled extensively along the unexplored east coast in search of new botanical specimens, which he collected for his nursery and sold to English farmers.

Bartram enlarged a small stone Swedish farm house in two stages. By the second stage, his taste was more sophisticated. He dressed the stone and laid it in roughly equal courses with thick mortar joints. This more formal ashlar work is paired with a two-story Ionic portico that looks out over the Schuylkill River. The rather novel columns are built up in horizontal courses of the same dressed stone. The windows are framed with carved volute surrounds in a rough imitation of Baroque curves. In true Georgian fashion, the facade is for show; around the corner, the walls are rubble and stucco.

The seed house, also on the grounds, is another delightful example of Bartram's handiwork. It is rubble with stone chips set decoratively in thick joints.

1751
Pennsylvania Hospital, first in America, founded

1752
First American fire insurance company: The Contributionship

1753
The Argo leaves Philadelphia; First Arctic expedition

1754
First American stock exchange opens

127

---

125 A,B,J *OP*
Carpenters' Hall, 1770–74
320 Chestnut St.
Robert Smith

In the 18th century, building trades in the city were dominated by members of the Carpenters' Company. The company was founded in 1724 and modeled after English builders' guilds. In addition to building design and construction, members assisted contractors and clients in determining the fair value of completed work. The company's Rule Book, published in 1786, contained principles for measuring and fixing prices. Only members were allowed to see it.

Robert Smith, a member, was chosen to design the company's meeting place. He created a cruciform plan based on one of Palladio's Italian villas and the town halls of his native Scotland. The building's details are Georgian, such as the pediments over the north and south doors and the cupola on the roof. The first floor was a large meeting hall; the second was divided into smaller meeting rooms. The members used the hall for their meetings, but also rented space to other organizations. The most famous group to use the hall was the Continental Congress in 1774.

---

126 G *OP*
Deshler-Morris House, 1750–72
5442 Germantown Ave.

David Deshler, a well-to-do merchant, built a summer home in Germantown, following the example of his uncle, John Wister. He finished the house in 1772 by adding a large front section facing the street. To dress up the facade Deshler covered the building with stucco ruled to look like stone. He added a classical frame around the doorway with Tuscan columns topped by a pediment, which was the fashionable custom in the city. On the first floor the rooms are divided by a center hall, an advanced plan for colonial houses in Germantown, where most rooms on the first floor had separate doors to the outside.

In the summer and fall of 1793, yellow fever devastated the city. President Washington moved his family to Deshler's elegant home and, having enjoyed his stay, returned the next summer.

---

127 K *OP*
Fort Mifflin, 1772–98/1870s
Fort Mifflin Road
Thomas Mifflin and Pierre Charles L'Enfant

Philadelphia had no military fortifications because William Penn had determined to live in peace with the Indians. In 1772, however, the British began to build a fort to protect the Delaware River. After the Revolutionary War began, the fort was completed by the colonial army, directed by Major General Thomas Mifflin. The British marched into Philadelphia to attack Washington's troops in 1777. A line of defense between Fort Mifflin and Fort Mercer, across the river, held off the British fleet long enough for Washington's troops to reach Valley Forge. In the process, the fort was nearly demolished.

Reconstruction of the fort was carried out in several phases. The major portions were planned by the French architect Pierre Charles L'Enfant, who designed the plan for Washington, D.C. He also designed the commandant's house. Other notable structures include the officers' quarters, the artillery shed and the bombproof underground shelters.

29

●
1757
*First streetlights installed;
designed by Franklin*

●
1759
*Southwark, America's first
theater, opens*

128

131

The Federal Style

*By 1770, Robert Adam and his brother were
the most prominent architects in England.
Adam continued the tradition of classical
investigation by publishing a book on
Roman architecture. Adam used new information about details and decoration and
the variety with which classical orders were
used in Roman domestic architecture to
form his own style.*

*The Adam style is known as the Federal
style in the colonies because it reached its
popularity in the period after the Revolution, when the new government was being
formed. The Federal style is light and delicate compared with the robust richness of
Georgian design. Columns, pilasters and
other moldings are narrow and flat. Windows are narrow, with slender mullions.
Exterior decoration is limited and usually
confined to doorways. Interior ornamentation is equally delicate, with an increased
used of curved and oval forms in the plans
of rooms, in bay windows or fanlight windows over the main door. The overall effect
is one of refinement and grace.*

---

128   A   OP
Hill-Physick-Keith House, 1786
321 South 4th St.

This house is the only remaining example
of the many freestanding mansions that once
existed within the row-house fabric of the
colonial city. It is also one of the finest examples of Federal-style architecture. Col-
onel Henry Hill, a prosperous wine merchant, built the house, which was later
owned by Dr. Philip Syng Physick, the
father of American surgery.

Federal-style ornamentation is more delicate than its Georgian predecessor. On the
Hill-Physick-Keith House, ornament is limited to projecting keystones and cornice
modillions. Brick courses, separating the
floors and outlining the main door, are
nearly flush with the wall surface. The

finely crafted double door, surrounded by
intricate carving and topped by an impressive fanlight, imparts a grace and monumentality more often found on country mansions. The spacious interior contains thirty-
two rooms, including a ballroom on the first
floor finished with elaborate woodwork.

---

129   K   PR
Reynolds-Morris House, 1786–87
225 South 8th St.

The Reynolds-Morris House was built by
William Reynolds, a doctor, and his brother
John, a gentleman bricklayer. It was later
purchased by Luke Wistar Morris, a merchant, whose family owned the house for
120 years.

The house was built on a double city lot,
allowing an elegant center hall plan. Although the Federal style was more popular
at the time, the Reynolds-Morris House was
designed in a Georgian manner, as seen by
the Flemish bond brickwork, articulated
with string courses between floors. The
heavy lintels with keystones, the cornice
modillions and louvered shutters all hark
back to the Georgian era.

130, 132   A,B   OP
Congress Hall, 1787–89
6th and Chestnut Sts.
U.S. Supreme Court, 1790–91
5th and Chestnut Sts.

As early as 1736, plans for the State House
complex included two buildings for county
and city government. The buildings were
not started until after the Revolutionary War,
when the Federal style was more popular
than the Georgian style of the State House.
The difference is especially visible in the
window treatments. The State House windows are held by a heavy wooden frame.
The windows on the new buildings have
thinner mullions, due to the use of a lighter
frame known as a reveal, which was re-

1765
First medical school in
colonies established

1767
First American play,
"Prince of Parthia," produced

1768
Regular street cleaning and
garbage collection begins

133

134

cessed into the wall. The first-floor windows
are particularly graceful. Another difference
between the two styles is the detailing of
the cornice. The heavy modillions of the
State House are replaced by delicate fret-
work and a tapering keystone shape.

While the federal government was in
Philadelphia, the buildings were used for
meetings of Congress and the Supreme
Court. Later, the buildings reverted to city
and county use until the new City Hall was
completed in 1894.

---

131 K
Woodlands, 1742/1788-89
Woodland Ave. and 40th St.

Woodlands is situated on the former estate
of Andrew Hamilton, a lawyer and designer
of the State House. The original mansion,
built by his son, was remodeled and expanded by Hamilton's grandson, William.
It was one of the finest mansions of the
period and an early example of the Federal
style.

William added the east and west wings,
which terminate in bowed walls enclosing
oval rooms. The informal interior has an
oval dining room and oval parlor opening
off a circular entrance hall. William's addition to the south front was one of the first
American domestic examples of a freestanding projecting portico. Other Federal-style
details are the giant Ionic pilasters on the
north front, the blind arches with Palladian
windows and the elliptical fanlight over the
central door. The slender proportions, delicate scale and stuccoed facade distinguished
Woodlands from neighboring country
mansions.

William also designed the grounds, one
of the earliest American examples of the
English romantic garden. The property was
sold to Woodlands Cemetery in 1843.

133 K
Pennsylvania Hospital, 1755/94-1805
8th and Pine Sts.
Samuel Rhoads/David Evans, Jr.
Center Pavilion Restored 1977,
Bartley Long Mirenda Architects

Pennsylvania Hospital, the first hospital in
the colonies, was founded by Dr. Thomas
Bond. Benjamin Franklin helped raise funds
for the first building, which was built on a
site far from the noises and smells of the
city. It was designed by Samuel Rhoads
using the same materials and proportions as
domestic architecture.

The center pavilion and west wing
specified in Rhoads's plan were not built
until after 1794. The center section, designed by Evans, is one of the finest examples of the Federal style in the country. The
facade shows a new sophistication in public
architecture. Monochromatic brick replaces
the checkerboard pattern of Flemish bond
and glazed headers. The first floor is faced
with marble, and giant Corinthian marble
pilasters stretch from the second floor to the
cornice. The center pavilion projects slightly
and has a fashionable oval window in its
pediment. Evans designed a circular amphitheater on the top floor, marked by an exterior balustrade. It was here that modern
surgery was first performed in the United
States.

---

134 A,J *OP*
First Bank of the United States,
1795-97/1901
120 South 3rd St.
Samuel Blodgett/James Windrim

After the Revolutionary War, the new federal government established a single form
of currency and an institution to handle its
extensive war debts. The First Bank was
created by Alexander Hamilton, who was
responsible for the country's initial mone-
tary policies.

As the first national bank building in the
country, the founders wanted to convey the
qualities of strength, dignity and security.

31

1770
Separate school for black children opens

1774
First Continental Congress meets

1775
*First U.S. carpet woven
First U.S. piano made*

138

Blodgett, a businessman and amateur architect, modeled his design on Thomas Colley's Exchange in Dublin. The bank was the most imposing structure of its day. The design incorporates typical Palladian motifs: a two-story Corinthian portico, hipped roof with balustrade, corner quoins and marble facing.

In 1901, James Windrim replaced the barrel vault over the banking hall with a skylit rotunda on Corinthian columns. The building was sold to Stephen Girard in 1812 and used as a bank until 1926; it was restored in 1957 by the National Park Service.

135 K *OP*
Loudoun, 1796–1801/1829/1850
4650 Germantown Ave.

Thomas Armatt first settled in Loudoun County, Virginia, before coming to Philadelphia. He was one of the many city dwellers who moved to Germantown following the yellow fever epidemics in the 1790s. He built a Federal-style house for his son, Thomas Armatt, Jr., who became a successful Philadelphia merchant and trader.

Loudoun stands on the summit of Naglee's Hill at the gateway to Germantown. From this prominent point one could see ships arriving on the Delaware. The outstanding feature of the house is the freestanding Corinthian portico on the south facade. This Greek temple front was added to the original mansion in 1850 by Armatt's son-in-law, James Skerrit.

136 G *OP*
Upsala, 1755/1797–1801
6430 Germantown Ave.
John Johnson 3rd, builder

Dirck Jansen, one of the early settlers of Germantown, built a house on land he later sold to John Johnson Sr., who bequeathed this property to his family. The front portion of the house was added by his grandson and is one of the finest examples of Federal architecture in Germantown.

By contrast with the Georgian style of Cliveden, directly across the street, Upsala is simpler and more delicate in scale and details. The facade is made of ashlar Wissahickon schist with marble trim. The windows are smaller than Cliveden's, and the doorway is marked by a refined Doric portico and pediment. On the interior, the house has four rooms to a floor, entered from a central hall. The rooms have fine woodwork, and there is a graceful stair leading to the second floor.

In the 19th century the house was named Upsala, after the Swedish university city. It remained in the Johnson family until 1941.

137 K *PR*
Sansom's Row, 1799
700 Blocks of Walnut and Sansom Sts.
Benjamin Latrobe/Thomas Carstairs

Early Philadelphia row houses were usually built one or two at a time. As more and more immigrants poured into the city, however, the need for rental housing generated the first speculative developments.

William Sansom's project was the first complete row of houses built at the same time. Latrobe designed 22 houses for Walnut Street, followed a few years later by 20 houses on Sansom Street by Carstairs. Because the site was on the outskirts of the city, Sansom paved the street at his own expense to help attract tenants. The simple plan of the row house and the repetition of identical units were the principal design determinants. The design implications of a unified block-long facade were suggested by paired doorways, contiguous beltcourses and battlements at the end of each pair. Except for 707 Walnut, the remaining houses have been substantially altered.

1776
Declaration of
Independence signed

1777
Battle of Germantown

1780
Pennsylvania first state
to abolish slavery

1781
First U.S. corporate
bank authorized

139

138 D *OP*
Lemon Hill, 1799
Lemon Hill Dr.

By 1774, Robert Morris, a prominent financier, had assembled 300 acres along the
Schuylkill River. He established a country
estate complete with a splendid mansion,
farm and greenhouses filled with lemon
trees. When his fortunes declined, Morris
sold 140 acres to Henry Pratt, who built the
present house, which he named Lemon Hill.
It is a lyrical example of the Federal style.

The house is rubble covered with stucco
and granite trim. It has a curved central bay
on the garden facade created by an oval
room projecting through the rectangular
plan. There also is an oval parlor and bedroom. The Palladian window was carried
over from the Georgian era, but is more
restrained, flush with the wall surface and
squeezed between the doorway and cornice.
Lemon Hill also had elaborate gardens that
attracted many visitors.

In 1844, Lemon Hill was purchased by
the city to protect the municipal water supply. It became the initial part of Fairmount
Park in 1855.

139 B *OP*
Arch Street Friends Meeting House,
1803–5/1810–11
330 Arch St.
Owen Biddle

William Penn and many of the original
settlers of Philadelphia were members of
the Society of Friends, commonly known
as Quakers. The Friends worshiped in
gatherings without a minister and shared
their spiritual thoughts. The meetinghouses
built for their services usually contained
two rooms: a large entrance and gathering
room and the meeting room itself.

The Arch Street Meeting House is the
largest in the city and second oldest. It was
built on land given to the Friends by Penn
in 1693 and initially used as a burial ground.

There are two rooms in the central structure
and two flanking wings used for annual
meetings, when men and women met
separately.

The building is a plain brick structure
with flat exterior surfaces, marble steps,
wood shutters and simple columned porticos
over the doors. The center structure and
east wing were designed by Owen Biddle,
author of the influential trade book, *Young
Carpenter's Assistant* (1805).

140 K *PR*
York Row, 1807
712–16 Walnut St.
Joseph Randall, carpenter

York Row was another speculative housing
development started by William Sansom.
The plan of the houses and the simple repetition of units are similar to his previous
project across the street. Certain details,
such as the splayed lintels with projecting
keystones above the windows, are typical
of Georgian design. But the absence of beltcourses and cornice modillions, combined
with the profusion of detail around the entrances and the delicate details and scale,
indicate that the overall design is based on
the Federal style.

141 K
Spark's Shot Tower, 1808
29–31 Carpenter St.
Thomas Sparks and John Bishop

Spark's Tower was the first shot tower in
the United States and is one of the last remaining examples. It was built by one of
the city's first "plumbers," makers of leaden
vessels, to manufacture shot for sport. Shot
was made by pouring molten lead through
perforated pans at the top of the 142-foot
tower. As the lead descended it spun into
droplets, which hardened when they hit cold
water at the bottom. The tower became a
munitions factory during the War of 1812,
and continued to produce shot up to 1907.
Since 1913, the structure has been part of a
recreation center.

1784
First U.S. daily
newspaper published

1786
Fitch demonstrates steamboat
on the Delaware River

1787
Constitutional convention
held

144

142 K *PR*
Franklin Row, 1809–10
236 South 8th St.
Robert Mills

Robert Mills was an active builder and the
first native-born American architect. His
designs were influenced by the neoclassical
ideas of Thomas Jefferson and Benjamin
Latrobe, but Mills interpreted these ideas in
an innovative manner.

Mills constructed a speculative row of
houses in the tradition of Sansom and York
rows, but only one structure remains. The
tripartite window and recessed arch on the
facade convey a monumentality that must
have been impressive when repeated across
a row of houses. The two remaining buildings of the Carolina Row, 925 and 929
Spruce Street, also attributed to Mills, have
a similar treatment.

143 B
Girard Warehouses, 1810
18–30 North Front St.

Early warehouses in Philadelphia were simple, four-story brick structures, built on
long, narrow lots, with one large room to a
floor. The west side of Front Street contains
some of the oldest and most beautiful
warehouses in the city. Numbers 18–30
were owned by Stephen Girard, who at his
death was the wealthiest man in the United
States. They are typical of early 19th-
century warehouses. The ground floor had a
store in front and a counting room in back.
The facade is brick on the upper floors, but
the first floor is granite, a popular material
for storefronts at that time. The Trotter
warehouses at numbers 36–44 are equally
handsome and have been occupied by the
same company since the 1830s.

144 D
Fairmount Waterworks, 1812–15
Fairmount, at Schuylkill River near 25th St.
Frederick Graff

The first city waterworks, designed by Benjamin Latrobe, were located on Center
Square. When a new system was required,
Graff, a draftsman on the original project,
became the architect and chief engineer.
The new facility was one of the most notable engineering accomplishments of its
day. The original steam pumping station
carried nearly four million gallons of water
every day from the Schuylkill River to re-
servoirs at the top of "Faire Mount" (now
the Art Museum), where it was gravity-fed
to homes and hydrants.

The complex, added to throughout the
19th century, was modeled after Roman
temples and arranged around paved courts
and walkways. Galleries inside the pump
rooms allowed visitors to view the machinery. The grounds were extensively landscaped, creating a very picturesque setting
that became one of the first parts of Fairmount Park. The waterworks, abandoned in
1911, were used for an aquarium until 1962.

The Greek Revival Style

*By the early 19th century, Roman architec-
tural models had been replaced by classical
Greek orders, available in England and the
colonies through such handbooks as Stewart
and Revett's* Antiquities of Athens. *The use
of Greek orders flourished in the United
States during the 1830s and 1840s because
of the new nation's identification with the
democratic ideals of ancient Greece.*

*The first Greek Revival building in the
country was designed by Benjamin Latrobe
in Philadelphia in 1798. But it was not a
popular style until after 1820. The first book
to include Greek orders was John Haviland's* The Builders Assistant, *published in
Philadelphia in 1818.*

● **1789**
City incorporated

● **1790**
Franklin's funeral attended
by 20,000

● **1792**
First U.S. mint begins
operation

145

147

Greek Revival buildings are easily recognizable through their use of the temple form, complete with pediments; heavy cornices; Doric, Ionic or Corinthian columns; and their use of white marble as the primary building material.

145 A,B,J OP
Second Bank of the United States,
1818–24
420 Chestnut St.
William Strickland

The Second Bank was founded in 1816. Nicholas Biddle, its most influential president, was a tireless champion of Greek architecture. When the bank held a competition for the design of its new building, Biddle required all architects to use the Greek style.

Strickland's design is one of the first Greek Revival public buildings in the country. Modeled on the Parthenon, it features plain Doric columns and little decoration except for the triglyphs and metopes on the entablature. The structure appears to be of solid marble, but really is brick faced with marble. In contrast to the Greek exterior, the interior is Roman. A barrel-vaulted ceiling covers the banking hall.

President Jackson's veto of the bank's charter in 1832 led to its demise. Strickland altered the building in 1844 for use as the U.S. Customs House, which it remained until 1935. It is now the National Portrait Gallery.

146 K
St. Stephen's Protestant Episcopal Church, 1822–23/1878–79/1888
19 South 10th Street
William Strickland/Frank Furness/
George C. Mason

Many new churches were constructed in the early 19th century to serve the changing population of the city. St. Stephen's, built on the site where Franklin flew his famous kite, was the first designed in the Gothic Revival style.

Strickland's Gothic designs, of which this is the only survivor, were neoclassical buildings with applied Gothic details. St. Stephen's is Gothic by virtue of the crenelations over the screen on the facade, the lancet windows in the twin towers and the pointed, arched windows on the screen. Originally, the octagonal towers were crenelated as well.

The church contains outstanding examples of religious works of art. These include the "Angel of Purity" by August Saint-Gaudens, two marble effigies and a baptismal font by Steinhauser and a richly carved marble reredos. Over the altar is a mosaic of the Last Supper, inlaid with 180,000 pieces of Venetian glass. Three Tiffany windows adorn the south wall.

The north transept and vestry room were added in 1878–79 by Frank Furness. In 1888, George C. Mason designed the parish house, west of the vestry room.

147 J
Eastern State Penitentiary, 1823–36
Fairmount Ave. at 21st St.
John Haviland

"The exterior of a solitary prison should exhibit . . . great strength and convey to the mind a cheerless blank indicative of the misery that awaits the unhappy being who enters within its walls." These were the directions to architects in the competition for the design of the Eastern State Penitentiary. Haviland's winning entry was a fortress with an austere granite facade and a forbidding iron portcullis.

The interior was based on Sir Samuel Bentham's 1787 radial plan, used for jails and insane asylums in England. The plan consists of seven long cell blocks radiating from a central surveillance rotunda. The cell blocks contained dark passageways lined with individual cells.

●
1793
First circus held;
First American balloon
flight

●
1801
Public waterworks opens;
Chamber of Commerce
established

150

The prison features such early Gothic details as lancet windows, square towers flanking the entrance and battlemented turrets at the corners. But the simple, massive forms are typical of Haviland's Greek Revival style. The design was enormously influential; it was copied in more than 500 prisons around the world.

---

148 C,J
Pennsylvania Institution for the Deaf and Dumb, 1824–26
320 South Broad St.
John Haviland; Renovated 1983,
F. Daniel Cathers and Associates

In 1820, Broad Street was a rural pastureland on the edge of town. Social and cultural institutions moved here to escape the noise of the city. One of the first, the Pennsylvania Institution for the Deaf and Dumb, was designed by John Haviland, then at the peak of his career as the most prolific Greek Revival architect in the city. Haviland adapted the Greek Revival style to the individual project, rather than imposing archaeological correctness like his contemporary, Strickland. The Doric portico and pediment on the granite facade are Greek Revival, as is the simple massing of forms, typical of Haviland's style. The exposed basement, however, resulting from the raised entrance, is a Roman feature, while the shallow inset arches on the wings, added in 1838 by Strickland, derive from the Federal style. The building was renovated in 1983 by the Philadelphia College of Art, now the University of the Arts, which has occupied it since 1893.

149 B *OP*
Franklin Institute (Atwater Kent Museum), 1825
15 South 7th St.
John Haviland

The Franklin Institute was founded by Samuel Merrick, a businessman and manufacturer who wanted to promote research, education and communication among scientists and inventors. The institute was involved in many important 19th-century scientific activities, including the first weather bureau, plans for the first coal gasification plant, standardization of machine parts and the promotion of the incandescent light bulb. It gave the first architectural courses in America, with such teachers as Thomas Walter and William Strickland. Haviland based the design of the building on the Greek Monument of Thrasyllus. Because of the restricted site, however, he compressed the elements into simple masses, austere surfaces and bold proportions.

The Franklin Institute vacated the building in 1933, and it was almost demolished. In 1938, A. Atwater Kent, an inventor, radio magnate and manufacturer, established a museum of the history of the city, which continues to occupy the building.

---

150 K
United States Naval Asylum,
1827–33/1844
Gray's Ferry Ave. and Bainbridge St.
William Strickland

The Asylum was built for the benefit of "disabled and decrepit" naval officers, seamen and marines. It was one of the largest Greek Revival hospitals in the country. The main building, Biddle Hall, contained public rooms, a domed auditorium, dining rooms and officers' quarters. Men's dormitories were located in the wings.

Strickland imposed an Ionic portico,

1804
Market Street bridge spans
Schuylkill River

1805
Pennsylvania Academy of
Fine Arts founded

1811
First medical textbook
in U.S. published

152

153

based on Stuart and Revett's illustrations of
an Athenian temple, onto a utilitarian building. The cast-iron columns on the balconies
were an early use of this new economical
and fire-resistant material. Their delicate
scale, continuing the graceful rhythms of
the portico columns, helps to lighten the
massive structure.

In 1844, Strickland added the governor's
and surgeon's residences. Each is brick
faced with stucco and features a verandah
with cast-iron supports. The ornamental
ironwork contains naval motifs of dolphins,
anchors and ropes.

The asylum was the first home of the
U.S. Naval Academy, and later a home for
retired naval personnel, until it was closed
in 1976.

151 K
Walnut Street Theatre, 1808–9/1827–28
829–33 Walnut St.
John Haviland

The first theater company in the United
States opened in Philadelphia in 1749.
Quaker opposition hindered the early devel-
opment of a permanent theater, but by 1820,
Philadelphia was the theatrical center of the
country.

When the Walnut Theatre was built, it
was at the western edge of the city. The theater was renovated in 1816 and again in
1828, when John Haviland added a Greek
Revival facade for Joseph Randall, the developer of York Row. Haviland's facade
was decorated with painted cast-iron details.
The facade was obscured by later renovations by J. C. Hoxie and Willis Hale, which
were removed when the building was
restored in 1970–72. The theater had a
national reputation and attracted great per-
formers of the period, including Forrest,
Booth, Bernhardt and Barrymore. It is the
oldest continuously used theater in the
country.

152 A PR
Girard Row, 1831–33
326–34 Spruce St.
William Struthers

Row houses were a favorite investment for
Stephen Girard, millionaire banker and merchant, who considered them a way of
beautifying his adopted city. He died before
this row was completed, but they were
finished by his estate.

In contrast to the uniform red brick of
earlier row houses, the ground floors of the
Girard houses are surfaced in marble, a
fashionable Greek Revival building material. The first residents of these townhouses
were goldsmiths, shoemakers, house carpenters, bricklayers and merchants.

153 K PR
Portico Row, 1831–32
900–930 Spruce St.
Thomas U. Walter

Portico Row is an outstanding block of early
19th-century row houses. It was built by
real estate speculator John Savage, who
hired the young architect Thomas U. Walter
to design sixteen houses for sale to upper-
middle-class lawyers, doctors and merchants. The houses were elaborately designed on both the exterior and interior. The
brick facades, with marble lintels, are distinguished by a series of projecting porticos
supported by marble Ionic columns. Each
portico provides entrance to two houses.
The interior rooms were spacious and richly
finished. Highly polished marble was used
for all fireplaces, walnut or mahogany for
doors and trim. Even the water closets were
built of walnut, and the bathroom floors
were marble.

Sarah Hale, editor of the fashionable
Godey's Lady's Book and one of the best-
known arbiters of 19th-century taste, lived
on Portico Row for several years.

●
1812
Philadelphia Academy of
Natural Sciences established

●
1817
First public building,
the State House, lit by gas

●
1818
Public school system
organized

154

154 A,J
Merchant's Exchange, 1832–33
143 South 3rd St.
William Strickland

When Philadelphia businesses became too
numerous to meet in coffee houses and
taverns, merchants formed the Philadelphia
Exchange Company. Strickland designed
their building, now the oldest stock exchange in the country, which was considered
to be one of the most beautiful structures of
its kind.

The building consists of a rectangular
main structure with a semicircular portico;
Strickland used the Corinthian order on the
colonnade, reflecting the evolution of a
more elaborate Greek Revival style. He
crowned the building with a lantern meticulously copied from the Choragic Monument
of Lysicrates, one of the most copied monuments of the period.

The Exchange Room, in the curved portion of the building, was sumptuous. It had
a mosaic floor, a domed ceiling supported
on marble columns and frescoes on the
walls. Real estate dealings, auctions and
business transactions of all kinds took place
in this room, where shipping news and
newspapers from all over the world were
posted.

The Exchange dissolved during the Civil
War. When wholesale food markets took
over the area, sheds were erected around
the east end of the building. These remained
until 1952, when the Exchange was purchased by the National Park Service.

155 K
Frankford Arsenal, 1816–1976
Bridge and Tacony Streets

Although the development of the Frankford
Arsenal took place over a 160-year period,
the first phase of construction occurred in
the early decades of the 19th century. The
arsenal was established by the U.S. Army
on a 20-acre site along the Delaware River

and Frankford Creek. Philadelphia was
selected as the site because it had an active
gunpowder industry, a sizable community
of skilled German gunsmiths and good access by water to iron and timber. Until 1850
the arsenal was an ammunition depot and
repair shop. The early buildings consisted
of officers' quarters, storehouses, kitchens
and the commandant's house. These are
clustered around a quadrangle, known as
the Parade Ground. Most of the buildings
completed by the 1830s are designed in the
Federal style, with fanlights, elliptical windows, stringcourses and restrained decoration. The cast-iron veranda of the commandant's house, added in the 1850s, was a
common feature of other buildings of that
time.

In the decade prior to the Civil War, the
arsenal began its transformation from a
depot to a munitions fabricator. New buildings were designed in a utilitarian version
of the Greek Revival style, with arched bays
on the facades, classical pediments and
decorative details. The most significant
building of this period, and perhaps the
most significant building at the arsenal, is
the Rolling Mill, designed by John Fraser
in 1865. The mill is constructed of iron
trusses supported by wrought-iron columns
strengthened with iron plates. These are
known as Phoenix columns and Fink
trusses. On the exterior the mill introduced
an Italianate style, which predominated at
the arsenal for the next 80 years.

Other buildings added before the two
world wars followed the industrial Italianate
style of the Rolling Mill. One exception is
the Ammunition Proof House, from 1917–
18, which has Gothic battlements, oriels
and hood moldings. Buildings constructed
after 1940 adopted simple functional forms
consistent with the modern movement in
architecture. When the arsenal finally closed
in 1977, it contained 246 buildings on its
110-acre site.

156

156 𝅘𝅥

Founder's Hall, Girard College, 1833–47
Girard and Corinthian Aves.
Thomas U. Walter

In his will, Stephen Girard, the first American multimillionaire, bequeathed $2 million for a school for "poor white male orphans."

The architectural competition held to select designs for the College was won by Walter, who had been practicing architecture for only three years. His design soon changed, however, under pressure from Nicholas Biddle, president of the board of trustees. Biddle believed that the two great truths in the world were the Bible and Greek architecture. He seized this opportunity to build the most correct Greek temple in America.

In response to this direction, Walter wrapped marble Corinthian columns around the entire building and raised the temple on a flight of steps that circled the peristyle. The roof and walls are covered with local Chester County marble. Inside, the four rooms to a floor, required by the will, are vaulted. Under the roof, pendentive domes with skylights make use of the space behind the entablature.

Founder's Hall, one of the most expensive buildings of its time, took fourteen years to build. It was the climax of the Greek Revival style in America. The building worked poorly and was abandoned as a schoolhouse in 1916. It remains a tribute to Stephen Girard, whose tomb is on the first floor.

Girard College was integrated in 1968, following years of significant civil rights litigation.

2

The
Industrial
Metropolis

1835–1905

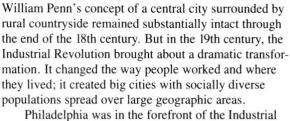

The Industrial Metropolis
1835–1905

Furniture influenced by the Gothic Revival had strong vertical lines and ornate detail. This cathedral chair from 1845–55 was made in New York and owned by a family on Spruce Street. It is black walnut with ash trim.

William Penn's concept of a central city surrounded by rural countryside remained substantially intact through the end of the 18th century. But in the 19th century, the Industrial Revolution brought about a dramatic transformation. It changed the way people worked and where they lived; it created big cities with socially diverse populations spread over large geographic areas.

Philadelphia was in the forefront of the Industrial Revolution in the United States. Many of the forces that transformed the city were initiated before 1840. The invention of the steam engine in 1803 allowed factories to locate anywhere and become larger than water-powered mills. Railroads brought coal and iron to the city but also enabled wealthy and middle-class residents to move out. By 1840, the majority of the 250,000 residents lived outside the city; by 1860, the population of 565,000 was distributed in 40 independent villages and townships scattered throughout the once rural countryside.

While the most extensive changes occurred in Philadelphia county, the city, laid out by Penn between Vine Street, South Street and the two rivers, was altered substantially. The port, second in size only to New York, continued to be an important center of economic activity, exporting iron, coal, steel, sugar, textiles and other manufactured products. But manufacturing businesses increased steadily, although most people still were employed in small establishments. Printing and publishing, textiles, and the manufacture of paint, chemicals and drugs were important businesses. In the 18th century, most people were individual entrepreneurs of similar economic status. Industrialization separated places of business and work, and created clear class distinctions between business owners, managers and employees.

By 1850, the fashionable neighborhood in the city was between Seventh and Broad streets, south of Walnut Street. The older areas east of Seventh Street deteriorated as a result of overcrowding by the poor and recent immigrants. New brick row houses, larger and more spacious than their predecessors, were heated by coal furnaces and had indoor plumbing. Most were built speculatively, but not in a continuous pattern. Open space existed east of Broad Street, and in 1850, the area west from Broad Street to the wharfs along the Schuylkill River was largely undeveloped.

Although housing expanded, the residential population of the city started to decline. Commercial development predominated and followed the westward growth of housing. Chestnut Street was the main street for fashionable shops and elegant hotels, while Market Street became a new manufacturing and commercial district. The market sheds at Second Street were removed in 1853 and a farmers' market created at 12th Street. Museums, an opera house, and theaters provided

By the mid-19th century, French design influenced dress as well as architecture. This silk taffeta wedding dress of 1854 followed Paris fashions with a three-tiered skirt supported by a stiff crineline hoop undergarment and bell-shaped sleeves trimmed with matching bands.

cultural activities. In 1855, Fairmount Park was founded on the edge of the city to provide a place of recreation and to protect the city's water supply.

The steady increase in construction encouraged the introduction of new architectural ideas, usually derived from English sources. London townhouses and clubs, modeled after urban palaces of the Italian Renaissance, became the predecent for similar buildings in the city. New churches were constructed in most new neighborhoods. Their design reflected the return to the Gothic style in England, resulting from a resurgence of interest in medieval liturgy and construction.

Commercial buildings also presented an opportunity for new architectural ideas. Loft buildings were designed in the Italian Renaissance style, but after 1850, businessmen who wanted to express their success adopted the more ornate Italianate style then popular for suburban houses. Commercial Italianate design flourished with the introduction of cast iron, which permitted the mass production of ornamentation at low cost. As a structural system, cast iron made it possible to use big windows to light large floor areas of commercial structures.

While these transformations were occurring in the city, even more dramatic changes were taking place in the county. Steam-powered plants, belching smoke, were widely dispersed throughout the county. Because transportation was predominantly by foot or horse, people of all economic classes lived close to their jobs. New residential areas surrounded centers of employment. Each area was an independent village or township with its own ethnic character, which made it easy to assimilate the different immigrants coming to the city.

While these settlements were a major factor contributing to the growth in the county, railroad lines and horse-drawn trolleys in the 1850s enabled middle-class

Growth of the City

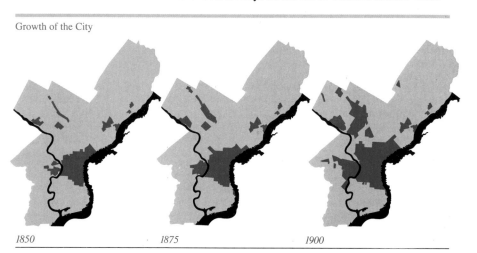

1850 *1875* *1900*

J. E. Caldwell and Co. made this silver pitcher in 1857 as a presentation piece. The pitcher is decorated with a water-lily motif and is similar to designs exhibited in England and Europe in the 1850s.

This chair was owned by James Dobson, co-owner of Dobson Mills. It is made of ebonized cherry and was originally upholstered in damask woven at the mills. The delicate scale, rocòco shape and carved rose and leaf motifs are indicative of the fine craftsmanship of its manufacturer, Gottlieb Vollmer.

residents to commute easily from Germantown, Chestnut Hill and West Philadelphia, east of 42nd Street. These areas, characterized by tree-lined streets, freestanding and twin houses with small yards, were a sharp contrast to the dense brick row houses of the city. The exodus to the countryside was part of the Romantic movement then prevalent in England and the United States. English architects responded by reviving the Gothic style, which seemed more appropriate for country houses because of its asymmetry and ornamentation. The Gothic villa started the picturesque movement; its popularity encouraged English architects to explore other sources of picturesque design, particularly the vernacular architecture of the Italian countryside. The Italianate style offered the same opportunities for informality and asymmetry. It was popular with wealthy families because of its elaborate detailing and ornamentation.

The development of the city during this period did not proceed without some difficulty. The abundance of cheap labor, at a time when industries were becoming increasingly mechanized, created competition for jobs between native-born residents and the new immigrants, particularly the large influx of unskilled Irish Catholics. Riots were common in the 1840s. Some were expressive of anti-Catholic sentiments; others directed against blacks and others caused by volunteer fire companies. The riots were difficult to control because of the absence of common police services outside the city. This difficulty, as well as the inability to provide uniform fire protection and water supply, led to the political consolidation of the city and county in 1854.

At the time of the Civil War, Philadelphia was a prosperous city. The war had a limited social impact on the city, since slavery had been eliminated by 1820. But it did have a substantial economic impact. As a major manufacturing center, the site of the U.S. Navy Yard and Frankford Arsenal and the first large city north of the Mason-Dixon line, Philadelphia was a major supplier of military goods. The war strengthened the city's economy and consolidated its position as a leader in industrial manufacturing. After the war, Philadelphia considered itself the "workshop of the world." It led the nation in the production of steam engines, locomotives, street cars, textiles, and steel ships. It was also a major producer of rugs, hats, sugar, cigars and the site of many breweries. Because of its industrial prominence, Philadelphia was selected to host the 1876 Centennial Exposition, which celebrated the new technology.

In 1870, the population of the city was 675,000; by 1876, it was 820,000. In the following decades immigrants poured into the city; by the end of the century more than 1,300,000 people lived in Philadelphia. The first wave of immigrants came primarily from Germany and Ireland, but there were also many blacks from the South. Toward the end of the century, the influx of Irish was matched by a sixfold increase in the Italian population. Other immigrants, many from Russia and Eastern Europe, contributed to the diversity of the city's population.

Building in the city boomed. More than 100,000 houses were constructed in the 1870s and 1880s. Most were built by speculative developers. The availability of cheap land, the dispersion of manufacturing plants, the extension of the street grid in 1858 and the introduction of street railway lines in the same year contributed to this rapid expansion. Newly created building and loan associations provided financial assistance, so that even working-class families could own their own homes. Houses in South Philadelphia, built for the poor and new immigrants, were small and crowded together. North Philadelphia was the focus of middle-class expansion. Mansions of wealthy individuals along North Broad Street encouraged the creation of large and distinctive row houses west of Broad Street. These thousands of row houses, in contrast to the tenements of New York, gave Philadelphia the reputation as a city of homes.

By 1890, 25 of the city's 125 square miles were urbanized, extending north to Erie Avenue, west to 49th Street, and south to Snyder Avenue. Chestnut Hill and Germantown also grew but remained separated

Frank Furness designed this desk and chair in 1875 for his brother's house. Both pieces have an architectural character and contain elements also found in Furness's buildings. The desk has a Moorish arch and ornamental details worked into the walnut similar to those found in the brickwork or terra-cotta panels of his buildings. The chair has a simple, rectangular form typical of English furniture of the 1870s.

from the rest of the city by undeveloped land. The physical pattern of separate villages disappeared, but neighborhoods were still segregated by ethnicity and race. The introduction of the electric street railways, in 1892, increased mobility and began to modify these patterns.

Within the central area of the city, fashionable residential areas moved further westward, focusing around Rittenhouse Square. Houses were even more spacious than earlier in the century, reflecting the common practice of live-in servants. Older residential areas east of Broad Street deteriorated as the downtown became an increasingly commercial district. The second half of the 19th century saw a substantial increase in the production of consumer goods. The mass production of clothing and other household goods created totally new types of stores, such as Lit Brothers and John Wanamaker's department store.

The westward growth of downtown influenced the decision to build a new City Hall on Center Square, set aside by Penn for civic buildings. The grandiose City Hall epitomized the self-confidence of the period. Its construction immediately shifted the financial and governmental center away from Independence Square. In response, the railroads created new terminals east and west of City Hall. These were followed by a new scale of commercial and office building, made possible by the invention of the elevator and the use of fireproof steel construction.

After the Civil War, American architects no longer felt confined to a single historical style. Many different styles were used and often mixed with one another. This eclectic attitude was the basis of Victorian design. The principal historical influence was Gothic, but the Gothic of Venice rather than England. John Ruskin, the English art critic, drew attention to the use of color in Venetian buildings. The High Victorian Gothic style followed Ruskin's suggestions, creating color and texture through the use of different materials or variations in the use of brick. The application of this style to speculative row houses, particularly in North and West Philadelphia, produced some of the most inventive and distinctive houses ever built in the city. Many outstanding commercial and civic buildings were designed in this style, which reached its apex in Philadelphia in the work of Frank Furness.

Architects who were tired of the heavy, somber Victorian style adopted the lighter and more informal Queen Anne style, which was based on houses built in England in the transitional period between medieval and Georgian design. Many houses were also built in the Second Empire style, derived from civic buildings. Row houses with mansard roofs, arched doorways and decorative arched lintels over windows were fashionable in many sections of the city.

Daniel Pabst made this night table for his daughter in 1875. It is decorated with floral motifs cut through the maple veneer to expose the walnut underneath. Pabst executed some of Furness's furniture and also drew upon English designs of the 1870s for the details and ornamentation of his own work.

This beautiful cream and dark-green silk dress of 1885 is typical of the late 19th century. It is draped in front and has a prominent bustle in the back to create the "receding silhouette" considered fashionable at the time.

This Renaissance Revival clock from 18 5–75 was sold by J. E. Caldwell and Co. It is made of marble with gilded bronze and contains architectural motifs found on Second Empire–style buildings.

Civic and commercial architecture, in the last decades of the century, sought a monumental expression consistent with the economic prosperity of the period. To achieve this effect, the great railroad stations, collegiate buildings and churches drew on a variety of styles ranging from the High Victorian Gothic to the Renaissance Revival, Gothic Revival and Romanesque Revival. The most impressive building of the period, City Hall, was designed in the Second Empire style derived from the monumental buildings created in Paris by Napoleon III. This return to classical forms reflected the dominance of the École des Beaux-Arts in Paris in architectural education. Virtually every important American architect of the late 19th century attended the École or worked for someone who did. The popular impact of neoclassical designs at the 1893 Columbian Exposition in Chicago gave impetus to a classical revival just at the time that modern architecture had its first beginnings in Chicago.

The end of the 19th century was one of Philadelphia's best periods. The city was a prosperous manufacturing center. Large portions of the city had been developed, but there was still ample land for future growth. The city was no longer the financial capital of the nation, nor the leading cultural center. But its place as an industrial center, and one of the major urban areas in the country, seemed secure. Philadelphians entered the 20th century content and optimistic.

Glossary of Architectural Terms

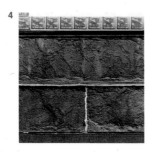

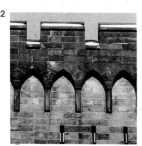

1 bargeboard
a decorative, often ornately carved board attached to the edge of a gable roof

2 battlement
a low wall, at the edge of a roof, which is broken by vertical slots

3 bracket
a small support of stone or wood under the eave of a roof or other overhang; more decorative than functional and usually quite elaborate on Italianate houses

4 brownstone
dark brown or reddish sandstone used on the facades of late 19th-century houses

5 cast iron
iron that has been smelted and shaped in a mold; used for interior columns and the facades of commercial buildings from 1860 to 1900

6 corbel
a projecting stone block or bricks supporting an arch, beam, roof or other feature on the exterior of a building

7 crocket
a carved projection in the shape of leaves; used on Gothic buildings to decorate the edges of spires or gables

8 **lancet window**
   a narrow window with
   pointed arch

9 **lantern**
   a small structure on a
   roof, with windows on
   all sides providing light
   to the interior of a
   building; commonly
   found on Italianate
   houses

10 **mansard roof**
   an attic roof with two
   planes, the lower one
   being steeper; named
   after its French inventor, François Mansart;
   a distinguishing char-
   acteristic of the Second
   Empire style

11 **oriel**
   a projecting bay win-
   dow on an upper floor

12 **pilaster**
   a flat representation of
   a column, attached to
   a wall

13 **terra-cotta**
   fine-grained, red-
   brown fired clay used
   for roof tiles and
   facade ornamentation;
   sometimes glazed to
   look like ceramic tile
   for decorative facades

202

201 A
**Philadelphia Contributionship for the
Insuring of Houses from Loss by Fire,**
1835–36
212 South 4th St.
Thomas U. Walter

The Contributionship, the oldest mutual fire
insurance company in the country, was organized by Benjamin Franklin in 1752. The
company originally met in coffee houses or
taverns and later in the home of the treasurer. The directors wanted their permanent
office to look like an elegant house and to
provide a residence for the treasurer. Walter
drew upon his Greek Revival design for
Portico Row. The building is a simple brick
structure with an elegant portico supported
by fluted marble Corinthian columns. Offices were on the ground floor, the kitchen
in the basement and the living quarters on
the top two floors.

In 1866 the portico had to be replaced.
Collins and Autenreith followed Walter's
design, but expanded the living quarters
with the addition of a stylish mansard roof.
A marble cornice also was added between
the third and fourth floors. The Contributionship's seal of four hands clasped in the
fireman's carry is located on both ends of
the building.

202 D,K OP
Laurel Hill Cemetery, 1836
3822 Ridge Ave.
John Notman

John Jay Smith, head of the Library Company, wanted to establish a nonsectarian
cemetery outside the city. He acquired 50
acres overlooking the Schuylkill River and
created a corporation to attract affluent
customers.

Laurel Hill is designed in the picturesque
English garden tradition. Notman based his
plan, selected through a design competition,
on the Kensal Green Cemetery, in London.

Roads and paths radiate from a central circular drive. Gazebos and lookout points
provide lovely views throughout the site,
which was planted with exotic trees and
shrubs. The gatehouse, also by Notman, is
modeled on the classical Palladian plan of a
central building flanked by colonnades. It
still retains the original wood paneling
painted to imitate stone.

The cemetery was the burial ground for
wealthy families, who built large mauso-
leums in various architectural styles. Many
were designed by such prominent architects
as Notman, Strickland and Walter. Originally, Laurel Hill was an important recreation area and tourist attraction, with up to
30,000 visitors a year.

203 A
Philadelphia Saving Fund Society,
1839–40
306 Walnut St.
Thomas U. Walter

PSFS, founded in 1816, was the first savings
bank in the United States. For its first headquarters the bank wanted a building that
would recall the treasury buildings of antiq-
uity. Walter's design is a modest Greek
Revival structure, made of brick faced with
hand-rubbed Chester County marble. The
two-story Ionic portico gives the small
building a monumental quality. Within the
building special fireproof precautions were
taken: the cellar was vaulted in stone and
brick and windows were covered with iron
shutters.

The pediment was added to the facade in
1881, when PSFS sold the building.

●
1836
*Philadelphia Gas
Works established*

●
1837
*Edgar Allan Poe
moves to city*

●
1838
*Central High School founded;
First U.S. Naval Academy opens*

204

204 A
The Athenaeum, 1845
219 South 6th St.
John Notman

A group of young men formed a social and
literary club in 1814 named the Athenaeum,
after Athena, the Greek goddess of wisdom
and learning. When they could afford to
build a library, they chose John Notman.
Notman's design reflected the work of the
English architect Charles Barry, who had
been influenced by the urban palaces of Italian princes. It was the first Renaissance Revival building in America.

The building is simple and symmetrical,
with corner quoins and a large overhanging
cornice. The floor-to-ceiling windows on
the second story are treated decoratively,
with entablatures supported by scroll brackets. The building was to be covered in marble, but brownstone, a new building material, was used to save money. Notman's
design and the use of brownstone influenced
a number of later residences and clubs, including the Union League.

The Early Gothic Revival Style

*The Gothic Revival began in England and
paralleled the development of the Greek
Revival style. It was advocated by those
who found the Greek orders too rigid and
uniform. The Gothic style was considered
more appropriate for country houses: its
asymmetry and ornate details were in keeping with the forms of nature. The Gothic
style also was a significant influence on
church design. The English Cambridge
Camden Society, founded in 1836, advocated proper Gothic design and construction
as the only appropriate ecclesiastical form.*

*Although the first American residence
incorporating Gothic details was designed
by Benjamin Latrobe as early as 1799, the
style did not become popular until the
1840s, when the romantic movement was at
its height in England and the United States.*

*The Gothic Revival style is distinguished
by the pointed arch and the vertical emphasis on most elements. Towers, steep
gable roofs, asymmetrical plans, window
tracery and ornamentation in the form of
foliage are common features of residential
and religious buildings.*

205 K
Church of St. James the Less, 1846–49
Clearfield St. and Hunting Park Ave.
Robert Ralston, from the drawings of
G. G. Place

Robert Ralston, a prominent Philadelphia
merchant and owner of a summer estate in
Falls of Schuylkill, decided to establish an
Episcopal church for the growing community of mill families and summer residents.
He obtained measured drawings of a 13th-
century English parish church from the
Cambridge Camden Society. These plans
were carried out faithfully by John E.
Carver, superintendent of construction,
whose only revision was the addition of one
bay to the nave.

The church has a steeply sloping roof, a
small attached chancel, a crowning bell-
gable on the west wall, buttresses and
rubble-textured granite walls. Many of the
interior details were made in England.

St. James the Less became the source for
subsequent Gothic Revival churches in
America. It remains unsurpassed for the
authenticity and completeness with which it
interpreted the English model.

51

●
1839
Saxon takes first
U.S. photograph

●
1840
First lager beer
manufactured in U.S.

206

208

---

206   C,J
Cathedral of SS. Peter and Paul, 1846–64
18th and Race Sts.
Napoleon LeBrun/John Notman

Although Catholics had always been present in the city, their numbers were not significant until after the Irish immigration in the 1830s. By 1844, the Irish population was large enough to support the building of a cathedral. The cathedral is the oldest building on Logan Circle, one of the original five squares in Penn's plan. It was one of the most sumptuous churches in the country when completed, and remains the center of Catholic life in Philadelphia.

The interior is designed in a grand Italian Renaissance style. The original plans were drawn by Reverends Mariano Maller and John B. Tornatore and reworked by LeBrun. Notable features include the domed baldachino (canopy) over the altar, the giant Corinthian pilasters encircling the nave and transept and the deeply coffered barrel vault over the nave. Notman and Reverend John T. Mahoney added the dome and the elegant Palladian facade after 1850. The facade uses brownstone, which Notman had introduced at the Athenaeum.

207   K
St. Augustine's Church, 1847–48
4th and New Sts.
Napoleon LeBrun

St. Augustine's is the fourth oldest Catholic church in Philadelphia. The original church was burned in 1844, when anti-Catholic sentiment was at its peak. The new building incorporated elements of the original plan. It is a strong Palladian form, with tall blind arches, a cornice with modillions and a staged tower, which was completed by Edward Durang in 1867.

The sanctuary is a Palladian design modified by renovations in 1895 and 1923. The ceiling frescoes, some of which were added by the Italian painters Nicola Monachesi and Philip Costaggini, give a neo-Baroque flavor. Especially notable are the arched, white marble altar, composed of a skylit dome resting on splendid Corinthian columns, and the organ facade painted in gold, bronze and ivory. Above the galleries are tribune boxes, a rare feature in church design.

The entrance was lowered during the 1920s to accommodate the construction of the Benjamin Franklin Bridge.

208   K
St. Marks Church, 1848–51
1625 Locust St.
John Notman

The founders of St. Marks were influenced by the Anglican reform movement, which advocated correct medieval Gothic design as a way of returning spiritual ardor to the church. Notman's plans were sent to the Cambridge Camden Society in England for review, to ensure correct Gothic construction.

The exterior of the church is in keeping with the 19th-century interest in picturesque design. Each of the elements is given separate expression, in contrast to the simple rectangular form of 18th-century churches. The tower and entrance door are set off from the nave, the center aisle and side aisles are expressed by different rooflines, and the chancel is a separate mass with a lower roofline.

As was typical of medieval churches, construction materials are left in their natural condition on the interior. This gives the church an unusually impressive character. The walls and ceiling are of hammer-dressed stone, and the exposed trusses are of oak. Gothic details are present in the pointed arch windows with tracery, the quatrefoil shapes of the piers and on the capitals of the piers, some of which were left uncarved to symbolize that the work of the church is never finished.

1842
Philadelphia and
Reading Railroad begins
operation

1842
First minstrel show
in U.S. at Walnut Street
Theatre

1843
First steamship with
screw propeller
launched

211

The church has been enriched by gifts of the faithful, of which the most impressive are the Lady Chapel, designed by Cope and Stewardson from 1899–1902, and the richly sculpted silver altar, both donated by Rodman Wanamaker.

209 K PR
1600 Block of Locust St., 1848–1908

In the 19th century, many of Philadelphia's finest families lived in elegant mansions around Rittenhouse Square or in fine townhouses nearby. This block of Locust Street is unique because of the number of houses designed by prominent architects.

Italian Renaissance Revival brownstones predominate on the south side of the block. Numbers 1604, 1620, and 1622 have been attributed to Notman. The brownstone at 1618 was altered at the turn of the century by Wilson Eyre. The frame of the first-floor window is carved in rich floral motifs with a human face emerging from the swirling leaves.

The two houses at 1631–33, by Cope and Stewardson, reflect the late 19th-century taste for Georgian Revival. Frank Miles Day designed the house at 235 South 17th Street in a medieval style with gables, bay windows and dark brick offset by limestone trim. The white limestone Beaux-Arts style house at 1629 Locust was designed by Horace Trumbauer.

210 B
St. Charles Hotel, 1851
60–66 North 3rd St.
Charles Rubican, builder
Renovated 1980 by Adaptive Design

American hotels of the 19th century were small and designed for middle-class patrons. They were often modeled after Italian Renaissance palaces. The St. Charles was designed in this style using cast iron, a new building material, rather than stone. The iron was cast in a foundry into smooth panels, which were then painted a stone color with sand added to the paint to create a granular texture.

Local newspapers covered the construction of the hotel, describing the innovative plan, which included a bar and reading room on the first floor, a second-floor parlor for women and three floors for the more than 50 hotel rooms. Later, the same newspapers commented on the crowds who came to see the cast-iron front that imitated stone. The building was converted to apartments and office space in 1980.

211 K PR
1800 Block of Delancey Place, 1853–80

After 1850, Philadelphia's elite families moved west of Broad Street, a section of the city that was still largely undeveloped. Speculative developers followed, building blocks of large row houses between Walnut and South streets for the affluent middle class. The size of the houses was indicative of rising economic conditions and the presence of live-in servants.

Delancey Place, one of the earliest of the new developments, was opened as a street in 1853 on a parcel of land granted by Christ Church. Most of the houses on the north side were completed by 1860, with the remainder finished by 1880. The Biddle family was the principal property owner. The houses were designed in the Italianate style, but later additions to several houses by Wilson Eyre and Cope and Stewardson have given the block a more Victorian appearance.

213

212   K
Gaul-Forrest Mansion, 1853–54
1346 North Broad St.
Stephen Button

For half a century, North Broad Street was one of the best addresses in Philadelphia, rivaling Rittenhouse Square. Many houses were built by wealthy, self-made men. This house was designed for William Gaul, a successful brewer. It is a fine example of an Italianate townhouse in brownstone, the popular building material of midcentury. The second owner was Edwin Forrest, a famous Shakespearean actor. Forrest added a new wing to house an art gallery and installed a private theater below.

In 1880 the house was purchased by the Philadelphia School of Design for Women, the first industrial arts school for women, and now the Moore College of Art. James Windrim was hired to enlarge the building. Along the Master Street facade, he used galvanized iron trim, pressed into ornate shapes and painted to look like brownstone.

213   C
Arch Street Presbyterian Church,
1853–55
1724 Arch St.
Joseph C. Hoxie

The Presbyterians were active church builders in the 19th century. As the population of the city moved westward, Presbyterian churches followed. The design of the Arch Street Church is a blending of several styles, a common practice at the time, and one at which Hoxie was particularly adept. Here, Baroque, Roman and Gothic forms are unified by the use of the Corinthian order. The exterior of the church is especially impressive, with a copper dome influenced by the design for St. Paul's Cathedral in London. The original building included a cupola, two bell towers and a balustrade with urns, all of which have been removed.

The sanctuary is a masterpiece of the Classical Revival style and one of the most beautiful interiors in the city. The Corinthian columns and pilasters are exquisitely scaled and detailed. The dome and ceiling over the altar and transepts are treated with coffers, some of which are faced with glass, allowing natural light to bathe the altar.

214   K
Tenth Presbyterian Church, 1854
17th and Spruce Sts.
John McArthur, Jr.

The Tenth Presbyterian Church is another example of the many churches built by the Presbyterians to serve the developing neighborhoods in the western section of the city. It was designed by John McArthur, one of its members. McArthur was the architect of City Hall and is chiefly remembered as a leading exponent of the Second Empire style. But he was firmly established in the eclectic tradition and designed competently in many styles. For this church he drew on three principal influences. The spire and recessed porches are reminiscent of French Gothic; the base of the tower and the walls of the church are paneled in colonial fashion; and the round-headed windows, pilaster strips and corbel tables are suggestive of the Romanesque style.

The Italianate Style

The Italianate style grew out of the continuing English search for the picturesque, which began with the Gothic Revival. Based on the rural Italian villa, it allowed flexible planning and elaborate exterior forms. In the United States, Andrew Jackson Downing popularized the Italianate style as an appropriate style for country homes. It became nationally influential in the decade before the Civil War. The application of the Italianate style to commercial buildings led to the mass production of certain decorative elements in cast iron and pressed metal.

1847
American Medical
Association formed

1848
First regular comic
paper published

1849
Wooden water pipes
replaced with iron

215

217

The first house in the Italianate style was designed by John Notman in Burlington, New Jersey. Residential buildings in this style usually have a square tower placed off-center within an asymmetrical grouping of other rectilinear shapes. Roofs are low pitched, with heavy overhangs supported by brackets. Houses usually have round-headed windows with elaborate frames, bay windows, porches or verandas. Most are wood-frame buildings covered with light-colored stucco. Commercial buildings are very ornate, with many of the details executed in marble, granite or cast iron.

215 H
Piper-Price House, 1854
129 Bethlehem Pike
Samuel Sloan

Chestnut Hill began its slow transformation from farmland to suburb with the extension of rail service to the community in 1854.

The Piper-Price House is believed to be the design of Samuel Sloan, based on its similarity to a villa published in Sloan's book, *The Model Architect* (1852).

Sloan's pattern books helped popularize the Italian villa, a style valued for its picturesque qualities as well as its generally affordable cost. The Piper-Price House is typical of the style. It is symmetrical in plan, with a simple square form and center tower from which to view the countryside. The house presents an image of strength and solidity through the simple massing of its cubelike parts, pieced together like building blocks, and by the contrast of dark trim set off against light-colored stucco. Only the round-arched windows and the rounded projection of the bays relieve the cubic severity.

216 B
Elliot and Leland Buildings, 1854–56
235–37 Chestnut St.
Joseph C. Hoxie

By midcentury, commercial buildings and warehouses were being designed by architects. The basic plan of the buildings remained the same as earlier warehouses on Front Street. The first floor was a store or office, and each upper floor was one large room used for storage or manufacture. In contrast to its shallow four-story predecessors, however, the 19th-century commercial building was taller and deeper.

The Elliott and Leland buildings are fine examples of the Italianate commercial style. Each has a granite facade and is five stories high. The depth of the buildings made it essential to open up the facade to gain as much light as possible. Hoxie achieved this by organizing the facade in response to the structural system rather than as a wall with windows placed in it. The window spandrels are recessed and the columns and capitals emphasized, producing a simple and direct form.

217 B
Farmers' and Mechanics' Bank, 1854–55
427 Chestnut St.
John M. Gries; Renovated 1984, 1993,
Bower Lewis Thrower

Commercial banks increased in the 19th century, locating near the center of government at Independence Square. So great was their concentration that the blocks between 3rd and 5th streets on Chestnut were referred to as Bank Row. The Farmers and Mechanics Bank illustrates the prevailing notion that banks had to look like Italian Renaissance palaces to convey an image of wealth and substance. The symmetrical marble facade has arched windows on each floor and ornate cornices and belt courses decorated with sculptural heads of sheep and other animals. The main banking room in

219

220

the rear of the building was three stories high and covered with a skylight. It was reached by a grand hall decorated with Corinthian columns.

The bank was technologically advanded for its time. Iron was used for the entrance doors, bank counters and skylight shutters. A wrought- and cast-iron truss supported the roof of the banking room. The bank had the most up-to-date sanitary facilities and a complex heating and ventilation system, which changed the air in the building once an hour.

218 B
Leland Building, 1855
37–39 South 3rd St.
Stephen Button

The Leland Building is one of the best remaining examples of the 19th-century utilitarian commercial building. It was designed for Charles Leland, a prosperous merchant. The building was very unusual for its time. The plan was imaginatively organized around an inner court to provide light and increase the size of usable interior space. The building also contained the latest in plumbing, heating and lighting systems.

On the exterior, Button emphasized the height of the building by an unorthodox arrangement in which the horizontal spandrels are recessed behind plain pilasters, which rise uninterrupted to the top floor. Button eliminated most of the typical Italianate ornament, giving the facade a simple appearance. This approach found immediate favor and influenced commercial building throughout the decade.

219 B
Smythe Buildings, 1855–57
101–11 Arch St.
Renovated 1984, Hans P. Stein Architects

The introduction of cast-iron facades made it possible to achieve the architectural effects of the popular Italianate style on commercial buildings in an economical manner.

The facade of the Smythe Buildings is the best example of cast-iron design remaining in the city. The facade was produced by the Tiffany and Bottom Foundry in Trenton, New Jersey, and probably designed by a company draftsman. The building originally extended half a block, with a continuous facade composed of the delicate cast-iron columns and arched windows. In addition to its rich appearance at relatively low cost, cast iron appealed to the commercial developer because of the ease of construction and the large amount of window area relative to the structural support required for the facade. The middle section of the facade was demolished in 1913 to make room for a trolley turn-around. When the buildings were converted to apartments in 1984 this section was reconstructed in fiberglass using old section molds.

220 C,J
Academy of Music, 1855–57
232–46 South Broad St.
Napoleon LeBrun and Gustave Runge

Philadelphia's musical development was slow compared with other cities, partly because of the dominant Quaker conservatism. Musical entertainment was provided in small theaters and concert halls, but by the 1850s the public was eager for opera on a grand scale. A site for a concert hall was acquired on Broad Street, a largely undeveloped, quiet location.

The plan, selected by a competition, was modeled after La Scala, in Milan. LeBrun and Runge fashioned the interior like a huge barrel, excavating a well beneath the parquet, ballooning out the ceiling in a dome, placing a sounding board in the orchestra pit and curving the rear walls of the auditorium. To allow the walls to settle, the building stood for a year without a roof. When finished, the Academy was acoustically unsurpassed.

•
1854
*City consolidation
act passed*

•
1855
*Fairmount Park
started*

222

The neo-Baroque interior is one of the most lavish in the city. Huge Corinthian columns mark the proscenium, and an immense Victorian chandelier hangs from a ceiling decorated with murals by Karl Heinrich Schmolze. The Academy is the oldest musical auditorium in the country still serving its original purpose.

221   K
Pennsylvania Hospital for Mental and Nervous Diseases, 1856
111 North 49th St.
Samuel Sloan

In 1841, Pennsylvania Hospital moved its psychiatric patients to a rural 37-acre site in West Philadelphia, two miles beyond the city limits. The new facility was supervised by Dr. Thomas Kirkbride. Isaac Holden won the competition for the first building with a design based on the echelon plan, which used extended wings to isolate the separate wards of the hospital. It was the first example of the echelon plan in the country and was so successful that it became the model for many other facilities.

Sloan's design for a second building, to be used exclusively for male patients, duplicated Holden's plan. The large structure has a central pavilion flanked by two L-shaped wings with pedimented pavilions at the ends. The small dome over the central pavilion held iron tanks, which supplied water to the entire building. The east facade has a broad pediment and is faced with cut-stone. A granite Doric portico is the only decoration. The west facade is similar but is stucco and has a smaller portico.

Sloan was the most prominent hospital architect of the period. At his death he was credited with designing 32 hospitals for the insane and three general hospitals.

222   H   *PR*
Watson House, 1856
100 Summit St.

George Watson, a carriage maker, built one of the first suburban houses in Chestnut Hill following the introduction of rail service to the area. During the next 20 years, others followed his example, constructing similar homes along Summit Street. Watson's house is an imposing Italianate villa with a tower, or campanile. The house is set back from the street and built on high ground. It is stuccoed, as were many houses in the Italianate style. One of its distinguishing features is the bracketing under the eaves, which looks like icicles and recalls the brackets on Swiss chalets.

223   G   *PR*
Mitchell House, 1856
200 West Walnut Lane

Joseph G. Mitchell, a bank president, is said to have built four houses in Germantown. He lived in this one for two years, then sold it for a quick profit. The house has been considered the work of Samuel Sloan, but no documentary evidence supports this claim.

The Mitchell house is an example of the Gothic villa, a house type popularized by A. J. Downing. Gothic villas were designed to blend into their natural settings by harmonizing with the shapes of nature, where few things are ever symmetrical.

The house is built of Wissahickon schist. It has a projecting tower entrance that gives the facade a picturesque asymmetry. The gable roof is steeply pitched with decorated barge boards; the crenelated tower projecting above the roofline was usually reserved for grander Gothic villas. Typical Gothic hood or drip moldings of stone surround the window openings.

●
1856
First Republican
National Convention
held

●
1857
Academy of Music
opens

●
1858
Street grid extended
to entire city

227

224 K
St. Clement's Episcopal Church, 1855–59
20th and Cherry Sts.
John Notman

Real-estate developer William S. Wilson
provided the land and some money for St.
Clement's, hoping it would attract buyers
to the speculative houses he was building
nearby. Notman was both architect and contractor. He used brownstone and the
medieval Romanesque style, characterized
by round arched openings. This style was
less expensive to construct and more flexible
than the Gothic style. Notman maintained
the eastern orientation of the chancel by
placing the doorway in the middle of the
block and the chancel on the street facade.
He emphasized the round shape of the chancel by rounded, individual stones and the
sloped wall.

After 1870, a Lady Chapel was added,
with wrought-iron gates by Samuel Yellin.
Later, the floor and ceiling of the chancel
were raised and small Gothic lancet windows added on the second story. In 1929
the church was moved forty feet west to
allow for the widening of 20th Street. Over
three days, the 5,500-ton stone structure
was moved an inch at a time with no dam-
age to the building.

225 K
Church of the Holy Trinity, 1856–59
Walnut St. on Rittenhouse Sq.
John Notman

The Church of the Holy Trinity was built at
the same time as St. Clement's by the same
architect, in a similar style and with the
same brownstone building material. Holy
Trinity, however, has a more dramatic
facade, made possible by placing the chancel at the west, rather than in the traditional
eastern location.

The church was one of the first accurate
renditions of the Romanesque style in the
country. The three doorways are deeply re-

cessed and carved with geometric and
foliate designs in typical Romanesque fashion. A rose window dominates the third
story, and a massive tower adds picturesque
asymmetry. The interior is relatively simple,
in keeping with the simple service of the
Low Church, but it has beautiful stencil
work on the vaulted ceiling. In the 19th century, Holy Trinity had a fashionable following from the well-to-do families who lived
around Rittenhouse Square.

226 B
Bank of Pennsylvania, 1857–59
421 Chestnut St.
John M. Gries

When the Bank of Pennsylvania was
formed, it selected a site on Chestnut Street
near the city's other major financial institutions. Gries recently had completed the adjacent Farmers and Mechanics Bank and
designed this building in a similar Italianate
style. The bank is based upon Renaissance
palaces of Venice, a highly ornate version
of Italianate design that prefigured the Victorian love for richness of detail. Like the
Farmers and Mechanics Bank, this bank
also had a rear banking hall that was originally covered by a cast-iron dome, which
was demolished from 1892–93.

The bank failed during the financial panic
of 1857, when the building was only half
completed. It was finished by the subsequent owner, the Philadelphia Bank.

227 K OP
Burholme, 1859
Burholme Park, Cottman and Central Aves.
Restored 1983, Vitetta Group

Burholme is one of the finest Italianate villas in Philadelphia. Joseph W. Ryerss, a
railroad entrepreneur, built the mansion and
matching carriage house on an 85-acre estate, which he named after his ancestral estate in England. The name means "house in
a woodland setting."

228

229

Burholme is an extravagant example of the Italianate villa. The building is stone covered with stucco and is surrounded on three sides by a veranda. Its richness of detail is exemplified by the crowning belvedere, with stained-glass windows, added after 1888. During the Civil War, Burholme served as a station on the underground railroad, aiding runaway slaves. Later, Ryerss's sympathy for stray animals led to the founding of the Ryerss Infirmary for Dumb Animals. Some of his adopted pets are still buried on the grounds.

228   G   *OP*
Ebenezer Maxwell House, 1859
200 West Tulpehocken St.

The extension of the railroad to Germantown in 1832 initiated one of the first suburban developments in the country. Tulpehocken Street was opened in 1850 and soon filled with pretentious houses. One of the most striking was the Ebenezer Maxwell House, built for a prominent dry-goods merchant. The design has been variously attributed to J. C. Hoxie, Samuel Sloan and an unknown carpenter-builder. The mansion is an early masterpiece of the eclectic tradition, skillfully blending elements of the French Renaissance, Gothic, and Italianate styles. Maxwell was a speculative developer, who built this house and three others on the street to be sold for profit. Much of the exterior woodwork is painted to look like stone. On the interior, inexpensive wood is grained to look like oak or mahogany, and the slate mantelpieces look like marble.

The house, in danger of demolition in the 1960s, was saved by Maxwell Mansion, Inc. It has converted the mansion into a museum, and the grounds have been replanted according to the principles of A. J. Downing, America's leading landscape architect in the 1850s.

229   J
Lit Brothers, 1859–1907
Market St., 7th to 8th Sts.
Collins and Autenreith; Renovated 1989, Burt Hill Kosar Rittlemann and John Milner Associates

By 1859, commercial development along Market Street had extended to the 800 block. Among the businesses were the J. M. Maris Co., a dry-goods company located in a modern five-story structure, and the J. B. Lippincott publishing company.

In 1891, the Lit family opened a small shop specializing in women's clothes at the corner of 8th and Market streets. Their advertising techniques were so successful that within a few years they established one of the city's largest retail stores. Between 1895 and 1907 they purchased the entire block and added the two large buildings at either end, designed to blend with the Renaissance style of the Maris, Lippincott and Bailey buildings.

The Lit Brothers store is the only complete block of Victorian commercial architecture in the city. The use of a common window unit with a classical arch and a single painted color creates the appearance of a single building with a cast-iron facade. There are several buildings, however, of which only the facade at 719–21 is cast iron. The others are brick with marble or granite sheathing on the front. The two end buildings with octagonal towers are brick with terra-cotta and galvanized iron trim.

After the store closed in 1977, the buildings were in danger of demolition for many years. A vigorous public campaign for preservation and the efforts of a local developer, Growth Properties, led to the renovation of the buildings for offices and stores.

230

231

230 K *PR*
1500–2300 Blocks of Green St., 1860–90

Green Street's principal growth occurred after the extension of the street railway system, when wealthy industrialists were building mansions along North Broad Street. This encouraged speculative builders to create high-quality row houses nearby for the rising managerial middle class.

By the end of the century, the row houses were joined by more elaborate houses of well-to-do industrialists. The grandest of these is the Kemble-Bergdoll Mansion. Other notable examples are 2223, designed by Willis Hale, with an unusual facade of brick enlivened by multicolored ceramic tile; 2220, a Romanesque revival house with a corner tower; and 2301, also designed by Hale. All were owned by the Fleisher family, wealthy textile manufacturers, who have lived in the area for three generations. The handsome brownstones at 2144–46 Green, with the ribbon carved in stone over the doorway, are attributed to Wilson Eyre. The generous brownstone at 1901–3 has been attributed to The Wilson Brothers. The house at 1708–10 is thought to be the work of Hale, and the distinctive, exuberant Queen Anne–style house at 1533 Green has been attributed to John Fraser.

There are also two notable churches on the street: the Romanesque Revival Lutheran church in the 1500 block, designed by Stephen Button, and St. Francis of Xavier Catholic Church in the 2300 block, a later and richer example of the Romanesque style, designed by the prominent church architect E. F. Durang.

231 F,J *PR*
Woodland Terrace, 1861
Samuel Sloan
500–520 Woodland Ter.

West Philadelphia also developed after the extension of the street railway system. Speculative builders created housing for the affluent middle class, who sought to escape the dense urban environment of the city.

The houses on Woodland Terrace were designed as Italianate villas. Because they were built as twins on narrow lots, they were more vertical in their massing than individual houses. A special feature of these houses is the terrace, or garden plot, separating the house from the street. Woodland Terrace is probably the best preserved example of this type of housing in the city. The most expensive and picturesque houses were placed at either end of the block, where they were most visible. They are built of stone, and each is graced with a curving Corinthian-columned porch and prominent tower. The houses on the interior of the block are built of stucco or brownstone and have a simpler appearance.

---

232 K
St. Timothy's Protestant Episcopal Church, 1862–66
5720 Ridge Ave.
Emlen T. Littell/Charles Burns

St. Timothy's is a handsome, country parish church set within a walled churchyard. It was designed in the High Victorian Gothic style and built in stages over 23 years. The gable-roofed sanctuary was designed by Littell, a New York church architect. The corner tower, added in 1871, has terra-cotta battlements similar to those on the Penn Library, suggesting it may have been designed by Furness. In 1874 the nave was extended and the parish house begun. These were further extended in 1885 by Charles Burns, architect of the Church of the Advocate.

● *1863*
*Olmstead designs
Central Park, New
York*

● *1863*
Abolition of slavery

● *1865*
*Lincoln's body lies
in state at
Independence Hall*

234

In spite of the many additions, the church appears to be a single design. Common materials unify the composition. Uncoursed ashlar, interlaced with rose-colored mortar, and brick string courses are the dominant materials. Particularly noteworthy are the hipped roof of red and gray slate shingles, the terra-cotta battlements on the clerestory tower and the bell tower, which is decorated with brick corbels and scalloped louvers.

The intimately scaled interior has a hammer-beam ceiling, delicate stenciled designs on the nave walls and an imposing pre-Raphaelite mosaic behind the altar.

233 F *PR*
William Montelius House, 1863–65
223 South 42nd St.
John D. Jones, builder

The Montelius House was built by John D. Jones, a speculative real-estate developer and builder. He constructed a group of houses on the east side of 42nd Street, which was the western edge of development until the end of the 19th century.

The Montelius House, named for the coal-shipping merchant who first owned it, is an Italianate villa similar to other suburban houses of the period in West Philadelphia and Chestnut Hill. It is made of brownstone rather than stucco, has a columned porch topped by a balustrade and a handsome corner tower.

The Second Empire Style

The Second Empire style was based on the monumental buildings constructed in Paris during the reign of Napoleon III. The style of these buildings was copied throughout Europe and introduced into the United States in the 1860s. In this country, the Second Empire style was closely associated with large public buildings, such as federal office buildings, post offices, courthouses and city halls.

The chief characteristic of the style is the mansard roof with dormer windows of all shapes and sizes, which permitted the attic to become a usable floor. Larger buildings have projecting pavilions in the center or at the corners and such heavily embellished classical elements as pediments, balustrades or windows flanked by paired columns. Residences are less decorative but always retain the mansard roof.

234 C,J
Union League of Philadelphia, 1864–65
140 South Broad St.
John Fraser

The Union League was one of many political clubs organized during the Civil War years. It was an outgrowth of the Union Club, organized by a group of aristocrats to raise funds and recruit troops for the Union cause. By 1865, the League had a membership of several thousand.

The brick and brownstone building was one of the few buildings erected in Philadelphia during the Civil War. It is an early example of the Second Empire style, which was to reach full Victorian exuberance in the City Hall. The design includes a mansard roof—the distinguishing characteristic of the Second Empire style—dormer windows, projecting pavilions and a monumental stairway. The original ornamental iron roof trim and asymmetrical tower were removed during the 1920s.

The large annex to the rear was added by Horace Trumbauer from 1909–11. Its formal Renaissance design is a startling contrast to the main building.

•
1865
*John Stetson begins
hat business*

•
1866
*Hires invents root
beer*

•
1867
*First merry-go-round
operated in U.S.*

236

235 K
Philadelphia Saving Fund Society,
1868–69/1897–98
700–710 Walnut St.
Addison Hutton/Furness Evans
and Company

For their second headquarters, PSFS sponsored a design competition, which was won by the firm of Sloan and Hutton. The building established the career of Hutton, who completed the design after his partnership with Sloan dissolved. It is a fine example of an Italianate bank, constructed of brick with granite ashlar facing. The flat roof is surrounded by a balustrade, and there are two round arched entrances on the facade.

The building was expanded by Hutton from 1885–86 and again by Furness from 1897–98. Subsequent interior alterations included work by Howe and Lescaze from 1929–31.

236 C *OP*
Masonic Temple, 1868–73/1890s
1 North Broad St.
James Windrim/George Herzog

Freemasonry prospered in Philadelphia from colonial times, despite the rise of anti-Masonic sentiment during the early 19th century. Several temples were built, culminating in this magnificent structure, one of the world's greatest Masonic temples.

The Masons held a competition and selected Brother James Windrim, a 27-year-old freemason, as the winner. Windrim's design was modeled on a medieval style known as Norman. This is reflected in the massive carved doorway that projects from the wall; the ashlar stone work; the fortresslike towers; and the corbel tables, a round-arch decorated cornice under the roofline. Many of the granite blocks for the temple weighed as much as six tons.

The temple took five years to build. The interior design was begun 14 years later and took 15 more years to complete. George Herzog, who had trained in the royal workshops of Ludwig I of Munich, was the primary designer. The spectacular interior spaces include seven lodge halls, each lavishly decorated in a specific style. The most renowned is the Egyptian Hall, replete with accurate hieroglyphics. The temple was one of the first buildings in the city to be lighted by electricity.

237 K *PR*
2000–2100 Blocks of Spruce St., 1868–80

Brownstone became a popular building material because it was cheap, attractive and easily carved. Many brownstone houses were built prior to 1880, when it was discovered that the stone fell apart over time. The brownstones on these two blocks are fine examples of the many found in the Rittenhouse Square area. They show the influence of the Second Empire style in the use of mansard roofs and round-headed windows with keystones and framing pilasters.

In addition to brownstones, the 2100 block has several houses by prominent architects. The house at 2111–13 was designed by Furness. Wilson Eyre designed 2123–25, an elegant Colonial Revival house. The unusual double house at 2132–34, attributed to Furness, is notable for its giant brownstone arch and pressed metal ornament. A colorful note is added to the block by the facade of 2129, which was resurfaced with Mercer tile in 1913.

At the corner of 21st and Spruce streets are four of the finest Victorian row houses in the city. The three brick houses were designed by George Hewitt, of which 2100 Spruce, built in 1883 for Lucien Moss, is the most interesting.

237

239

The High Victorian Gothic Style

*High Victorian Gothic reached its peak of
popularity in England in the 1860s. The
development of this style was influenced by
the writings of John Ruskin, a prominent
art historian and architectural critic. Ruskin
advocated the use of color on buildings,
emanating from the natural color of building materials. He directed attention to the
buildings of Venice, in contrast to the exclusively English medieval base of the early
Gothic Revival. Architects designing in this
style were not so much concerned with
beauty as with forceful character.*

*The High Victorian Gothic style was
popular in the United States after the Civil
War. The buildings of Philadelphia architect
Frank Furness are among the finest examples of this style in the country.*

*High Victorian Gothic is very colorful in
its use and combinations of materials. Two
kinds of stone are often used in the same
wall: brickwork is banded with stone, usually pink or gray granite or limestone, and
combined with terra-cotta panels. Brick is
laid in many patterns and textures, with
heavy ornamentation. Rooflines are broken
by a profusion of dormer windows, often
giving buildings a top-heavy appearance.*

---

238 K

Second Presbyterian Church, 1869–72/
1900
2036 Walnut St.
Henry Sims/Frank Furness

The Presbyterians kept pace with the westward development of the city, erecting new
churches as fashionable neighborhoods expanded. They were always designed in the
latest style, making it possible to trace the
history of 19th-century church architecture
through a chronology of Presbyterian
churches.

Second Presbyterian was the most socially prominent. It was a major landmark
in a neighborhood of fashionable homes
designed by Chandler, Trumbauer and Cope
and Stewardson. Sims, a founder of the
Philadelphia AIA chapter, designed the
church in the High Victorian Gothic style.
This differs from the early Gothic Revival
in its grander scale, bulkier details and proportions, flamboyant decoration and mixed
use of materials—brownstone, with granite
trim. The tower and addition to the chapel
were designed by Furness in 1900.

---

239 E

University of Pennsylvania, College Hall,
1871–72
Locust Walk, between 34th and 35th Sts.
Thomas W. Richards

In 1870 the university decided to move from
Ninth and Market streets to the Hamilton
estate in West Philadelphia. A competition
was held to select a design for the first
building to house the Collegiate and Scientific departments. It was won by Richards,
an instructor in mechanical drawing, who
had worked for Samuel Sloan and placed
second in the Academy of Fine Arts competition. The trustees were so pleased by College Hall that they promoted him to profes-
sor and asked him to design three more
buildings.

College Hall set the standard for Collegiate Gothic design on campus. The exterior is characterized by a picturesque
massing of volumes, which once included
towers and pinnacles. In typical late Gothic
fashion, a variety of contrasting surface materials is used, including a brownstone base,
cornices and gables of Ohio stone, polished
red granite columns and walls of green ser-
pentine ashlar stone.

241

---

240 B
**Pennsylvania Company for Insurances
on Lives and Granting Annuities,** 1871–73
431 Chestnut St.
Addison Hutton

This building is the last remaining post–
Civil War banking structure on Bank Row.
It was built at the same time as Frank Furness's two flamboyant banks on the same
block, both of which have been demolished.
The squat columns at the third-floor windows are reminiscent of Furness's style and
may have been influenced by his neighboring buildings. In contrast to early banks,
Hutton placed the main banking room in the
front, with light entering through a vaulted
ceiling from skylights above.

---

241 C,J *OP*
Pennsylvania Academy of the Fine Arts,
1872–76
See page 65.

---

242 C,J *OP*
City Hall, 1871–1901
See page 67.

243 K
Dobson Carpet Mills, 1872–73
4041 Ridge Ave.

From 1870 to 1900, Philadelphia was one of
the country's largest industrial centers. Factories and mills were developed throughout
the city. Many located in Falls of the
Schuylkill, of which Dobson's Mill is the
only one still standing.

James Dobson and his brother emigrated
from England in 1854. They established
their first mill at Ridge Avenue and Wissahickon Creek, where they made woolen
blankets for the Union army. When it was
demolished to extend Fairmount Park, a
new mill complex was built on Scott's
Lane.

Dobson's mill was one of the largest textile complexes in the city. The main building
is patterned after English factories of the
same period. It is made of closely laid stone
blocks, with brick jack-arches above the
windows. Spinning, weaving, combing,
carding and spooling took place in the main
building, while adjacent buildings were used
for a printing yarn room, coloring and dye-
ing. Dobson's complex closed in 1927. Portions of the complex were renovated for
apartments in 1991, by Cassaway Albert
and Associates.

241

241 C,J *OP*
Pennsylvania Academy of the Fine Arts,
1872–76
Broad and Cherry Sts.
Furness and Hewitt: Restored 1976,
Day and Zimmermann Associates

The academy, founded in 1805, was the first art school and museum in the country. Its most famous student was Thomas Eakins, who became a dominating presence as a teacher from 1876–86. Originally located at 10th and Chestnut streets, the academy moved to Broad Street after the start of the new City Hall. The new building was planned as part of the 1876 Centennial. The building committee wanted a two-story, fire-proof building with two entrances: one for students and one for the public. Students' rooms were to be on the first floor, with skylighted galleries on the second floor, accessible by a main stairway.

The academy is the most outstanding example of Furness's work and one of the most magnificent Victorian buildings in the country. In contrast to the somber tones of previous Victorian architecture, the interior is an explosion of color: the walls have gilt floral patterns incised on a field of Venetian red; the cerulean blue ceiling is sprinkled with silver stars; the gallery walls are plum, ochre, sand and olive green. Furness's work is characterized by overscaled and unusually proportioned structural details and the extensive use of carved floral patterns. These can be seen throughout the interior in the form of cast-bronze foliation along the stair rail,

compressed iron columns in the galleries and the use of dwarf columns supporting massive arches. In answer to the building committee's fireproofing specifications, Furness laced the building together with brick, stone and iron. Some of the I-beams and columns were left exposed, making this an early example of expressed iron construction.

The facade is an amalgam of historical styles, fused in an aggressively personal manner. The pointed arches, floral ornament and use of color are derived from English Gothic design, while the mansard roof, projecting central pavilion and panels of incised tryglyphs come from French sources. This riot of forms is executed in rusticated brownstone, dressed sandstone, polished pink granite, red pressed brick and purplish terra-cotta.

For many decades the academy was considered to be an unattractive building, and its ornamental brilliance was obscured. A comprehensive restoration in 1976 returned the building to its original appearance.

244

242

244   K
Victory Building, 1873−75
1001 Chestnut St.
Henry Fernback

The Victory Building, a branch office of the
New York Life Insurance Company, was
the first commercial building in the city designed in the Second Empire style. Originally the building was three stories high
with a mansard roof. When it was enlarged,
the mansard roof was removed and then set
back in place after three floors were added.
A balustrade on the facade marks the division between the old and the new. The lower
three stories are richly textured with classical pilasters and columns; the upper floors
are more restrained.

The building was designed to be fireproof.
The exterior is faced in granite, and the interior has iron posts and girders and iron
frames around the windows and doors. The
windows also had iron shutters. The corridors were lavishly outfitted with ornate ironwork and marble, making the Victory Building an elegant office building for its time.

245   K
Ridgway Library, 1873−78
901 South Broad St.
Addison Hutton

In 1727, Benjamin Franklin organized a club
known as the Junto, whose members met in
taverns to discuss scientific, social and
moral issues. Their discussions led to
Franklin's proposal for the Library Company, the country's first subscription library.
Its first permanent building was at Fifth and
Chestnut streets.

Dr. James Rush, a leading physician and
one of the company's directors, bequeathed
a million dollars for the construction of a
new library, to be named after his wife,
Phoebe Ridgway. The Library Company
raised strong objections to the proposed site
on South Broad Street, despite the assur-
ances of Rush's executors that the continued
southward expansion of the city would guar-

antee a central location for the library. Not
only did this vision fail to materialize, but
from the outset the new building presented
practical problems.

Although Hutton chose the Parthenon as
his model, he abandoned its graceful elegance for a pompous and forbidding assem-
blage of pedimented porticos, heavy columns, blank ashlar walls and hard-edged
details. The resulting tomblike structure
was impossible to heat. When the Library
Company moved to Locust Street, in 1964,
it sold the building to the city for use as a
neighborhood recreation center.

The Beaux-Arts Style

*The École des Beaux-Arts, in Paris, was
the world's preeminent architectural school
in the late 19th and early 20th centuries. Its
curriculum required students to work in the
studio of an architect, developing designs
for hypothetical projects of monumental
scale. Emphasis was placed on the study of
Greek and Roman structures and on drawing and rendering skills. The best students
were awarded the Grand Prix de Rome,
which allowed them to continue to study in
Rome for three additional years. Many
prominent American architects studied at
the École or worked for someone who did.
Their designs for large-scale public buildings, such as libraries, railroad stations,
museums and exhibition halls, reflected the
enormous impact of Beaux-Arts training.*

*Beaux-Arts classicism is characterized by
the use of paired columns on the facade,
monumental flights of stairs and the use of
figurative sculpture on the facade and along
the roofline. Buildings are symmetrical in
plan, with clearly expressed central bays
and supporting wings.*

242

City Hall, 1871–1901
Broad and Market Sts.
John McArthur, Jr., with Thomas U. Walter;
Alexander Milne Calder, sculptor

Penn set aside Center Square as a site for public buildings, but it was not used as such until the city expanded westward, justifying the relocation of the city hall from Independence Square. City Hall is the largest municipal building in the country and the finest example of the Second Empire style. It contains 14½ acres of floor space, occupied by city and county offices, courtrooms and several ornately detailed public spaces.

The building is organized around a central public courtyard, which is reached through monumental arched portals on all four sides. Second Empire motifs are combined with an abundance of sculpture to give the exterior a rich yet intimately scaled appearance. Among the most prominent features are the projecting corner pavilions; the towered pavilions over the entrance portals; the mansard roof with dormers, connected to one another by curved frames; and the large-scale paired columns, which help to make the building's eight stories look like three. Solid granite, 22 feet thick in some portions, forms the first floor and supports a brick structure faced with white marble.

Calder created all the sculpture on the building. There are groups of figures representing the seasons, continents, arts and science, as well as allegorical figures, heads and masks. Calder also designed the 27-ton cast-iron statue of Penn atop the tower, which is the largest single piece of sculpture on any building in the world. The 548-foot tower is the world's tallest masonry structure without a steel frame. It is granite up to the clock, then cast iron painted to look like stone.

Public spaces within the building are among the most lavish in the city. The City Council chamber is larger than the House of Lords in London; it is ornately detailed and uses such expensive materials as alabaster on the walls. The Mayor's Reception Room is extremely handsome; it has a blue and gold ceiling, beautiful woodwork and red Egyptian marble columns. Conversation Hall, restored to its original elegance by Day and Zimmermann Associates in 1982, is dominated by a magnificent chandelier. John Ord, chief architect from 1890–94, is thought to have been responsible for much of the interior detailing. Other notable features are the octagonal cut-stone staircases in each of the four corners and the Supreme Court Room, which was designed by George Herzog.

The tower is open to the public and affords a wonderful view of the city.

● **1874**
Blue Law bans
Sunday liquor sales

● **1875**
Thomas Eakins paints
The Gross Clinic

246

247

---

246 D
Memorial Hall, 1874–76
West Fairmount Park
Hermann Schwarzmann

In 1876, the Centennial Exposition of the United States was held in Philadelphia. The exposition displayed the achievements of the industrial era at a time when Philadelphia was the country's leading industrial city. When the original building designs proved too costly, Schwarzmann, an engineer with Fairmount Park who had never designed a building, was sent to Vienna to study the 1873 Exhibition. On his return, he designed five of the exposition buildings.

Memorial Hall, the principal building of the exposition, is an excellent example of Beaux-Arts design. The facade contains three colossal, arched doorways that open onto a central exhibit space, which is covered by a glass and cast-iron dome topped by a bell tower. The dome was originally lit with gas jets to glow at night, an effect that has recently been recreated. In the Beaux-Arts tradition sculptural figures were placed along the skyline; the statue on top of the dome is of Columbia holding a laurel wreath.

Memorial Hall was the Pennsylvania Art Museum until the city's Art Museum opened in 1926. It influenced the design of many other museums in this country, including the Metropolitan Museum in New York, and was one of the first American buildings to be influential in Europe. It was a model for the German parliament building, designed in 1882.

247 J
Ridge Avenue Farmers' Market, 1875
1810 Ridge Ave.
Davis E. Supplee

Farmers markets have been a tradition in Philadelphia since colonial days. Open markets were gradually replaced by market houses, of which the Ridge Avenue market is a rare, surviving example. The market, originally the commercial focus of its middle-class neighborhood, remained in continuous use until the 1960s.

The building was designed in the High Victorian Gothic style by an architect about whom little is known. Many of its features led to a mistaken attribution of the market to Furness. The building has a steep jerkinhead roof, pointed arched windows, and brick walls, coursed with polychrome and molded brick on a rusticated brownstone base. The interior features an open trusswork ceiling and cast-iron piers.

---

248 C,J
Pennsylvania Institution for the Deaf and Dumb, 1875
320 South Broad St.
Furness and Hewitt

Fifty years after the completion of Haviland's building for the Pennsylvania Institute for the Deaf and Dumb, Furness designed an addition on the 15th Street side that more than doubled its size. It is a fine example of Furness's mature work in the Victorian Gothic style. Patterns in the brickwork produce contrasts of texture and shadow, while the placement of chimneys, gables and dormers results in a rich clustering of forms. The Philadelphia College of Art, originally the Pennsylvania Museum School and now the University of the Arts, has occupied the building since 1893.

● **1876**
Centennial Exposition opens;
First telephone demonstrated

● **1877**
John Wanamaker opens
new-style department
store

249

251

249 K *PR*
Thomas Hockley House, 1875/1894
235 South 21st St.
Frank Furness

Thomas Hockley, an influential lawyer, was
an early supporter of Frank Furness. He
assisted Furness in obtaining commissions
for a number of his later buildings. Furness
designed this house when he was just
emerging as a leading architect.

The house has the standard Victorian
forms, such as the mansard roof, pointed
dormers and projecting bay window. But
the ornament and the variety of brick patterns is distinctively Furness. There are variations of cut, pressed, diapered and diago-
nally laid brick; string-courses and stepped
corbels; and a blunt-headed chimney, which
seems to grow out of the wall from corbeled
stems. The oversized, formalized flower
designs in the porch tympanums resemble
Furness's use of similar motifs on the facade
of the Pennsylvania Academy.

The use of brickwork to create rich textures and patterns was copied in many other
houses of the period.

250 E,J
Centennial Bank, 1876
32nd and Market Sts.
Frank Furness

The Centennial Exposition sparked a building boom in West Philadelphia. The site of
the Pennsylvania Railroad's main depot, at
32nd and Market streets, was a key intersection. Of the many commercial buildings in
that area, only the Centennial Bank remains.

The bank is characteristic of Furness's
style. The symmetry of the facade is emphasized by a projecting bay with hip roof
that is penetrated by a window stack, which
terminates in a crocketed gable. The facade
includes all the typical Furness devices:
squat columns, pointed windows, oversized
ornamentation and decorative patterns of
cut and pressed red brick. Although less
colorful than some of his other designs, the

exterior uses the unusual glass tiles also
found at the Pennsylvania Academy. Furness devised the glass tile to give permanent, vivid color to the facade. Light pene-
trates the painted tile to a backing of gold
and silver foil, whose reflective properties
intensify the color. The interior of the bank
was brilliantly colored and lit by skylights.

251 K
Kensington National Bank, 1877
Frankford and Girard Aves.
Frank Furness

Furness designed many banks throughout
the city, most of which have been demolished. This is the only remaining one
still in use as a bank. The stonework and
projecting central bay, which corbels out
over the entrance, are similar to his other
buildings but more subdued. Also typical of
his style are the incised geometric floral patterns, the ironwork and variety of textures
in the materials. The design is unusual because of its incorporation of classical details
based on an ornamental style developed in
France in the 1840s, which Furness may
have acquired from his teacher, Richard
Morris Hunt. The original interior, of which
nothing remains, was brilliantly colored
and lit through a coved iron ceiling.

252 J
Church of the Gesu, 1879–88
18th and Stiles Sts.
Edwin F. Durang; Exterior Restored 1991,
John Blatteau Associates

When St. Joseph's College outgrew its
original quarters, the Jesuit fathers decided
to create a grand church and ecclesiastical
college in North Philadelphia. Father Bur-
chard Villeger directed the move. A chapel
and rectory were built in 1868, but as the
surrounding area developed, a new church
was required. Villeger decided to model the
church after the Gesu in Rome, and hired

1878
First telephone book
published

1879
First Salvation Army
corps in U.S.
organized

1880
Abner Doubleday
invents baseball

253

254

Durang, who had designed the chapel and was the foremost architect of Catholic churches of the time.

The church has a breathtaking scale and magnificent sanctuary, reminiscent of Baroque churches of Europe. The most notable aspect of the church is the interior space. The enormous nave, once the widest unobstructed nave in the country, is covered by a barrel vault, which spans 76 feet and rises to a height of 72 feet over the altar. It is then topped by an aspidial dome. The rich interior decoration includes gilded plaster in the nave coffers and monumental sculptured figures in the nave and galleries.

The exterior reflects the Second Empire style through the use of superimposed classical orders and heavy sculptural ornament.

---

253 K *PR*
William H. Rhawn House (Knowlton),
1879–81
8001 Verree Rd.
Frank Furness

Furness designed this unusual rural retreat for Rhawn, a banker, who was one of his early patrons. The house was built on a 12-acre hilltop site purchased from the estate of Isaac Livezey. It is one of Furness's few remaining suburban designs.

Furness based the complex design on the domestic Queen Anne style, which was compatible with his interest in irregular forms and eccentric detail. Sheds, jerkinhead dormers, arched gables, verandas, carved chimneys and bracketed balconies are standard Queen Anne features. The walls are faced with slate, frame clapboards and fieldstone, which was quarried on the grounds.

The interior has been altered, but still preserves the original stained glass, light fixtures and elegant woodwork. The woodwork in the stairhall shows the influence of Charles Lock Eastlake and the geometric designs of Japanese woodcuts, which Furness might have seen at the Centennial Exposition.

254 C
A. J. Holman Factory, 1881
1222–26 Arch St.
The Wilson Brothers

Bibles have been published continuously in Philadelphia since 1743, when Christopher Saur of Germantown printed a German bible, the second bible published in America. Andrew J. Holman formed his bible publishing company in 1872 with two members of the renowned William J. Harding Company, with which he had trained. Within a decade Holman's company had outgrown its headquarters.

The new building is one of the few commercial loft buildings of the period that has been well preserved in its original form. The facade is faced with brick. It is more embellished than the Leland Building, but is still restrained compared with the ornamental treatment of The Wilson Brothers' other projects, such as the nearby Reading Terminal.

---

255 H
Gravers Lane Station, 1883
Gravers Lane near Stenton Ave.
Frank Furness

When the Philadelphia and Reading Railroad extended commuter rail service to northwest Philadelphia in the 1870s and 1880s, Frank Furness designed many of its commuter stations. This is the only surviving example. The building has a simple rectangular plan, with waiting rooms on the first floor and the station manager's residence above. Its complicated appearance is created by a porte cochere jutting out to the rear, a shed porch extending over the platform and a conical ticket tower, which terminates in a complex grouping of shed and gable dormers. The apparently awkward proportions, contrasting materials and the heavy brackets and trusses are characteristic of Furness's work. The station was restored in 1982 and painted with its original cream and brown colors.

1881
*Electric street
lighting introduced*

1882
*Walt Whitman's
Leaves of Grass
published in city*

1883
*Phillies baseball
team founded*

255

257

The Queen Anne Style

*The Queen Anne style was developed by the
English architect Richard Norman Shaw.
He was inspired by older, rural structures
built during the transitional period when
Georgian motifs were overlaid on medieval
forms. Shaw's work was published extensively in architectural journals and greatly
admired in the United States.*

*The style was introduced in this country
in two staff residences built by the British
government for the 1876 Centennial. These
buildings were notable for their picturesque
qualities and lightness, in comparison with
the heavy-handed Victorian Gothic style.*

*The Queen Anne style is characterized by
the use of contrasting materials: brick or
stone on the first floor, with stucco, shingles
or horizontal paneling above. Large medieval chimneys, often made of molded brick,
are common. Bay windows or projecting
bays are used to break up the massing of
the houses, which are topped with gables or
high-gabled roofs.*

---

256 H *PR*

Anglecot, 1883/1910
Evergreen Ave. and Prospect St.
Wilson Eyre;
Renovated 1983, Greg Woodring and
Associates

Anglecot was built for Charles Adam Potter,
a manufacturer of oil cloth and linoleum,
and so named because of its angle to the
street. It was designed in the Queen Anne
style by Eyre when he was 25. The Queen
Anne style favored by American architects
was based on colonial design, particularly
early buildings in New England.

Anglecot was altered by Eyre a number
of times. Many original details are gone,
but some typical Queen Anne motifs remain, such as the corbeled chimneys, the
broad gables across the front and the whimsical eyelid dormer window in the attic.
Eyre's interest in seaside resort buildings is
reflected in the informal plan and the way
the house appears to ramble over the site.

The interior contains a living hall, a room
that combines the function of the hall and
staircase with that of a living room, complete with fireplace and built-in sitting area.
The house has been subdivided and converted to condominiums.

---

257 H

Wissahickon Inn, 1884
500 West Willow Grove Ave.
G. W. and W. D. Hewitt

The Wissahickon Inn was built by Henry
Howard Houston, a shipping executive and
financier. Houston used his influence as director of the Pennsylvania Railroad to have
service extended on the west side of Germantown Avenue, where his real-estate
holdings were located. He built the inn as a
vacation spot for city dwellers, whom he
hoped would be encouraged to purchase
houses he was building in Chestnut Hill.

Hewitt had worked with Notman and Furness before opening a firm with his brother
William. They were the principal architects
for all of Houston's work. The inn was designed in the picturesque Queen Anne style.
It had 250 rooms and was completely surrounded by a generous porch. The exterior
woodwork is particularly rich, with sun-
flower relief panels on the corner bay windows and half-timbered dormers. The windows on the upper floors are typical of the
Queen Anne style, with a large lower pane
and small upper panes.

The inn became the home of Chestnut
Hill Academy in 1898.

---

258 G

St. Vincent's Parish Hall, 1884
109 E. Price St.
Victor Briannd de Morainville

St. Vincent's is the oldest Catholic parish in
Germantown. By the mid-19th century, the
importance and growth of the parish was
reflected in the construction of a large,
Italianate church completed in 1851. The
dome, added in 1857, is a prominent
landmark.

●
1883
Ladies Home
Journal *first*
published

●
1884
*First steel-frame
skyscraper built in
Chicago*

●
1884
*First black
newspaper started*

258

260

Briannd de Morainville, a member of the
parish, was a civil engineer who supervised
construction for the Reading Railroad, including buildings by Furness. His design
for the parish hall is a distinctive example
of High Victorian Gothic design, obviously
influenced by Furness. The main facade is
divided into three bays reflecting the interior
plan, where a central stair leads to the large
auditorium. The steeply pitched pyramidal
roof over the western bay, corner turret,
pressed-metal cornice and arched windows
enrich the design, but the side facade is even
more dramatic. Three very large, wide dormers with steep gables add to the complexity of the roofline, and the wall is broken
into several surfaces, with strong horizontal
bands of trim similar to those of the main
facade. The building is stucco, lined to look
like stone, with terra-cotta and wood trim.

259　E

Tabernacle Presbyterian Church,
1884–86
3700 Chestnut St.
Theophilus Parsons Chandler; Renovated
1988, Hugh Zimmers and Associates

The Tabernacle Presbyterian Church was
once the center of a wealthy neighborhood
and had a sizable congregation. The church
was designed in the English Decorated
Gothic style, a favorite of Chandler's,
which is characterized by profuse decoration. The heavily rusticated exterior of the
church is detailed in precise Gothic terms,
as evidenced by the corbel tables around the
cornice and above the second stage of the
tower, the elaborate window tracery and the
multiple pinnacles and gables. The interior
contains an outstanding hammer-beamed
ceiling decorated with wood-carved flying
angels bearing shields.

The growth of the University of Pennsylvania and changes in adjacent neighborhoods reduced the size of the supporting
congregation. The church has been converted to a theater without altering either
its exterior or interior character.

260　K

First Unitarian Church, 1885–86
2125 Chestnut St.
Furness, Evans and Company

The Reverend William Henry Furness was
instrumental in having his son selected to
design a new church for his growing congregation. Furness created a two-story,
cruciform structure with gable-roofed nave
and transept. The exterior of the church has
been significantly altered. The massive carriage porch has been removed. The south
porch, decorated with carved ferns, sur-
vives, but the original rough-face stonework
has been smoothed.

The interior of the church has fared better.
The sanctuary is covered with an elaborate
hammer-beam ceiling, composed of iron
rods and wood timbers. Skylights along the
ridge illuminated the sanctuary, but these
are now covered. Simple wood wainscoting
surrounds the plaster walls, which were
painted cerulean blue. The ceiling is painted
a rust red and stenciled with gold-leaf daf-
fodils, one of the few remaining stenciled
designs by Furness. The oak pews and chancel area are also notable, especially the
carved altar and reading desk.

261　H　*PR*

Houston-Sauveur House, 1885
8205 Seminole Ave.
G. W. and W. D. Hewitt

Henry Howard Houston built close to one
hundred houses within a few years after the
Pennsylvania Railroad opened its Chestnut
Hill line. Houston wanted control over his
neighborhood, so rather than make an immediate profit on cheap housing, he built
fashionable, solid and substantial houses
both for sale and to rent.

This house was originally rented, then
sold to Louis Sauveur. It is a magnificent
example of the Queen Anne suburban
house. The design contains typical medieval
motifs, such as the steeply pitched roof and
half-timbered gables. These are enhanced

261

262

by classical details, including a swan's-neck pediment over the second floor and a Palladian-style window on the front. The house is built of several materials, principally rough-textured stone and wood shingles, and is distinguished by a generous double-decked porch surrounded by delicate railings.

262　H　*PR*
Druim Moir and Brinkwood, 1885–86
West Willow Grove Ave.
G. W. and W. D. Hewitt; Renovated 1982, DACP Associates

Henry Howard Houston was once the largest single landholder in Philadelphia. His estate, Druim Moir, which means "great crag" in Gaelic, was set on 55 acres of virgin woods.

The house was designed to look like a Scottish baronial castle. It has heavy stone walls of Wissahickon schist, projecting bays and a massive porte cochere. Druim Moir was substantially altered in the early 1940s by Robert McGoodwin, who removed turrets, gables and some floors to make the house easier to maintain.

Houston also built a more informal house for his son. Brinkwood was executed in the shingle style. The basement is coursed in Wissahickon schist, while the two stories above are sheathed with stained cedar shingles, staggered to create a checkerboard pattern. A dentil molding along the eaves and some of the woodwork on the porches draw on 18th-century classical details.

Like many large estates, Druim Moir became too expensive to maintain as a single family residence. Its subsequent development is a model for saving large houses on large estates. The main house was converted to three attached houses without altering the exterior appearance. New houses, designed in a revival style, based on early 20th century houses in the area, are grouped together, leaving half the estate undeveloped and in common ownership.

263　K　*PR*
Houses for a Moravian Community,
1885–89
1600 St. Paul St., corner Rowan St.

William F. Shaw, a devout Moravian, built these houses for the small Moravian community in the Nicetown section of Philadelphia. Shaw was a transplanted Englishman, and he wanted the development to look like a cozy English village. He chose the Queen Anne style, simplifying its normally complex shapes but retaining the picturesque tower, steep gables and front porches. As a further amenity, he turned the center of Rowan Street into garden plots. The houses were restored in the late 1960s by the existing homeowners.

264　J　*PR*
1500 Block of North 17th St., 1886
Willis Hale

P. A. B. Widener and William Elkins became wealthy industrialists through their monopoly over the street railway system. They used their wealth to develop significant portions of North Philadelphia for middle-class families working in the growing manufacturing centers of the city. Widener and Elkins used Hale to design a number of blocks in the area, including the 1800 and 2300 blocks of West Thompson Street. This row of houses on 17th Street is typical of Hale's exuberant style. The 29 twin houses are of brick with molded brick details, terracotta panels and brownstone trim. Heavy, rough-textured stone surrounds the windows and arched entrances. Particularly flamboyant are the mansard roofs with stepped gables supported by projecting corbels.

265

265 F,J *PR*
4206–18 Spruce St., 1886
G. W. and W. D. Hewitt

William Kimball followed John D. Jones as the developer of the area around 42nd Street. He directed his efforts to middle-class homeowners and retained the Hewitt brothers to design several projects, probably including the 200 and 300 blocks of South 42nd Street.

This row on Spruce Street is the most distinguished block of late 19th-century houses in the city. It was designed as a unified composition in the Queen Anne style. The center is marked by a large gable; second-floor bay windows, projecting out at either end, visually frame the rambling structure. The Queen Anne style is exuberantly exploited for its picturesque effect through the steeply pitched gables, the wooden, stick-style porches and the variety of building materials, which include hung tiles and cut-brick details.

266 F *PR*
Poth Mansion, 1887
216 North 33rd St.
A. W. Dilks

Powelton was one of the earliest settlements in West Philadelphia. Many of the houses were built in the 1850s in the Italianate style, including several designed by Samuel Sloan. After the Centennial Exposition, the area attracted wealthy homeowners, such as Frederick A. Poth, a brewer, for whom this house was built.

Dilks had worked for the fashionable architect T. P. Chandler. This house was probably his first independent commission. The design reflects the High Victorian love of rich colors and details and the visual prominence wealthy industrialists sought for their homes. The walls have semicircular and polygonal bays and towers of red brick and brownstone trim in a variety of textures. A large porch, with delicate wood detailing, sweeps dramatically across two sides of the house.

267 G *PR*
Charles Lister Townsend House, 1887
6015 Wayne Ave.
G. W. and W. D. Hewitt

Charles Lister Townsend, a broker and president of the Philadelphia Stock Exchange, built this 12-bedroom castle from which he commuted to downtown Philadelphia. The house was modeled after Druim Moir, the castle the Hewitt brothers had designed the previous year for Henry Howard Houston. Like Druim Moir, the Townsend house has a large, round-arched porte cochere and is built of coarse-textured Wissahickon schist. It has stepped Flemish gables and a corner tower topped with a curving mansard roof.

268 C
Keystone National Bank, 1887/1890
1326 Chestnut St.
Willis Hale

The Keystone Bank was built in an era when self-made millionaires used architecture to express their success. Willis Hale, according to his obituary, was fortunate "to have as clients a number of men whose desire to spend their easily gotten millions was not controlled by education or inherited standards of taste; and to this fact should be attributed some of the lack of restraint that marked his work."

The bank is a fine example of Hale at his flamboyant best. The design is derived from the French Renaissance revival, based on chateaux of the Loire Valley, which combined both classical detail and Gothic verticality. Classical details include the pilasters, brackets and frieze; the tower, steep roof

•
1890
*Roman Catholic
High School opens:
first free Catholic
high school in U.S.*

•
1890–91
*Louis Sullivan
designs Wainwright
Building, St. Louis*

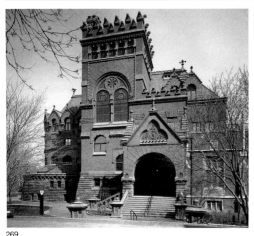

269

pitch, chimneys and decorations on the wall and dormer are clearly Gothic. The elaborate facade is made of sharply outlined, rock-faced limestone. The high mansard roof is even more elaborate, with dormers and chimneys creating an almost chaotic jumble of shapes.

---

269 E,J *OP*
Anne and Jerome Fisher Fine Arts Building, University of Pennsylvania, 1888–90
34th and Walnut Sts.
Frank Furness; Restored 1991, Venturi Scott Brown and Associates with Clio Group and Marianna Thomas Architects

The library is one of the finest remaining examples of the work of Frank Furness. When completed it was the most innovative library building in the country. It was one of the first to separate the reading room and book stacks. Books were kept in a separate wing, which was designed so that the rear wall could be removed on jack screws and new bays added as additional space was needed. Within the book stacks, translucent glass floors allowed light to penetrate from the sloping glass roof.

The most impressive interior spaces are the catalog room and the reading room. The catalog room is dominated by a monumental fireplace. The reading room is surrounded by study alcoves and lit from windows above. Curved iron beams radiate from the center of the ceiling to delicate terra-cotta leaves on top of the brick pilasters.

Like most of Furness's buildings, the exterior was highly controversial. It contains a rich use of brick and stone with terra-cotta panels, short heavy columns and unusual details, such as the scalloped crenelations on the tower and gargoyles on the north end.

Robert Venturi was one of the first contemporary architects to recognize the importance of Furness's work. It was fitting, therefore, that Venturi Scott Brown and Associates was chosen to restore the building.

270 K *PR*
Bedell House, 1889
22nd and Chestnut Sts.
Wilson Eyre

Although Victorian architects had to design row houses for the same narrow lots as Georgian houses, they wanted to break up the monotony and symmetry of traditional row house design. The Bedell House is a fine example of Eyre's eclectic style. Eyre imaginatively selected elements from colonial and medieval sources to create his own version of Queen Anne domestic design. In this house he placed the door off center, created an irregular pattern of windows and designed a very visible chimney rising the height of the building. Eyre often lavished attention on the doorway, where a building is seen most closely. Here he placed medieval sculptural figures, probably designed with his sister, at either end of a ribbon stretching over the doorway. Carved in the ribbon is the date of the house.

---

271 K
Mother Bethel African Methodist Church, 1889–90
419 South 6th St.
Hazelhurst and Huckel

In 1787, when black members of St. George's congregation were discriminated against, Richard Allen and other black members of the church formed what eventually became the mother church of the African Methodist Church.

The church was in the center of the principal black residential area of the city. The site is the oldest piece of land continuously owned by blacks in the United States. The present building, the fourth church built on the site, was designed in the Romanesque Revival style. The stone and brick structure features a generous semicircular arched doorway with a large stained-glass window directly overhead. The rough texture of the stone and the recessed openings that reveal

● **1891**
First commercial skyscraper

● **1891**
Drexel Institute established

● **1892**
Electric trolley cars introduced

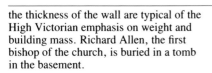

273

274

the thickness of the wall are typical of the High Victorian emphasis on weight and building mass. Richard Allen, the first bishop of the church, is buried in a tomb in the basement.

272   K
Baptist Temple, 1889–91
Broad and Berks Sts.
Thomas P. Londale

Russell H. Conwell, a pastor of the Grace Baptist Church, was one of the greatest orators of his time. He is best known for his "Acres of Diamonds" speech, which he delivered more than 6,000 times. Conwell also provided educational programs for students of limited means and in 1888 established an urban college, which is now Temple University.

Conwell's enormous following necessitated a larger church. Lonsdale adopted the Romanesque style for the building, which was a combination church, meeting hall and community center. The exterior has the appearance of a conventional church, but the interior is a large auditorium with excellent acoustics, accommodating up to 4,200 persons.

The temple is constructed of rock-faced granite set as coarsed ashlar with wide joints. The main facade is flanked by two towers capped with large, copper-covered domes and has a prominent stained-glass half-rose window in the center. Round-headed, clerestory windows to light the interior are located below the eave of the main roof, which is also topped with two copper cupolas.

273   E
Drexel Institute, Main Building, 1889–91
32nd and Chestnut Sts.
The Wilson Brothers

Anthony J. Drexel, one of the nation's prominent philanthropists and bankers, founded Drexel Institute to offer courses in art, domestic science, commerce, technology and shopwork. For the site, he chose the corner where he and George W. Childs met every morning for their walk into town. Joseph Wilson was selected as manager of the institute as well as its architect.

Wilson considered this his most important commission. He chose a composite Renaissance style for the exterior, applied in the form of highly decorative, terra-cotta detailing. Especially noteworthy are the high-relief medallion portraits within the tall entrance portal.

The building focuses around a central court, which is one of the finest interior spaces in the city. It is a rococo blend of red tile, pink marble, white enameled brick and once gold-tinged wrought-iron balustrades. The building is also notable for its early use of poured-in-place reinforced concrete in the first-floor slab and the supporting piers of the court.

The auditorium contains a huge Haskell organ, one of the largest pipe organs in the city, which has superbly carved wood pilasters decorated with gold.

274   C
Clarence Moore House, 1890
1321 Locust St.
Wilson Eyre

Clarence Moore was a wealthy merchant and amateur archaeologist. Eyre's design for his house is an imaginative essay in eclectic picturesque design. The pointed arched openings are Gothic, the top floor loggia is Venetian and the tower is French, derived from the chateaux along the Loire River. The exterior is a rich study in the

275

276

contrasting textures. Rusticated limestone is used for the basement, smooth limestone for the door and window trim, elongated Roman brick for the walls and slate on the roof.

Each side of the building has its own character. The facade is compact, with a sculptural chimney squeezed between the entrance and the tower. The side elevation is nearly symmetrical, bracketed by end towers with a bay of windows sheathed in limestone in the center. The elevation along the alley is treated with as much care as the facade and contains sculptured human figures and gargoyles.

---

275 J *PR*

Kemble-Bergdol House, 1890
2201–5 Green St.
James Windrim with George Herzog

William H. Kemble, a financier, built an elaborate mansion, which he later sold to the Bergdol family, owners of one of the city's largest breweries. Bergdol descendants have inhabited the house ever since.

The house is one of the city's finest examples of Italianate brownstone design, a style whose rich and elaborate carving appealed to late 19th-century industrialists. The symmetrical facade is very imposing and has a generous portico entrance. Porches on the rear and west elevations are constructed of copper, iron and glass. The lavish interior was principally the work of Herzog, interior designer of the Masonic Temple. It has richly carved woodwork and plaster walls, hand-stenciled with designs in gold leaf.

---

276 K *PR*

Neill and Mauran Houses, 1890
315–17 South 22nd St.
Wilson Eyre

John Neill, a real-estate agent, commissioned Eyre to design two speculative houses a few years after he had completed the Bedell House. Once again, Eyre drew

freely on the colonial and medieval sources of the Queen Anne style. These houses show Eyre's increasing predilection for simplified shapes and materials. Wall surfaces are plain brick, interrupted only by windows of different sizes and shapes. The only ornamentation is around the paired doorways, which have Gothic-arched openings and are separated by a buttress over which stands a medieval figure. Of special interest are the finely crafted doors, which are well-preserved examples of Arts and Crafts wood construction.

The huge gambrel roof, which makes the two houses look like one, is colonial in inspiration but Victorian in its exaggerated scale.

---

277 K

Germantown Cricket Club, 1890–91
5140 Morris St.
McKim, Mead and White

The Germantown Cricket Club, founded in 1854, is the second oldest institution of its kind in the country. When the club merged with the Young America Cricket Club in 1889, the board decided to build a new clubhouse and retained Charles McKim of New York to design it.

McKim, Mead and White were the leading advocates of a return to classical models, in contrast to the complex and heavy forms of the Victorian era. The Cricket Club was one of the first examples of Georgian Revival, a style for which they became the national authorities. The building has a symmetrical facade, a quiet roofline, and uses the red brick and white trim typical of colonial design. Although the overall scale is much larger than any colonial building, the details are carried out in a similar, elegant and delicate manner. The clubhouse is named Manheim, after the street that connects it to Germantown Avenue.

278

280

278 C,J
Reading Terminal, 1891–93
Market St., between 11th and 12th Sts.
The Wilson Brothers; Head House
Renovated 1985, Cope Linder Associates,
Bower Lewis Thrower and John Milner
Associates; Train Shed Renovated 1993–94,
Thompson Ventulett Stainback Associates
and Vitetta Group

The Reading Railroad was created in 1840
to bring coal and iron from western Pennsylvania. The railroad also provided passenger
service to many areas north and west of the
city. When steam locomotives eliminated
the fear of fire from wood-burning engines,
the Reading built an inner-city terminal on
a site occupied by the Franklin Farmers'
Market since 1860. The market was given
space under the train shed, where it remains
to this day.

   The terminal is actually two buildings:
the Head House, which contained waiting
rooms and offices, and the shed covering
the train platforms.

   The Head House is constructed of
wrought- and cast-iron columns, wrought-
iron and steel beams and brick floors. Its
Italian Renaissance exterior was applied
over the structural system by a consulting
architect, Frank Kimball of New York. Ornate cream-colored terra-cotta details are
set off by pale pink walls and framed by a
heavy copper cornice.

   The shed is the only surviving single-
span, arched train shed in the country. It
was the largest single-span structure in the
world when completed. Trains stopped
using the shed after the commuter rail tunnel
was completed in 1984. To preserve this
important engineering landmark, the shed
was incorporated into the design of the Convention Center. The Ballroom, meeting
rooms and Grand Hall are located on several
levels under a spectacular skylight in the
shed roof.

279 K
Mount Sinai Cemetery Chapel, 1891–92
Bridge St., west of Cottage St.
Furness, Evans and Company

This chapel is one of the most successful
small-scale designs of Furness's later career.
Furness designed many buildings for the
Jewish community, in which he demonstrated a preference for Moorish motifs.
The chapel reflects this in the shapes of the
window and door openings. The interior is
dominated by a massive hammer-beam ceiling similar to Furness's design for the First
Unitarian Church.

280 K
Church of the Advocate, 1891–97
18th and Diamond Sts.
Charles M. Burns

The Church of the Advocate was the high
point in the career of Charles Burns, principal architect for the Episcopal church at the
end of the 19th century. It was built to serve
the growing middle-class neighborhoods of
North Philadelphia, much like the Church
of the Gesu, a few blocks away. The church
was made possible by gifts of the South
family in honor of George W. South, a
merchant and public official.

   The church is a wonderful interpretation
of French Gothic design. Certain features
recall the Cathedral of Amiens, such as the
soaring spire on the roof at the juncture of
the nave and transepts, the flying buttresses
and the treatment of the chancel. The interior is richly ornamented, with beautiful
stained-glass windows and fine stone carvings. The nave conveys the monumental
dignity of European cathedrals through the
use of stone vaulting for the ceiling, a feature rarely found in American churches.

● **1894**
Statue of William Penn
installed on City
Hall tower

● **1894**
Broad Street paved
with asphalt

281

281 G
Cummings House, 1892
240 West Tulpehocken St.
Frank Miles Day

Harry Cummings, a grain merchant and feed dealer, lived in suburban Germantown. His house was built at a time when architects comfortably combined different European styles into an eclectic composition.

Day was particularly adept at this approach. For this house he combined three different sources. The decorative details on the balcony are Italian, as are the sculptured cherubs and open loggia above the port cochere. Germanic influences are present in the steep slope of the roof, which was originally red tile, and in its generous eaves, tile-covered dormers and once tall chimneys. The semicircular portico recalls Roman designs. None of these styles predominates, however, and the result is a balanced composition that looks familiar but is fresh and sophisticated. Day was also creative in his use of color. The pink tint of the stucco walls is offset by buff-colored Pompeian brick that outlines the windows and forms the water table around the house and the quoins at the corners.

282 C
Joseph Leidy House and Office, 1893–94
1319 Locust St.
Wilson Eyre

The Leidy House was designed three years after its neighbor, the Moore House, for an antiquarian who was interested in early American history. It is an early urban example of the Georgian Revival style carried out in an imaginative, rather than historically correct, manner.

Such Georgian details as the blocks of stone that surround the arched windows and door are large and overscaled. The walls are brick with brownstone window trim of the Victorian era, rather than the colonial palette of brick and light stone. The promi-

nent gable, with its steep pitch, and the bay windows recall medieval rather than Georgian precedents.

Eyre was a fine draftsman, and his drawings of this and the Moore house were displayed at the Columbian Exposition in Chicago in 1893.

283 K
Overbrook Farms, 1893
Overbrook Ave. and Drexel Rd., between 59th and 66th Sts.
Frank and William Price, Boyd and Boyd, Thomas Lonsdale, Horace Trumbauer, Addison Hutton, et al.

Overbrook Farms is a delightful example of a planned Victorian community. Wendell and Smith, the developers, hired a number of young architects to prepare sketches of houses according to prescribed guidelines. A few model homes were erected also. Potential residents could select the design they preferred or mix features from several samples.

The houses provide a fair sampling of turn-of-the-century eclecticism; Queen Anne, Georgian Revival, Arts and Crafts, Shingle and Italianate styles are represented. Thomas Lonsdale designed Our Lady of Lourdes Cathedral, at the center of the development, as well as 5871 Drexel Road. Charles Barton Keen and his partner, Frank Mead, designed the twin house at 6380–84 Overbrook Avenue. Addison Hutton designed the Presbyterian church at Lancaster and City Line avenues. William Price, working alone and with his brother Frank, is probably best represented. His own house, at 6323 Sherwood Avenue, served as one of the original model homes.

284

285

284 B *OP*
The Bourse, 1893–95
11 South 5th St.
G. W. and W. D. Hewitt
Renovated 1982, H2L2

The Bourse, an impressive testimony to the
city's industrial and financial community,
was developed by George Bartol, a local
businessman. It originally accommodated a
variety of financial institutions, including
the Maritime Exchange and the Stock Exchange, as well as grain-trading activities.
Modeled after European bourses, it was at
the time the only institution of its kind.

The block-long building is steel-frame
construction with bowed steel trusses spanning the trading floor. The exterior is clad
with red sandstone and Pompeian brick.
Giant columns and piers define the entrances
on Fifth and Fourth streets. The facade is
enlivened with terra-cotta decoration and
topped by a large cornice.

The trading floor was a two-story skylight
interior court. The court was formed by
eight stories of offices.

After the stock exchange moved and the
financial district relocated to the City Hall
area, the Bourse declined. In 1982 it was
extensively renovated to create a three-level
retail shopping mall with offices above. The
original skylight at the second-floor level
was removed and replaced by a new structure at the top of the interior court. Ornate
plasterwork, iron and brass fittings and colored floor tiles were restored. A modern
glass curtain wall sheathes the offices overlooking the interior space.

285 E,J *OP*
University Museum, 1893–1926/1969–71
3320 South St.
Wilson Eyre, Frank Miles Day and brother,
Cope and Stewardson/Mitchell/Giurgola
Associates

In 1886 the city gave the University of
Pennsylvania 12 acres to build a museum to
house the rapidly expanding department of
archaeology. Three local firms collaborated
on the design, which was generally under
the direction of Eyre.

The museum is a brilliant example of the
19th-century eclectic tradition: many historical styles are combined in a unified and
original composition. A Japanese gate forms
the entrance to an intimately scaled courtyard, created by the main building and
wings of the museum. The monumental
arched entrance has a stone hood supported
by figures carved by Alexander Milne Calder. A prominent rotunda dominates the
otherwise horizontal tile-covered roofs of
the main building. Eyre's interest in Arts
and Crafts design is reflected in the brickwork, laid in an unusually thick mortar bed,
coarsened with pebbles to achieve a handmade character. White and colored marble,
colored brick and varying brick patterns
enrich the wall surface; the eaves of the
main building are decorated with mosaics.

The interior of the building contains galleries for the museum's outstanding collection and includes an enormous single room
in the rotunda, which is lit by arched clerestory windows. Because the museum was
never completed, interior circulation was
awkward until the addition of a new wing,
designed by Mitchell/Giurgola. The new
wing blends with the red brick and tile-
roofed exterior of the original building, but
on the interior, glass and reinforced concrete
are clearly expressed in a successful jux-
taposition of old and new styles.

● **1896**
W. E. B. Du Bois writes
The Philadelphia
Negro

● **1897**
Fairmount Park
trolleys in service

286

286 E,J *PR*
Men's Dormitories, 1895–1902
Spruce St. between 36th and 38th Sts.
Cope and Stewardson; Renovated 1983–
1987, Davis Brody and Associates

American universities grew rapidly at the
end of the 19th century. To accommodate
new students, the University of Pennsylvania commissioned a new dormitory,
stipulating that it be designed so that it could
be built in stages and still look complete.
The dormitories were inspired by the residential colleges of English universities.
They are an outstanding example of the
Jacobean Revival style, which was derived
from English architecture in a transitional
phase from medieval to classical forms.

The dormitories have a rambling, informal plan organized around a series of courtyards of different sizes, which are connected
to one another by archways. The most
prominent of these is the tower entrance at
39th and Spruce streets, built in 1901 in
honor of the men who served in the Spanish-
American War. The buildings are made of
hard-burnt brick laid in Flemish bond and
offset by Indiana limestone. Gargoyles,
gables and bay windows of a medieval style
embellish the buildings, which also contain
classical balustrades, quoins and Palladian
windows. Stone sculptures in the second-
floor string course contain whimsical features, such as a monkey with a diploma.

287 C
Crozer Building, 1896–98
1420 Chestnut St.
Frank Miles Day

The Crozer Building was built for the
American Baptist Publication Society and
named after one of its principal benefactors.
It is an interesting contrast to its neighbor,
the Land Title Building. Although the building has a modern steel structural frame, the
exterior is derived from French and Italian
sources. It is made of Pompeian brick and
terra-cotta, with heavily decorated window

frames reminiscent of Renaissance townhouses. The top of the building, which
looks like a French chateau, was deliberately designed to make looking up worth-
while. Steep pitched roofs, chimneys, and
giant multistory dormer windows, with
pilasters and statues tucked into niches, are
combined to make a fascinating
composition.

288 K
Fell-Van Rensselaer House, 1896–98
1801–3 Walnut St.
Peabody and Stearns

Rittenhouse Square was once surrounded
by elegant mansions, many owned by the
Drexel family. Sara Drexel Fell, a widow,
built this mansion for Alexander Van Rensselaer of New York, who married her
shortly thereafter.

The architects were Peabody and Stearns,
a Boston firm whose clients were the social
elite of Boston, Newport and Philadelphia.
The mansion, considered to be one of the
finest examples of Beaux-Arts design in the
country, is characterized by such French
motifs as paired columns, ornamental crests,
projecting bays and grand staircases. The
slightly overdone effect was both desired
and admired at the time.

The interior was sumptuous, but all that
remains is the stained-glass skylit dome over
the central hall and the Doges Room, in
which Mrs. Van Rensselaer covered the ceiling with portrait medallions of the popes.
The family lived in the mansion until 1942,
after which it went through a succession
of owners before being converted to a
retail store.

●
1898
*Delaware River mined
to keep out Spanish
navy*

●
1899
*Philadelphia
Electric Co. created*

●
1900
*Philadelphia
Orchestra founded*

289

292

289   K
Overbrook School for the Blind,
1897–1900
64th St. and Malvern Ave.
Walter Cope

Philadelphia's first school for the blind was established in 1837. When the school decided to expand, the director wanted the buildings designed in the California Mission style. Cope, while honeymooning in Spain the previous year, had sketched many buildings.

The Overbrook School was one of the first successful adaptations of the Spanish Renaissance style in the United States. It is more informal than the Italian or French Renaissance styles because of the use of stucco instead of stone and the use of strong, contrasting colors.

The entrance is dominated by a pair of bold towers, behind which is a shallow dome buttressed by conically shaped supports. The building was planned with two cloisters flanking the central administration building—one for the female dormitory, the other for the male—to facilitate use by the blind. The picturesque massing of the complex is best seen from the cloister courtyard, where the stepped, red tile roofs descend abruptly to the serenity of the arcaded cloister.

290   C,J
Land Title Building, 1897
See page 83.

291   B
Corn Exchange, 1900–1901
Second and Chestnut Sts.
Newman, Woodman and Harris

When the city's fashionable residential areas moved westward, Dock Street became the center of the wholesale food market. Businesses active in the food market located in the surrounding area.

The Corn Exchange was established to serve merchants trading in grain and groceries. The original building consisted of an elaborate exchange room and supporting offices. The clock tower at the corner and second-floor offices were added later.

The exchange is a brick building based on the Georgian style of its colonial neighborhood. It is enriched, however, with elaborate, Baroque stone carvings. This is particularly apparent on the round windows above the first floor, which are surrounded by heavy wreaths and draped with stone swags. The exchange room has elegant classical pilasters and columns and a handsome recessed ceiling with skylights, which can be seen above the renovations made when the exchange was converted to a bank.

292   B   *PR*
**Tutlemann Brothers and Faggen
Building,** 1830–36/1900–1901
56–60 North 2nd St.

The Tutlemann Building, now called Little Boys Way, may have been the last cast-iron facade erected in this country. The original building was a store in the early 19th century, but over the years additions were made, and at one point the building housed a manufacturer of buttons and trim. The side that faces the alley is strictly factory utilitarian; brick piers alternate with generously sized windows to maximize light inside. But the main facade, added in 1900, is a handsome cast-iron grid, formed by simple but decorative piers and spandrels, similar to late 19th-century commercial architecture in Chicago. The building was one of the first renovated for loft apartments when the renewal of Old City began in the 1970s.

290

290 C,J
Land Title Building, 1897
Broad and Chestnut Streets
D. H. Burnham and Co.

The Land Title Building was one of the city's first major structures designed by a non-Philadelphia architect. Daniel Burnham was an early pioneer in the development of modern American architecture. His designs for tall buildings in Chicago were important landmarks in the evolution of the skyscraper and the Commercial style. Burnham also became a leading advocate of the Beaux-Arts movement and the Neoclassical Revival after his work on the 1893 Chicago Exposition.

The Land Title Building, built for the oldest title insurance company in the world, is the finest example of early skyscraper design in Philadelphia and the earliest east-coast example of this style by a major Chicago architect. It demonstrates Burnham's ability to combine classical elements with a simple expression of steel-frame construction. The sixteen-story structure, faced in buff brick, is divided into three parts. The two-story base, faced with granite, is unified by a rusticated Ionic arcade; the central portion of the building has alternating strips of projecting and flat windows, typical of the Chicago Commercial style. The continuous vertical piers, terminating in arches at the top, express the steel frame and were stan-dard devices used to emphasize the building's height. The top is treated as a separate unit, with a prominent overhanging roof and elaborate cornice.

Although built as a speculative office building, the interiors were finished in expensive materials, including marble and hardwood floors and marble wainscoting in the corridors. By setting the tower back from the base on the south side, Burnham created a well to ensure light and ventilation for the office floors. In 1902 a second office tower was added to the south, designed by Burnham with Horace Trumbauer. This building is taller, has a flatter facade and more overtly classical ornamentation.

●
1901
*Mummers Parade moved
to Broad Street*

●
1902
*Horn and Hardart's
opens first automat
restaurant*

293

294

293   K
St. James Apartment House, 1900–1904
1226–32 Walnut St.
Horace Trumbauer

At the turn of the century, most Philadelphians lived in individual homes. The elegant apartment buildings built in the fashionable neighborhoods along Broad Street and surrounding Rittenhouse Square, however, attracted many wealthy families.

Their style was eclectic, influenced by the Beaux-Arts movement and the neoclassical revival popular at the time. The St. James was typical. More substantial than some, it offered restaurants and other services specifically designed to draw wealthy tenants. Horace Trumbauer's ability to combine several architectural styles on a grand scale can be seen in the combination of such Second Empire motifs as the enormous mansard roof and the classical details of overscaled, voluted brackets supporting the balconies at the third and seventh floors.

This building firmly established Trumbauer's career as architect to the well-to-do families of Philadelphia.

294   C,J
The Bellevue Stratford Hotel, 1902–13
Broad and Walnut Sts.
G. W. and W. D. Hewitt
Remodeled 1980, 1989, Day and
Zimmermann Associates/Vitetta Group
with RTKL Architects

George Boldt, the son of a German immigrant, founded the Bellevue Stratford. He began his career as a dishwasher in New York, then moved to Philadelphia to become a headwaiter at the elite Philadelphia Club. When he opened the Bellevue Stratford in 1904, it immediately became one of the leading hotels of the world. Its amenities included Turkish and Swedish baths, a library, two in-house orchestras, three ballrooms and an outdoor rose garden on the roof. Rooms were decorated in Colonial, French, Italian and Greek styles.

Although the building was constructed of steel in the most modern method, the exterior was inspired by the sophisticated architectural style of the French Renaissance. The picturesque roofline consists of a slate-covered mansard roof with large overscaled dormers and chimneys. The main portion of the hotel is sheathed in terra-cotta, and the base is of rusticated stone. The Broad Street facade is enlivened by windows that are alternately flat and projecting, similar to Burnham's treatment of the Land Title Building.

The hotel closed in 1977 after an outbreak of Legionnaires disease among guests. A 1980 renovation reduced the number of rooms from 1,000 to 545, but this proved too large for the city's needs. A second renovation reduced the hotel to 165 rooms organized around a central atrium extending from the 12th to 19th floors. The original ballroom and Rose Garden were preserved and the remainder of the building converted to offices with retail stores on the first two floors.

295   E
Franklin Field, 1902–4/1913/1922
33rd and South Sts.
Frank Miles Day and brother

At the end of the 19th century, collegiate athletic departments began to serve all of the students and not just a few select varsity men. In response to this, the University of Pennsylvania decided to build a new gymnasium and a stadium for spectator sports. Day had worked on a number of collegiate buildings. He was supervising architect for Yale, Penn State and the University of Colorado, and designed several important buildings at Princeton.

The gymnasium closes off the open end of the horseshoe-shaped stadium, which was added in 1913 and enlarged in 1922. Both buildings are designed in the Collegiate Gothic style. Brick, laid in a Flemish bond with limestone trim, and battlements along the roofline help to unify the gymnasium and stadium into a single complex.

296

298

296 C,J *OP*
John Wanamaker's Department Store,
1902–11
1300 Market St.
D. H. Burnham and Co. with John T.
Windrim; Renovated 1991, Ewing Cole
Cherry Brott

John Wanamaker began selling ready-made clothing in 1861. By the time he moved his store to 13th and Market streets, it had become a full-fledged department store, one of the first in the country.

When Wanamaker decided to construct a new store on the same site, he also wanted the existing store to remain in operation. As a result, the building was constructed in three stages, which required considerable care to make sure that the joining of the stages was invisible. As the first phase of construction was completed, the settlement of the building was measured and used to determine the design of the next addition.

The exterior has little ornament or detail; it is a simple block, organized in three horizontal divisions much like Burnham's design of the Land Title Building. The handsome granite and limestone facade is an adaptation of the Renaissance palace, greatly enlarged in scale. Inside, the selling floors are organized around a spectacular central court that rises five floors. It is the most impressive interior space in any commercial building in the city. With two million square feet of usable space, Wanamaker's is the largest building in the city. When the department store could no longer fill the entire building, upper floors were converted to offices.

297 F,J *PR*
3500 Powelton Ave., 1902–8
Willis Hale and Milligan and Webber

Real-estate development in West Philadelphia prospered after the introduction of the electric streetcar in the 1890s. Frederick Poth, a wealthy brewer who lived in the area, started this block as a row of specula-

tive houses. He sold the uncompleted project to a new owner, who converted the houses to apartments. Milligan and Webber ingeniously filled in the spaces between the houses with stair towers, which are marked on the exterior by the double-story granite arches. They unified the block by placing a tower in the middle to create an appearance of planned symmetry.

The buildings are made of buff-colored brick and originally had copper sheathing on the bay windows.

298 C
Jacob Reed's Sons Store, 1903–4
1424–26 Chestnut St.
Price and McLanahan

At a time when department stores were emphasizing ready-made clothing, Jacob Reed's Sons prided itself on custom services and personalized care. This attitude was reflected in its finely detailed building.

Price's later work was influenced by the Arts and Crafts movement and his interest in the use of reinforced concrete. For the Reed store, he drew on the urban palaces of northern Italy. The facade has a loggia on the top floor, a high arched entranceway and is topped with a red tile roof. But the details show his Arts and Crafts interests in the dark brown brick set in thick mortar and the handmade Mercer tiles under the eaves and soffit, which depict crafts related to the garment industry.

The store was one of the first commercial uses of reinforced concrete in the city. Concrete columns, with Mercer tile in the capitals, support a high concrete barrel vault over the central sales space, which is flanked by two side aisles. Clerestory windows between the columns were lit from behind to give the illusion of a freestanding building.

3

The Contemporary City

1905–1993

The Contemporary City

Philadelphia entered the 20th century a major manufacturing center and the third largest city in the country. During the early decades of the century, continued economic prosperity attracted large numbers of foreign immigrants. New mass transportation systems, automobiles and an abundance of undeveloped land allowed the city to continue the outward expansion begun in the late 19th century. But, after 1940, many of these same factors contributed to the city's problems. Manufacturing industries declined, went out of business or moved to different areas of the country as part of a national shift of economic activities away from older, northern cities to the South and West. By midcentury such large manufacturing companies as Baldwin Locomotive, Disston Tools, Stetson Hats and the Cramp Shipyard were gone. After 1960 the population of the city began to decline. More significantly, the composition of the population shifted dramatically. More and more of the city's residents were black, reaching close to 40 percent of the population by 1980, and a large portion of that population was poor.

Between 1900 and 1920 the city's population increased from approximately 1,300,000 to 1,800,000. Most of the new immigrants were poor and unskilled Poles, Eastern European Jews, and Italians, who initially located in South Philadelphia. Although many of the Italian families remained, most of the others dispersed throughout the city, usually to neighborhoods of a similar ethnic background. As foreign immigration declined after World War I, black migration from the South began to increase; between 1900 and 1920, the black population doubled.

European and black immigrants were both attracted by economic opportunities. Manufacturing industries were large and extremely diverse; the port was still one of the country's largest, and the construction of substantial civic projects required many laborers and masons. As in the past, most working people lived within walking distance of their jobs, but by the 1920s the vast majority worked in large groups, in contrast to the many small independent businesses that characterized much of 18th- and 19th-century employment.

As new immigrants moved into older neighborhoods close to their jobs, middle-class residents moved steadily outward. Beginning in 1907, subway-elevated lines, supplementing electric trolleys and the commuter railroads, opened up new sections of the city. After the completion of the Market Street subway-elevated from 69th Street to downtown, the area west of 50th Street was transformed from farmland to substantial neighborhoods, doubling the population of West Philadelphia. The Frankford elevated opened up the near northeast; the north Broad Street subway shifted the direction of growth from Ridge Avenue to neighborhoods like Olney and Logan. More than 100,000 houses were built along these transportation routes in the 1920s. In con-

Peter Behrens was an important turn-of-the-century German architect. His buildings represent a transition between 19th-century historical styles and the unornamented style of 20th-century architecture. This oak chair was designed by Behrens in 1902. Its simple shape is in sharp contrast to 19th-century furniture; the curved lines of the back and legs suggest an Art Nouveau influence.

After 1912, the stiff formal dresses of the Victorian era were replaced by designs that had a simpler silhouette and were made of softer, looser materials. This ivory cut-and-uncut velvet dress is trimmed with beading, lace, silk and velvet flowers. The deep-cut neckline was very controversial at the time.

trast to the older areas, these new neighborhoods were exclusively residential, with no factories in their midst; residents commuted to their jobs, many of which were located downtown.

In the 19th century, downtown Philadelphia had become increasingly commercial. By the early 20th century only the Rittenhouse Square area remained a stable residential neighborhood. Offices and banks began to cluster in the area adjacent to the new City Hall and railroad terminals. Retail shopping extended from Wanamaker's to Lit Brothers; the wholesale food markets dominated the area around Dock Street. The concentration of employment brought thousands of people into downtown each day. Trolleys and a growing number of cars and trucks caused great congestion. Between 1918 and 1930 the number of cars in the city increased from 100,000 to 250,000. So great was the congestion around City Hall that a traffic signal was installed on the tower. New roads and bridges were overlaid on the grid of narrow streets; the Roosevelt Boulevard increased access to the northeast, the Benjamin Franklin Parkway led to the northwest and the completion of the first bridge across the Delaware River, in 1926, provided access from New Jersey.

Congestion and chaos were characteristic of most major cities and led to an expression of concern at a national level. The first city planning conferences were held before 1910, and the idea of zoning controls were introduced. Most cities wanted to have the spacious character and gleaming white classical appearance of the 1893 Chicago Exposition. The resulting City Beautiful movement swept the country. In Philadelphia, this led to the creation of the Benjamin Franklin Parkway, modeled after the Champs-Élysées, and the construction of prominent neoclassical buildings to house major cultural institutions.

Growth of the City

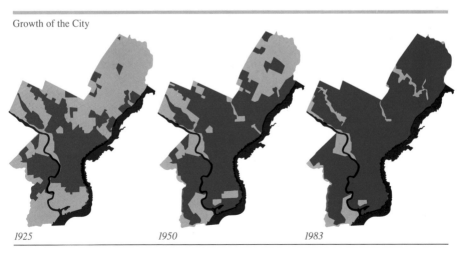

1925   *1950*   *1983*

Joseph Hoffman also was an important transitional architect, whose work in Austria influenced the development of the International style. This very simple frame chair of lacquered beech and leather, designed in 1907, anticipates the stripped-down functional style that would dominate furniture design later in the century. Hoffman's design also shows an Art Nouveau influence in its gentle curves and the decorative balls on the arms and legs.

Short skirts became the fashion in women's dress in 1925. The flapper style featured a flat, bustless design, low waistlines and skirts at knee length. This sleeveless dress from 1925 was very fashionable; it is made of magenta silk georgette and trimmed with beads.

Architectural styles were influenced by the exposition and by American architects who studied at the École des Beaux-Arts in Paris. A revival of historical styles became very popular, ranging from Greek and Roman for civic buildings to Gothic for collegiate buildings and early skyscrapers. Residential design was modeled after picturesque English, French and Italian country houses seen by American architects traveling in Europe. New houses, particularly in Chestnut Hill, used local stone, pitched roofs and simple forms to create a handsome, pastoral residential style unique to Philadelphia.

The residential building boom of the 1920s was accompanied by a similar boom in commercial development. Tall office buildings, banks, hotels and apartment buildings transformed the city skyline. Conservative Philadelphia lagged behind New York and Chicago in the development of skyscrapers. But from 1928 to 1932, many tall buildings were constructed. They were designed in a variety of styles, indicating the transitional nature of the period. Foremost among these was the PSFS building, the first International style skyscraper in the country.

By 1930 the city's population had grown to nearly 2,000,000, where it would generally remain for the next 40 years. The Depression brought the building boom to an end. Fifty banks in the city failed, but Philadelphia fared better overall than many other places due to the diversity of its industry. The troubled times made people eager for entertainment. Lavish movie theaters were constructed and eight radio stations were established. The Depression made people more conscious of their jobs, leading to the rise of labor unions. The Depression also encouraged the city to turn attention to the housing problems of the poor. Even before federal programs began, Philadelphia organizations sponsored housing for low- and moderate-income families. When the U.S. Housing Authority was created, the city responded promptly, completing its first project in 1937. But changing administrations and conservative mayors had mixed feelings about continuing such programs.

In 1940 the city covered 90 square miles, stretching south to Oregon Avenue, west to 69th Street, north to Olney Avenue, northeast to Cottman Avenue and northwest through Manayunk, Germantown and Chestnut Hill. Two- and three-story row homes predominated, extending block after block in all directions. The decline of manufacturing during the Depression created major financial problems and high unemployment, which only came to an end with World War II. Private industries, the Navy Yard and the Frankford Arsenal operated at capacity, producing tanks, ships, arms, textiles and other products for the war effort. This revitalization of industry, combined with the large percentage of the male population in the armed forces, created a labor shortage. Although many jobs were filled by women, immigrants were drawn to the city from rural areas of the country, contributing to an increase in the black population, which continued during the following decades.

During the war years many civic leaders expressed concern about the physical condition of the city. In spite of the new buildings of the late 1920s and early 30s, downtown Philadelphia had a Victorian appearance. The 18th-century neighborhoods east of Sixth Street were the city's worst slums. Civic leaders were also concerned about political corruption in the city government. The many reform efforts finally succeeded with the adoption of a new city charter in 1951, and with the election of new political leadership, which took the improvement of the city's physical environment as one of its major objectives.

Tubular chrome furniture was a distinguishing characteristic of the International style in Europe in the 1920s. This elegant chaise longue by the French architect Le Corbusier has a lacquered steel base, curved chrome-plated steel supports and ponyskin upholstery. It is as much a piece of sculpture as it is furniture.

At this time the city began to experience a dramatic shift in its economic character. Manufacturing industries declined, went out of business or moved to other sections of the country. Factories closed in the older neighborhoods, leaving downtown as the principal center of employment. The new city government placed a strong emphasis on downtown renewal and revitalization. A major exhibit in 1947 outlined ideas that were later formalized in the 1960 Comprehensive Plan and 1963 Plan for Center City. Many buildings were demolished to provide opportunities for new construction. A very ambitious program was begun to redevelop Society Hill. In an effort to attract affluent residents back to the city, virtually all the buildings in the 18th-century area east of Fifth Street were publicly acquired. At the same time, the federal government began to restore Independence Hall and related historic structures of national importance, creating the Independence National Historical Park. The rehabilitation of these buildings and the recreation of the historic residential character of Society Hill transformed the area into an affluent neighborhood but resulted in the displacement of many black residents, who had lived there for decades. The demolition of the Broad Street Station to create the Penn Center office complex was an equally ambitious undertaking. Other renewal projects were initiated in North and West Philadelphia to remove deteriorated housing and provide

Olaf Skoogfors designed this silver teapot in 1956 on the principle that the design of objects should directly reflect their function. Its handsome proportions and delicate craftsmanship are typical of fine contemporary silverwork.

The Barcelona chair, designed by Ludwig Mies van der Rohe in 1929, is one of the most famous and popular pieces of contemporary furniture. It is a fine example of International style design. The chair consists of stainless-steel supports and leather cushions minimally decorated with a grid of seams.

new housing for low- and moderate-income families. Philadelphia was a national leader in the urban renewal movement, and its projects influenced development in many other cities.

These efforts resulted in the first major construction in the city since the 1930s. Most architecture of the 1950s was based on the principles of the International style. Buildings had little ornamentation but were simple, direct expressions of their structural system. Modern glass, curtain-wall office buildings transformed the area west of City Hall.

In 1950 the city's population was still around 2,000,000, but the population of the suburban areas was 1,500,000 and growing at a more rapid rate. By 1960 it would exceed that of the city. This rapid regional growth was fostered by government-supported mortgage financing for veterans and middle-class families, combined with an ambitious highway progam that allowed easy access to the suburbs. Middle-class families moved outward as they had done since the early 19th century. In Philadelphia this led to the rapid development of huge tracts of land in the northeast section of the city, which attracted many residents from older ethnic neighborhoods, particularly South Philadelphia. As people moved to suburban areas or the outer parts of the city, the growing black population moved into the older neighborhoods. Most of West and North Philadelphia were black by the 1960s, as well as portions of South Philadelphia and Germantown.

Although the city had established a successful downtown revitalization program that continues to the present day, it was not until the federal government created the Model Cities program in the late 1960s that serious attention was given to the deteriorating conditions in older neighborhoods of North and West Philadelphia. These areas had many vacant factories and thousands of abandoned houses. Many were demolished, leaving vast undeveloped vacant lots. Despite the fact that new rental housing was built and many rehabilitation programs were launched in the 1970s, the dilapidated character of most of these neighborhoods remained relatively unchanged.

Philadelphia's leadership in urban renewal and restoration attracted many architects to the city, including several whose work has had international impact. By the 1960s, American architects were beginning to question the simple plain forms of the Modern style. Although most buildings continued to be designed in this manner, Philadelphia was the center of new and divergent ideas, particularly through the writing and teaching of Louis I. Kahn and Robert Venturi. Kahn emphasized heavy masonry construction; Venturi gave attention to popular influences. Both reintroduced historical influences in their work. By the late 1970s the desire for a richer, more ornate form of expression had given rise to a post-Modern movement.

The total absence of ornament is as much a characteristic of modern furniture as of buildings. This waste receptacle by Paul Mayen, from the 1960s, is typical of the simple, abstract industrial quality of many objects designed for offices and public buildings.

Post-modern furniture, like architecture, incorporates references to historic styles without creating reproductions. This molded laminated plywood chair by Robert Venturi, applies the painted image of the Sheraton style to an industrially produced object.

Throughout the 1980s and into the 1990s, the population and economic trends that began in the 1960s continued to influence Philadelphia. Population in the city declined to 1,585,557 in 1990—less than the population in 1920—while that of the suburban area increased to over 3,650,000. By the 1990s, for the first time in its history Philadelphia contained fewer jobs than the surrounding region. The decline in population was accompanied by a change in composition as well. Although the black population of the city remained relatively constant, during the 1980s the city experienced an influx of southeast Asian immigrants and a growth of the Hispanic community. By 1990, these three minority groups represented 45% of the total population. A large portion of this minority population was poor and lacked the education necessary to adapt to the change from a manufacturing to a service economy. Living conditions in many inner-city neighborhoods continued to decline, complicated by problems of drugs and crime, in spite of the efforts of a growing number of non-profit community development corporations. Large sections of the inner-city were characterized by vacant land, vacant and deteriorated houses as residents who could move to more stable neighborhoods did so. Homelessness appeared as a more dramatic urban phenomenon than it had in the past.

In contrast to the decline in inner-city neighborhoods, downtown Philadelphia appeared to be thriving. During the early 1980s, conversion of historic commercial buildings to housing, a dramatic new retail shopping complex along Market Street, a renaissance of restaurants and the completion of several new hotels indicated a renewed vitality. This increased significantly at the end of the decade and in the early 1990s. Four new office buildings were constructed exceeding the traditional height limit of the City Hall Tower, dramatically changing the city skyline and symbolizing a new sense of purpose and direction in leadership. A new convention center was completed and new cultural and performing arts facilities initiated to transform South Broad Street's Avenue of the Arts into a multi-faceted cultural district. Carried out with architectural distinction and exuberance, these new developments added to the city's character while transforming it.

By 1994, the 350th anniversary of William Penn's birth, Philadelphia had grown far from his initial vision. It was no longer a "greene country town" confined to a narrow band between two rivers, but a sprawling, complex social and economic environment struggling to find its way into the twenty-first century.

Glossary of Architectural Terms

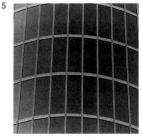

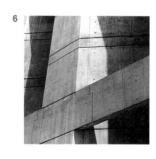

1 **atrium**
a large interior space,
usually extending the
height of a building
and covered with a
skylight

2 **cantilever**
a beam or other projec-
tion that is unsupported
at its projecting end

3 **chevron**
an ornamental zigzag
pattern of molding,
found on Art Deco–
style buildings

4 **Chicago window**
a wide window, often
a projecting bay, with
a fixed central glass
panel and two smaller
double-hung side
windows

5 **curtain wall**
a nonstructural exterior
wall, usually of glass,
steel or aluminum,
that is hung on the
frame of a building

6 **formwork**
wood or metal forms
into which concrete is
poured for walls or
columns; after the
formwork is removed,
the concrete is im-
printed with its patterns
and textures

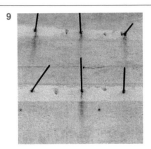

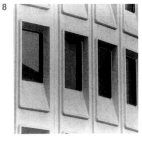

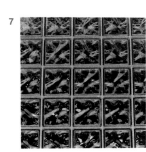

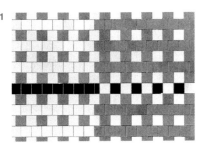

7 **glass block**
glass that has been
poured into structural
blocks

8 **precast concrete**
concrete columns,
beams or panels that
are poured and cast in
molds in a factory

9 **reinforced concrete**
a structural system in
which steel rods are
placed in the formwork
before the concrete is
poured to add strength

10 Sculptural panels were
a common feature on
the facades of impor-
tant buildings in the
1920s and 30s.

11 The use of color and
decorative patterns is
characteristic of many
buildings designed in
the post-Modern
manner.

301

302

The Neoclassical Revival

The popularity of the Beaux-Arts movement, after the 1893 Columbian Exposition in Chicago, prompted a revival of classical styles that lasted into the 1920s. Unlike previous historical styles, which were derived from English or European movements, this was solely an American phenomenon. Most cities tried to reproduce the clear, classical images of the exposition. So many large public buildings were created that more marble was used in the United States in 20 years than had been used in all of ancient Rome. Many architects designed neoclassical buildings, but McKim, Mead and White were the acknowledged leaders of the movement.

Most neoclassical buildings are based on the Greek orders, but they are larger than the Greek Revival buildings of the 19th century and less ornate than their Beaux-Arts predecessors. Stone or marble buildings are characterized by large, plain wall surfaces, flat pilasters, pedimented porticos and the use of single rather than coupled columns.

301   C,J
Girard Trust Company, 1905–8
34–36 South Broad St.
McKim, Mead and White; Furness Evans and Co.

The 1893 Columbian Exposition in Chicago introduced a revival of neoclassical design in the United States. The Girard Trust building is the city's best example of this neoclassical style. Furness originally attempted to design the bank in his heavy Victorian manner. The bank resisted, however, and the final design is a combination of Furness's plans with detailing by Stanford White, whose firm was responsible for much of the work at the Chicago Exposition.

The Girard Trust building is a small jewel surrounded by tall skyscrapers. With its gleaming white marble walls, handsome portico and distinctive dome, it has all the characteristics of a classical temple. Typically, however, the building used modern construction techniques, and behind the marble exterior is a steel-frame structure. The expansive dome, with skylit oculus in the center, is constructed of marble tiles using the technique developed by Rafael Gustavino. The adjacent office building, also in white marble, was added in 1923 by McKim, Mead and White.

302   K
Church of St. Francis de Sales, 1906
4625 Springfield Ave.
Henry Dagit

As late as 1890 this section of West Philadelphia was farmland. After electric trolleys were extended west of 42nd Street, the neighborhood began to grow, and a Catholic church was built to serve the area.

The rock-faced limestone facade of the church is designed in a Romanesque manner, with round arched openings. In contrast, the interior is one of the finest examples of Byzantine architecture in the country. It is richly decorated with marble and yellow, green and white tiles, and dimly lit by a series of windows that surround the huge dome. The dome was constructed in the Gustavino manner, similar to the Girard Trust building. Layers of terra-cotta tiles laid along the curve of the vault allowed a large dome to be built inexpensively.

304

305

303 H *PR*
100–102 West Mermaid Lane, 1909
Wilson Eyre

Dr. George Woodward, the son-in-law of Henry Howard Houston, continued Houston's practice of building houses in Chestnut Hill. He retained many creative architects to design innovative housing projects, primarily for rent to moderate-income families.

Eyre's design for this pair of houses was strongly influenced by the Arts and Crafts movement then popular in England. These English houses covered the entire exterior wall surface with a smooth, even stucco finish. Eyre adapted this approach to the simple shape and fenestration of the Pennsylvania farmhouse and produced houses to meet functional needs rather than to provide fancy show.

304 G *PR*
Adelbert Fischer House, 1909
6904 Wissahickon Ave.
Milton Medary

Adelbert Fischer came to Philadelphia from Germany to establish a branch of his father-in-law's machinery company. He commissioned Medary, a young German architect just beginning practice, to design a house based on 1907 books of German interiors.

The Fischer house is one of the few buildings in the city designed in the Art Nouveau style. Art Nouveau was popular in Europe at the turn of the century, but had limited impact in the United States. It was a decorative style, featuring dynamic forms and curving lines, and was particularly influential on interior design and furnishings.

Art Nouveau details visible on the exterior of the Fischer house include the curved dormer window and the door and window frames with curved corners. The interior of the house has a handsome tile floor in the entry hall and ornate Art Nouveau decoration on the fireplace hoods.

In recent years the period character of the house has been revived by Robert Venturi and Denise Scott Brown, with wall stencils and an eclectic combination of period and contemporary furnishings.

305 K
Packard Motor Car Company, 1910
317–21 North Broad St.
Albert Kahn; Renovated 1986, Bower Lewis Thrower and John Milner Associates

In the early 20th century, many motorcar companies located their offices and showrooms on Broad Street, which became known as "automobile row." The Packard Motor Car Company's building was designed by Albert Kahn, an engineer from Detroit who became one of the country's foremost designers of industrial buildings.

Kahn's design was one of the earliest uses of reinforced concrete in a commercial structure. The concrete columns and beams are inset with large industrial windows and covered with decorative terra-cotta panels, which give the facade a rich appearance. Additional ornamentation is provided by the handsome canopy over the entrance and a prominent overhanging roof. The showroom, remodeled in 1927 by Philip Tyre, was lavishly designed with a beamed ceiling and a Spanish tile floor.

● **1913**
*Congress Hall restored
and rededicated*

● **1914**
*First Tastykake
packaged*

307

306 H *PR*
Benezet Street Houses, 1910-16
28-34 Benezet St. and 25-33
Springfield Ave.
Duhring, Okie and Zeigler

Dr. Woodward's residential projects for
middle- and lower-income families often
took the form of grouped houses, of which
the ones on Benezet Street are among the
most innovative.

To achieve economy each unit contains
four houses under one roof. The stucco
houses have spacious living rooms, skylit
stairways, ample front yards and trellised
"drying yards." Woodward built the houses
for rent; they were so popular he had a long
waiting list of lower-income tenants. They
are still owned by the Woodward family.

In addition to the quadruple houses,
Woodward built twin houses on Benezet
Street, which are also fine examples of high
quality and economical design. Each house
has the same plan but different exterior materials and details.

20th Century Revivals

*In the late 19th century American architects
reacted against the heavy, ornate forms of
the High Victorian period. Several historical styles were revived to restore order and
simplicity to building design. Although the
Neoclassical Revival was the most popular,
the Georgian Revival, Jacobean Revival
and Late Gothic Revival all carried over
into the 20th century.*

*The Late Gothic Revival was extremely
popular for collegiate buildings and
churches, but was also an important influence on the design of such early commercial
skyscrapers as the Woolworth Building in
New York. The style, based on the English
Perpendicular style, placed strong emphasis
on the expression of vertical elements.
Churches and collegiate buildings were usually of stone, with finely crafted Gothic details. Similar details on skyscrapers were
generally executed in terra-cotta.*

307 C
Robert Morris Hotel, 1914-15/1921-22
1705 Arch St.
Ballinger and Perrot; Ballinger Company

New methods of construction did not deter
architects from using historic styles for
modern buildings. Gothic was a favorite for
skyscrapers. For the Robert Morris Hotel,
originally the Wesley Building, Gothic was
also consistent with its first use as offices
and a hotel for the Methodist church. The
building was constructed in two stages; the
top eight floors were added six years after
completion of the first six. The original cornice, with Gothic tracery, is still visible
above the sixth floor.

The facade is an impressive example of
the use of terra-cotta as a decorative material. Because it was malleable, terra-cotta
could easily duplicate rich details at low
cost. The detailing of the facade reflects
differences in the internal functions. Broad,
basket-handle openings and rich ornament
on the ground floor indicate its public use.
Large pointed-arch windows on the second
floor light an impressively detailed ballroom. The Gothic detailing continues inside
the lobby, which has a ribbed, groined vault
and a main stairway of marble with carved
and gilded railings.

308 H *PR*
High Hollow, 1914

See page 100.

1917
U.S. enters World
War I

1918
Benjamin Franklin
Parkway completed

1920
19th Amendment
ratified: women
given right to vote

309

309 D,J
Philadelphia Museum of Art, 1916–28
Benjamin Franklin Pkwy. and 26th St.
Horace Trumbauer, C. Clark Zantzinger,
Charles L. Borie, Jr.

By 1893, Memorial Hall was considered no
longer suitable for the city's art museum.
After many years of discussion, a site for a
new museum was selected on the hill known
as Faire Mount, at the end of the recently
completed Benjamin Franklin Parkway.
Trumbauer's chief designer, Julian Abele,
the first black graduate of the University of
Pennsylvania architecture school, returned
from Greece with the idea of building three
temples on a solid rock base. The final design is a compromise among his ideas and
those of the other architects.

At the start of construction not enough
money had been raised to build the entire
building. Eli Kirk Price, one of the fund-
raisers, suggested building the two wings
first, on the correct presumption that
Philadelphians would not leave the museum
unfinished.

The museum is reached from the parkway
by a monumental flight of stairs flanked by
cascading fountains. The stairs lead to a
large terrace with a spectacular view of the
city. The museum consists of three intercon-
nected temple structures with very tall porticos, topped by finely detailed pediments.

The pediment of the north temple contains a
brilliantly colored terra-cotta sculpture with
13 figures, representing sacred and profane
love. The warm, yellow Minnesota Man-
kato and Kosota ashlar on the facade and
gabled blue tile roof give the building
a distinctive appearance.

In addition to its outstanding art collection, the museum contains a number of
rooms representing different architectural
periods, most of which were built as WPA
projects during the 1930s. They include a
medieval cloister, a Japanese teahouse, a
Chinese temple, an Indian temple, a French
Empire room and many others.

● **1920**
Prohibition begins

● **1920**
John B. Kelly wins
Olympic gold medal
in single sculls

308

311

308 H *PR*
High Hollow, 1914
101 West Hampton Rd.
George Howe

Howe designed High Hollow for himself,
based on one of his final projects at the
École des Beaux-Arts. It was the first of
many beautiful country homes he would
design over the next decade.

High Hollow is built of red and dark
brown Chestnut Hill ledge stone, obtained
from an abandoned quarry reopened especially for Howe. It is beautifully sited on a
steep slope overlooking Fairmount Park,
with broad terraces linking the house and
landscape. The facade is enriched by red
brick stringcourses and frames around doors
and round-arch windows. Although not
based on any specific historic style, a
French influence is apparent in the steep
pitch of the hipped roof and the corner turret
between the main house and service wing.

The interior is organized around a spacious center hall. The principal rooms have
glass doors that slide into the masonry wall
and give access to balconies with dramatic
views of the park.

309 D,J
Philadelphia Museum of Art, 1916–28

See page 99.

310 H *PR*
Lincoln Drive Development, 1917–26
Lincoln Dr. from Springfield Ave. to
Pastorius Park
Robert McGoodwin, Herman Louis Duhr-
ing, and Edmund B. Gilchrist

Dr. Woodward, impressed with the planned
residential community around London's
Hyde Park, wanted to create a similar community in Philadelphia. He acquired untilled
farmland around Pastorius Park and hired
his three favorite architects to draw up a
general plan. The plan, designed to provide
housing for both affluent and middle-class
families, includes large single-family
houses, court houses, twin houses and
row houses.

Each architect carried out a portion of the
plan. Duhring designed the Half Moon
Houses at 7919–25 Lincoln Drive, a distinctive example of court houses sharing a common sunken garden. McGoodwin designed
a similar court at 131–35 Willow Grove
Avenue. The stucco-covered brick homes
along the 8000 block of Crefeld Street and
the brick rowhouses at 103–13 West Willow
Grove Avenue, known as Linden Court,
were designed by Gilchrist, one of the most
innovative of the Chestnut Hill architects.

The house at 200 West Willow Grove
Avenue is a replica of George Washington's
ancestral home in England. It was built for
the Sesquicentennial Exposition and subsequently moved and reconstructed here by
Duhring.

Most of these houses are still owned by
the Woodward family.

311 K *OP*
Free Library of Philadelphia, 1917–27
Vine St. between 19th and 20th Sts.
Horace Trumbauer

In the 18th and 19th centuries, Philadelphia
libraries were privately owned. The first
free library, conceived by Dr. William
Pepper, began operating out of City Hall
in 1894.

312

The library's rapid growth made it a logical institution to occupy one of the sites on Logan Circle, designated for civic buildings in the parkway plan. Since the parkway was modeled after the Champs-Élysées, it was logical for the library to take its form from the twin palaces on the Place de la Concorde, which occupied a similar position on the boulevard. This choice was probably influenced by the recent trips to France of Julian Abele, a black architect who was Trumbauer's chief designer.

The library was one of the largest and most modern in the world. It was considered the ultimate in fireproof construction, with steel and aluminum furnishings and trim throughout the building. The spacious interiors are treated in neutral tones and materials, except for the use of pink Tennessee marble in the halls and Welsh quarry tile and terrazzo on the floors. Each of the principal rooms has an unpainted, decorative plaster ceiling.

312   H   *PR*
Pepper House, 1920
9120 Crefeld St.
Willing and Sims

Chestnut Hill houses of the 1920s and 30s were influenced by French, Italian and English country houses. Many local architects developed a distinctive form of residential design based on these sources, which became known as the Philadelphia style.

Willing and Sims was one of the prominent firms of the time. Their houses were notable for the fine use of rough stone and for the sensitive relationship of interior spaces to exterior gardens and terraces. The Pepper House, one of the most charming houses in Chestnut Hill, is an excellent example of the firm's work.

From the street the house appears quite simple. A round tower at the corner is the only distinguishing feature. The L-shaped plan, however, focuses on a small but beautifully designed formal garden with terraces overlooking Fairmount Park and

High Hollow, immediately below. A living room with beamed ceiling and the dining room enter onto the garden through French doors. The house achieves its distinctive character by its simple volumes and materials. There is little ornamentation except for the decorative details on the iron balconies, the use of heavy cornices and an elaborate dormer window on the garden facade.

313   B
Public Ledger Building, 1924
6th and Chestnut Sts.
Horace Trumbauer

The Public Ledger was Philadelphia's first penny journal and the city's leading newspaper until 1940. It was founded in 1836 by Cyrus H. K. Curtis, publisher of many of the country's leading magazines, including *The Saturday Evening Post*. When the *Ledger* moved to Independence Square, it joined several other publishing firms already in the area, including the Curtis Publishing Company, immediately adjacent. Although the new building was designed in a grandiose Georgian Revival style, its general form, height and materials were similar to the Curtis Building.

Marble and arched openings define the ground floor and the top floors of the building; the central portion is brick with simple, rectangular windows reflecting the basic office use. A shallow Ionic portico marks the entrance. Typical of Trumbauer's elaborate style are the decorated coffers around the doorways, the lobby with its coffered barrel vault and the ornate reception room.

●
1924
*Curtis Institute of
Music founded*

●
1925
*First woman judge,
Violet E. Fahnstock*

314   315

314   K
Reading Company Grain Elevator, 1925
411 North 20th St.

In the 18th and 19th centuries, Philadelphia
was a distribution center for grain grown in
the rich farmlands of Pennsylvania. For a
long time grain elevators were a common
sight in the city, but only this one remains.
Grain was delivered by wagon to the entrance on 20th Street, then stored in the silos
until it was loaded onto trains and taken to
the port.

The simple, low-cost industrial structure
was designed by staff architects of the Reading Railroad. Concrete was economically
poured in place in a process known as continuous pour, which required the building to
have a simple shape. The windowless grain
silos comprise most of the building, with
machinery towers on top; lower levels terraced down to the railroad tracks.

In 1976, Kenneth Parker, an interior designer, purchased the grain elevator and
converted the lower floors to offices. The
silos were left untouched, but the machinery
towers were transformed into a penthouse
apartment with landscaped terraces, giving
the appearance of a garden in the sky.

315   F,J
Philadelphia Divinity School, 1925–26
42nd and Spruce Sts.
Zantzinger, Borie and Medary

The Philadelphia Divinity School was
founded in 1857 to educate Episcopalian
priests. In 1917 the school purchased the
Clark estate to establish a theological
college as an adjunct to the University of
Pennsylvania.

Although never completed, the school
complex was considered one of the most
significant architectural undertakings of the
time. The buildings, located on a dramatic,
hilly site, were designed in the Gothic style
then popular for collegiate buildings.

The most impressive building is the
chapel, located on the highest point on the
site. Its interior is a masterpiece of Gothic
design and one of the most beautiful religious spaces in the city. The plan follows
the Oxford tradition, with choir stalls for
students and faculty, an antechapel for the
laity and a rear sanctuary leading to the
altar. Gothic ornamentation of superior
craftsmanship embellishes the stone structure, which has a hammer-beam ceiling
decorated with polychrome figures. A European atmosphere is created by the Gothic
detailing of the choir stalls, the ornamental
iron screens by Samuel Yellin and the
stained-glass windows by Nicholas
D'Ascenzo.

316   C
Drexel and Company Building, 1925–27
135–43 South 15th St.
Day and Klauder

Francis M. Drexel was a portrait painter
turned banker. The company he founded in
1837 quickly became the city's most important financial institution. In the early part of
this century, the company was headed by
Edward T. Stotesbury, one of the most influential financiers of his day.

For the new building Stotesbury wanted
an Italian palazzo worthy of the Medicis.
The design is based on the Strozzi Palace in
Florence. It is a solid fortress of rusticated
granite blocks, relieved only by massive
doors with hammered-steel hinges. Most of
the interior was taken up by a single, two-
story room opulently decorated to convey
the company's prosperity. Above the fourth
floor, offices with ornate mahogany paneling
faced onto a stone courtyard.

In 1980 the building was converted to
offices by J. Nathan and Company. Although the main room was subdivided, the
hand-carved, coffered, walnut ceiling is
still visible from the second-floor mezzanine. The original vault, with its massive
steel lock, is in the basement and is worth
seeing.

●
1926
*Sesquicentennial
Exposition opens in
what is now F.D.R.
Park*

●
1926
*Franklin Bridge spans
Delaware River*

●
1927
*Philadelphia General
Hospital dedicated*

317

318

317 G
Alden Park, 1920
Wissahickon Ave. and School House Lane
Edwyn Rorke; Renovated 1988–93, SRK
Associates and John Milner Associates

Alden Park was the first apartment complex
in the country built in a parklike setting.
The developer, Lawrence Jones, was a
wealthy manufacturer who wanted to create
a luxury cooperative for families who desired the amenities of a pastoral setting
without the responsibility for maintenance.

The complex consists of three buildings
located on 30 acres overlooking the Wissahickon Valley. Each building is designed
differently, but all are based on the Jacobean
Revival style. The Manor is the most elaborate. It has three separate towers linked by
an elaborate lobby. Each tower is a reinforced concrete structure finished with
rough-textured brick walls offset by pink
terra-cotta detailing. The lobby is decorated
with reproduction period furniture and has
a massive fireplace and wrought-iron
chandelier.

Among the original amenities of the complex were a nine-hole golf course, a year-
round swimming pool with roll-top roof,
formal gardens and individual garden plots
for residents.

318 H *PR*
French Village, 1925–28
Elbow and Gate Lanes, off Allens Lane
Robert R. McGoodwin

Just as Dr. Woodward's trip to London led
to the creation of the Lincoln Drive development, his trip to Normandy in 1923 inspired
the creation of French Village. The village
consists of a series of large houses built
along three private lanes. The overall plan
and most of the individual houses were designed by McGoodwin, Woodward's favorite architect, who had studied at the École
des Beaux-Arts.

Gatehouses flank the ends of Gate Lane
and Emlen Street. These private residences
mark the entrance to the village with archways that extend over the sidewalks. All
of the houses are built of local stone and
designed with a common vocabulary of distinctive forms: octagonal and circular stair-
towers, hipped roofs with overhanging
eaves, tall French doors and broad masses
reflecting the spacious interiors. The sensitive and varied relationships of the houses
to the landscape and to each other make
French Village one of the period's most
interesting developments.

Art Deco

*Art Deco began as a European movement,
taking its name from the International Exposition of Decorative Arts, held in Paris in
1925. The exposition emphasized design
that deliberately rejected historic influences
and expressed the new machine age. During
the decade of its popularity, Art Deco had
an enormous impact on the design of such
diverse elements as jewelry, trains, furniture
and movie sets.*

*Art Deco's sleek appearance is often re-
ferred to as streamlining. Primarily a style
of ornamentation, it was influenced by
Cubism and by North and South American
Indian art. Linear patterns of parallel lines,
zigzags or chevrons predominate. On buildings, exterior materials of smooth stone and
metal are contrasted by accents of terra-
cotta, glass and colored mirrors. Sculpture
and lettering were also integrated directly
into the architecture. Most Art Deco buildings have a unity of design that carries
through to the interior fixtures and furniture.*

● *1928*
Broad Street Subway
opens; First autogiro
in U.S. flown at
Willow Grove

● *1928*
Baldwin Locomotive
closes

319

320

319   D
Fidelity Mutual Life Insurance Company Building, 1925–26
Pennsylvania and Fairmount Aves.
Zantzinger, Borie and Medary; sculptor
Lee Lawrie/Renovated 1983 Environmental
Design Corp. and David N. Beck

The Fidelity Building was planned in conjunction with the Benjamin Franklin Parkway. In contrast to the parkway's neoclassical civic buildings, the Fidelity Building was designed in the Art Deco style, popular for commercial buildings in the 1920s and 30s. The sleek appearance, lavish materials, color and ornamentation conveyed a sense of prosperity and confidence in the future.

The Fidelity Building is a fine example of the best characteristics of the Art Deco style. Sculpture and decoration are concentrated around the two massive arched portals, the window spandrels and the cornice. Figures of the father and the mother, symbolizing work and home, crown the pilasters. Other figures on the arch symbolize the seven ages and twelve labors of man, and a variety of images decorate the spandrels and cornice. The building was renovated in 1983 for the offices of the Reliance Standard Life Insurance Company.

320   K
Lasher Printing Company, 1927
1309 Noble St.
Philip Tyre

During the 1920s many industrial buildings located on North Broad Street. The Lasher Printing Company was designed by Philip Tyre, an industrial architect who was remodeling the nearby showroom of the Packard Motor Car Company. Tyre designed a concrete urban fortress to accommodate the heavy machinery that the printing industry then required. It is a unique example of an Art Deco industrial building. The building's rough-textured concrete and straightforward expression of structure and service elements, such as the concrete fire escape, give it a very contemporary character. But the zigzag pattern at the top and bottom levels, originally unpainted, is a clear expression of Art Deco ornamentation.

321   K
N. W. Ayer Building, 1927–29
204–12 South 7th St.
Ralph Bencker

Although most new office construction was occurring around City Hall, N. W. Ayer and Son, a prominent advertising firm, located its headquarters on Washington Square, near the concentration of publishing companies. Bencker wanted the building to harmonize with its historic surroundings without using borrowed forms. He achieved this by a subdued Art Deco style similar to that of the Fidelity Building.

The blocky mass is given a vertical emphasis by the use of tall, narrow windows and setbacks on the upper floors. This simple form is embellished in the Art Deco manner with decoration based on symbolism related to the building's function. The pylons, extending through the top three floors, terminate in monumental figures symbolizing truth, holding the open book of advertising. Carved birds in flight decorated the lobby and carved bronze panels on the entrance doors depict Egyptian-looking figures in robes, working in various phases of the advertising industry. Egyptian motifs gained popularity after the opening of King Tutankhamen's tomb in 1922.

322   K   *OP*
Rodin Museum, 1927–29
22nd St. and Benjamin Franklin Pkwy.
Paul Philippe Cret and Jacques Greber

The Rodin Museum houses the largest collection of Auguste Rodin's work outside France. The museum and collection were the gift of Dr. Jules Mastbaum, who asked Jacques Greber to prepare preliminary

323

324

plans. Greber, a French landscape architect who drew the final plans for the parkway, invited Paul Philippe Cret to collaborate.

The gateway to the museum is a replica of the Chateau d'Issy, reconstructed by Rodin for his own home in Meudon, France. It leads to a formal garden beyond which the architects placed a small, well-proportioned classical temple on a high podium. The interior walls are decorated with murals by the well-known Philadelphia painter Franklin Watkins.

Several of Rodin's most popular sculptures are incorporated into the architectural composition, including *The Thinker* and *The Gates of Hell*, the bronze doors located at the entrance to the museum.

323 C
WCAU Building, 1928
1620 Chestnut St.
Harry Sternfeld and Gabriel Roth;
Renovated 1983 Kopple Sheward and Day

Art Deco was an extremely popular style for places of entertainment and, by association, the appropriate style for a radio station. Although Sternfeld studied the Beaux-Arts style under Paul Philippe Cret, he was a master of Art Deco design.

The facade creatively expresses the building's uses. Large glass windows on the ground floor originally displayed a Woolworth's store. Horizontal strip windows above light the office floors. At the top, the radio studio was expressed by a tower of glass, which glowed blue at night when the station was on the air. Glass and metal chevrons decorate the facade on either side of the tower. The whole composition is tied together by a wall surface of blue glass chips set in plastic.

Roth, a student of Sternfeld's, designed the lobby, which has a coffered ceiling and marble walls with metal strips. The brushed-metal elevator doors and the mailbox are wonderful examples of Art Deco design. The building was renovated in 1983 for the Art Institute of Philadelphia.

324 K
Rodeph Shalom Synagogue, 1927
615 North Broad St.
Simon and Simon

The Mikveh Israel Synagogue, founded in 1740, was the focus for Philadelphia's Jewish community. In 1802 a group of German Jews founded a second synagogue, later known as Rodeph Shalom. It is the oldest Ashkenazic congregation in continuous existence in the United States.

The new synagogue, built on the site of an earlier building by Fraser, Furness and Hewitt, is an outstanding example of the Byzantine style. Both the exterior and interior walls are covered with painted and carved geometric designs executed by the D'Ascenzo Studios. They also were responsible for the stained glass in the main sanctuary and the mosaic floor of the vestibule. The sanctuary has a large pendentive dome and contains a beautiful ark, supported on marble columns, with intricately carved doors of painted copper, bronze, steel and glass.

325 G *PR*
Abraham Malmed House, 1929
1021 Hortter St.
Mellor and Meigs

Although architectural design was moving away from historically derivative styles, many wealthy persons still preferred traditional homes. Even after George Howe left the firm, Mellor and Meigs continued to design fine country homes in the pastoral style. This house, built for Abraham Malmed, a manufacturer, is typical of the many beautiful homes they designed in Chestnut Hill and surrounding suburban towns.

A narrow drive, lined by high stone walls, leads into a small forecourt formed by wings of the house. This entrance gives little indication of the building's large size and complexity. The division of the plan into several wings breaks down the size and allows the house to follow the contours of

● **1930**
Summer concerts
begin at Robin Hood
Dell

● **1930**
Great Depression
begins

● **1931**
Convention Hall
opens; Empire State
Building completed

326

327

the steep site overlooking Fairmount Park.
The facade, of local stone set in tan-colored
mortar with brick courses over the windows,
blends into the natural setting. The design
achieves a medieval character by the steep-
pitched roof, polygonal chimneys, gabled
dormers and a tower on the facade facing
the park.

326 C,J
The Drake Hotel, 1929
1512–14 Spruce St.
Ritter and Shay

The Drake Hotel was one of many tall buildings constructed west of Broad Street in the
late 1920s. The overall form was influenced
by the emergence of zoning laws in the
1920s, which required setbacks on the upper
floors of tall buildings. Even today, the ta-
pered silhouette of the Drake is a striking
feature on the city's skyline.

Ritter and Shay, one of the city's most
versatile architectural firms, covered the
steel-frame structure with Pompeian brick
and terra-cotta decoration. The Spanish
Baroque ornamentation is based on themes
related to Sir Francis Drake. Terra-cotta
motifs of dolphins, shells, sailing vessels
and globes cover the ground floor and re-
appear on the piers, which rise to an elaborate series of cornices and culminate in a
distinctive terra-cotta dome.

327 K *OP*
30th Street Station, 1929–34
30th St. and John F. Kennedy Blvd.
Graham, Anderson, Probst and White;
Restored 1991, Dan Peter Kopple &
Associates

In exchange for land required by the city
for the construction of the Benjamin
Franklin Parkway, the Pennsylvania Railroad was given tunnel rights from the
Schuylkill River to 15th Street. The railroad
then built two new stations: Suburban Station, near City Hall, and 30th Street Station,

in West Philadelphia. Both buildings were
designed by the successor firm to D. H.
Burnham and Co.

Only a few railroad stations as grand as
30th Street Station remain in the country
today. Like others of the time, it has an
enormous interior waiting room. This room
is faced with marble and covered with a
coffered ceiling painted in red, gold and
cream. Natural light enters through glass
walls at both ends, which contain catwalks
connecting the flanking wings of the
building.

The exterior has monumental, columned
porte cocheres on the east and west facades.
Although classical elements are used on the
facade, their simple form indicates a compromise between historical and emerging
modern styles.

When completed the station contained a
chapel, a mortuary, over 3,000 square feet
of hospital space and a landing deck for
small aircraft on its reinforced concrete roof.

328 C
One East Penn Square Building, 1930
1–21 North Juniper St.
Ritter and Shay

One East Penn Square was built for the Market Street National Bank when Art Deco
was at the peak of its popularity. The building is typical of the Art Deco approach to
office buildings. The facade is divided into
three parts, with a strong vertical emphasis
in the brick curtain wall. Ornamentation,
derived from Mayan designs, is concentrated around the base and along the skyline.
The decision to place the banking room on
the second floor and reserve the first floor
for shops was unusual at the time, and may
have influenced the design of the PSFS
building.

●
1932
*Cornerstone of Franklin
Institute laid;
International style
exhibit at Museum of
Modern Art*

328

331

---

329 H
Schofield Andrews House, 1930−32
9002 Crefeld St.
Tilden, Register and Pepper

Tilden, Register and Pepper was a very successful architectural firm in the 1920s and 30s. They designed several major Philadelphia buildings, including the University of Pennsylvania Hospital, the Art Deco office building at 1616 Walnut Street and, with Rankin and Kellog, the 30th Street Post Office. Their specialty, however, was residential design.

One of their clients was Schofield Andrews, a resident of Chestnut Hill, for whom they designed several homes. This house is designed in the English country style similar to that used by Mellor, Meigs and Howe. It is beautifully sited on the edge of Fairmount Park. Certain features make the house unique. The doors and gates were imported from Italy, and the courtyard is laid in Belgian block patterned around an ancient grindstone centerpiece. Other notable features, such as the solarium at the end of the drawing room and the automated bowling alley in the recreation room, were added by the second owner, Mrs. Eleanor Widener Dixon, who acquired the property in 1949. In 1969 her son, Fitz Eugene Dixon, gave the property to Temple University for a conference center.

The International Style

In the 1920s, European architects created a new architectural style that was an even more dramatic departure from the past then was Art Deco. Many of the originators of this new style taught at the Bauhaus, an important German school of design. Three of its most influential teachers, Walter Gropius, Ludwig Mies van der Rohe and Marcel Breuer, moved to the United States in the late 1930s and became prominent American architects.

This new approach to design was recognized in the United States and named the International style by the 1932 exhibition of architecture at the Museum of Modern Art. Until after World War II, it was the dominant influence in this country and the source of subsequent modern styles.

International style is characterized by a total absence of ornamentation. Most residential buildings have a horizontal emphasis, with flat roofs, ribbon windows and smooth wall surfaces, usually painted white. Commercial structures are also devoid of ornament, emphasize horizontal elements and use such new industrial materials as aluminum or stainless steel for interior and exterior finishes. In addition to its impact on architecture, the International style had a strong influence on the design of furniture and household objects.

---

330 C,J
**Philadelphia Saving Fund
Society,** 1930−32
See page 108.

---

331 K *PR*
Midvale Avenue Row Houses, 1931−33
3421−75 Midvale Ave.
Robert J. McCrudden

Midvale Avenue was opened in 1889, when Falls of the Schuylkill was a mill town. The area was forested with poplar trees and as late as 1920 was still known as the Midvale woods. McCrudden, a local developer, began constructing houses in 1925 and continued until he went bankrupt during the Depression.

This beautifully designed row was advertised as studio homes because of the English Tudor-style living room with a balcony and 14-foot-high beamed ceiling. A large, leaded-glass bay window floods the room with light and adds to the distinctive Tudor character of the half-timbered facade.

330

330   C,J
**Philadelphia Saving Fund
Society,** 1930–32
12 South 12th St.
Howe and Lescaze

When PSFS decided to build a new headquarters, the directors chose a site near the
Reading Terminal and Wanamaker's department store, where they already had a successful branch bank. George Howe was
retained as architect. Howe had a national
reputation for his pastoral suburban houses
but recently had become an advocate of the
International style emerging in Europe.

PSFS marked Howe's break with his past.
He left Mellor and Meigs and entered into
partnership with William Lescaze, a Swiss
architect. Together they designed the first
International style skyscraper in the country.
James Wilcox, president of the bank, supported the design and persuaded the conservative board to accept it.

PSFS is a masterpiece; it is the finest
20th-century building in the city and one of
the most important examples of the International style in the country. The exterior form
is a sophisticated expression of the different
functions within the building. The base contains a retail store on the first floor, with the
banking room located above, following Ritter and Shay's successful use of a similar
arrangement in the Market Street National
Bank building. Bank offices above are set
back from the facade of the office tower,
which rises to a complicated roof structure
and prominent sign. At the rear of the building, elevator shafts and service elements

form a separate unit. To emphasize further
the contrasting elements of the design, different materials and colors were used.
Highly polished gray granite covers the
base; sand-colored limestone is used for the
facade of the bank offices. The office tower
has exposed vertical columns covered with
the same limestone and gray brick spandrels. The huge rear wall of the service core
is made of glazed and unglazed black brick.

Even though PSFS was built at the height
of the Depression, expensive materials and
furnishings were used throughout. The
stainless steel hardware and most of the furniture were custom designed by the architects, as there was no inventory of modern
fixtures in the United States. This was also
the second building in the country to be air
conditioned. The most dramatic interior
space is the high-ceilinged banking room.
Subdued colors; polished materials like marble, glass and stainless steel; and gently
curved balconies give the room an exceptional quality. The PSFS building was
beautifully maintained by the bank. However, in 1992 PSFS was purchased by
another bank which became insolvent. This
resulted in reduced use of the building for
banking purposes and the removal of some
of the original furnishings. Nonetheless, the
PSFS building remains as striking today as
when it was built.

•
1933
First dried blood serum developed; First Girl Scout cookie sale

•
1933
Philadelphia Eagles football team founded

•
1935
30th Street Post Office opens

332

333 Demolished

332 K
Federal Reserve Bank, 1931−35
10th and Chestnut Sts.
Paul Philippe Cret

The Federal Reserve Bank of Philadelphia, founded by Congress in 1913, is one of 12 regional banks that make up the central bank of the United States. These banks are responsible for managing the nation's supply of money.

This building is a fine example of Cret's later style, which was based on classical principles rather than the use of correct classical details. Cret placed the public banking room in a Greek temple form with a Doric front and placed the private offices in a three-story "attic" above. The original bronze light fixtures, gently vaulted ceiling and bronze grilles of the lobby retain a classical spirit and are examples of Cret's meticulous attention to detail.

This facade is enriched by monumental figures, sculptured by Alfred Boitteau, which depict Athena, the goddess of wisdom, and a mighty oak. There are also symbols of the nation's economic foundation: agriculture, industry and trade.

Cret added the formal garden in 1941. His successor firm, Harbeson, Hough, Livingston and Larson, added the recessed seventh story from 1952−53.

333 (Demolished)
White Tower, 1932
159 North Broad St.
Charles J. Johnson

White Tower, founded in 1926, was America's first fast-food chain. The company became successful by selling five-cent hamburgers and coffee. It was dedicated to simplicity, cleanliness and economy, qualities conveyed by the company name and the appearance of its buildings.

The Philadelphia store, designed by White Tower's in-house architect, is an example of the standard building erected throughout the country. It has a white porcelain-enamel facade (originally glazed brick), with a square tower over the entrance, large windows, gooseneck lamps at the roofline and minimal decoration. The interior had simple white surfaces trimmed with shiny stainless steel.

334 K
Carl Mackley Houses, 1933−34
M and Bristol Sts.
Oscar Stonorov and Alfred Kastner

Although there had been much public concern about housing conditions for lower-income families around the turn of the century, the provision of housing was considered a private responsibility until the Depression. Even before the U.S. Housing Authority was created, John Edelman, an official of the Philadelphia local of the Hosiery Workers Union, initiated the construction of cooperative housing for factory workers.

Carl Mackley Houses, named for a union member killed in a strike, was located near the mills of Kensington and Frankford. It was the first of many socially responsive housing developments designed by Stonorov. The complex is organized in four parallel rows of three-story buildings, arranged around courtyards connected to one another by walkways passing through the ground floors. The simple structures, influenced by International style housing in Europe, where Stonorov was trained, are enriched by recessed balconies and the use of buff-colored brick and yellow terra-cotta tiles. The architects were particularly sensitive to the tenants' needs and included such amenities as a swimming pool, rooftop laundries, a cooperative grocery, collective kitchens and dining rooms and a nursery school.

● **1936**
Frank Lloyd Wright designs "Falling Water," Bear Run, Pennsylvania

● **1936**
Democratic National Convention held in Philadelphia; First public housing opens

● **1937**
Celebration of 150th anniversary of the U.S. Constitution

334

335

335 K
U.S. Naval Hospital, 1933–35
1400–1909 Pattison Ave.
Walter T. Karcher and Livingston Smith

The Naval Hospital was built, by an act of Congress, to replace the existing hospital in Philadelphia. The main building is now the center of the complex that extends over 48 acres. It is one of the finest Art Deco buildings in the city and a major landmark in South Philadelphia.

The building design deviated from the standard practice of housing naval facilities in several small, related structures, and concentrated hospital activities in one 13-story structure. Like other tall buildings of the period, the structural steel frame is covered, in this case, by walls of limestone, brick and hollow tile. Recessed windows and continuously rising piers that break the roofline give the building a vertical emphasis. Although ornamentation is minimal, a rich appearance is achieved through subtle contrasts of color, derived by setting limestone and aluminum trim against a background of cream and buff brick.

336 K
Mayfair Theater, 1936
7300 Frankford Ave.
David Supowitz

Streamlining was a favorite mode of design in the 1930s. It was an important aspect of the Art Deco style and reflected America's growing preoccupation with speed and transportation machines. Streamlining had little impact on building design in Philadelphia, but even in conservative cities movie theaters were often designed in this popular style.

The Mayfair was the first movie theater in the city designed in a streamlined manner. Supowitz, the city's outstanding theater designer of the 1930s, transformed the building into a giant sign. The horizontal bands of the curved marquee are repeated in decorative horizontal bands on the wall below, broken by circular display windows. To achieve a sleek appearance, Supowitz used modern materials, including porcelain, structural glass and stainless steel. The Mayfair influenced the design of many subsequent theaters in the city.

337 H *PR*
Charles Woodward House, 1939
8220 Millman St.
Kenneth Day

The Woodward House is one of the few houses in the city designed in the International style. Kenneth Day, the son of Frank Miles Day, received a Beaux-Arts education at the University of Pennsylvania and worked for the neoclassical architects McKim, Mead and White. But in the 1930s his interests in city planning and large-scale housing developments introduced him to the International style then evolving in Europe.

The Woodward House combines International style elements with local building methods and materials. The plain, white, painted exterior wall surfaces and narrow windows are typical of the new style. But the pitched slate roof and foundation of local stone are acknowledgments of Chestnut Hill building traditions. On the interior, Day gave each function a separate, spacious room, in contrast to the open plans of contemporary European designers, and linked the two floors with a dramatic freestanding spiral staircase.

● **1938**
*Philadelphia enacts
first U.S. wage tax*

● **1940**
*Republican National
Convention held in
Philadelphia*

340

338 K

Mill Creek Housing, 1946–54; 1959–62
Fairmount Ave. between 44th and 47th Sts.
Louis I. Kahn and Associates
(Kenneth Day, Louis McAllister, Ann Tyng
and Christopher Tunnard)

Mill Creek was one of the city's earliest
urban renewal areas. Large parcels of land
were acquired by the city over the bed of
a former creek in the center of a predominantly black neighborhood. The development plan was based on the concept of
creating pedestrian greenways that would
link new housing and recreational facilities
with the older parts of the neighborhood.

Kahn and his associates were responsible
for the design of the public housing project
as well as the overall plan. The first phase
consisted of three apartment towers and a
group of two-story quatrefoil units, all built
of exposed reinforced concrete. This combination of high and low buildings was characteristic of the city's early public housing
projects. The plan of the complex is distinguished by a careful siting of buildings
around intimately scaled landscaped areas.

The brick row and twin houses and the
community center were added by Kahn in a
second phase. Massive concrete elements
over the windows and the recessed entrance-
ways give the buildings an austere, overscaled quality. The use of brick and concrete
and the interior plan of the community center were influenced by Kahn's design for
the Richards Laboratory.

339 K

Philadelphia Psychiatric Center, 1949–53
Ford Rd. and Monument Rd.
Louis I. Kahn

Shortly after completing the Mill Creek
project, Kahn designed two wings for the
Philadelphia Psychiatric Center: the Pincus
Occupational Therapy Building, 1949–50,
and the Samuel Radbill Psychiatric Hospital, 1950–53. Both buildings demonstrate

Kahn's early experiments with structural
systems as determinants of building form.

The Pincus Building is built of steel lally
columns and exposed open-web steel joists,
with unplastered cinder-block partitions. It
was Kahn's last use of metal construction
systems. The Radbill Building features a
facade that reflects the building's internal
functions. The ground floor has large glass
areas for the administrative and public
rooms, and the upper floors have smaller
windows for the nursing and treatment
rooms. Cantilevered sunshades above the
windows are perforated with collared flue
tiles, through which the sun makes patterns
on the walls.

Both buildings are interesting examples
of Kahn's work during a transitional phase
of his career.

340 J

Parkway House, 1952–53
22nd St. and Pennsylvania Ave.
Gabriel Roth and Elizabeth Fleisher

Parkway House was one of the first postwar
luxury apartment buildings in the city. It is
an exceptionally fine design, with elements
from both the Art Deco and International
styles. The form of the building is derived
from a remarkable response to the shape
and location of the site. Two side wings of
the U-shaped plan step down toward the
parkway, creating generous terraces for
many of the apartments. Other apartments
have curved-glass projecting window bays,
which are organized in vertical rows on the
main facade. These elements create the only
decoration on an otherwise plain brick structure and are more characteristic of buildings
of the 1930s than the 50s, reflecting Roth's
Art Deco background. The building is also
noteworthy because it was one of the first in
the city designed by a woman architect.
With its large apartments, fine design and
wonderful views of the city, Parkway House
is still one of the city's finest residential
buildings.

•
1941
*Pearl Harbor: U.S.
enters World War II*

•
1945
*Atomic bomb dropped;
First electronic
computer operated at
University of Pennsylvania*

341

The Modern Style

*Most American architecture designed since
the mid-1940s is called modern, a term that
encompasses many different approaches to
architectural design. Modern architecture
is an evolution of the International style
into several different modes of expression,
often associated with an individual architect. For example, Ludwig Mies van der
Rohe's emphasis on structural expression,
particularly exposed-steel construction, and
a uniform curtain wall has been the basis
for almost all tall office buildings erected in
this country from 1950 to the present. The
extensive use of exposed concrete in modern
buildings derives from the work of the
French architect Le Corbusier.*

*Among the few common characteristics
of most Modern buildings are the absence
of ornamentation, the direct expression of
structural systems and the use of muted
colors.*

---

341 C,J

Penn Center Complex, 1953–82
15th to 18th Sts., between Market St. and
John F. Kennedy Blvd.
Vincent G. Kling and Assoc./Emery Roth
and Sons/Kohn Pedersen Fox; Renovations
to #2 and #3, 1989, 1986, Ueland Junker
McCauley

In 1953 the Broad Street Station and
"Chinese Wall" of elevated railroad tracks
behind it were demolished to make way for
the city's first new office buildings since the
Depression. The original concept for Penn
Center was developed by Edmund Bacon,
his City Planning Commission staff and
Vincent Kling. They proposed a lower-level
pedestrian area, open to the sky, that would
connect the subway station and suburban
train station with the new shops and office
buildings. Real estate considerations by the
Pennsylvania Railroad modified the plan,
resulting in a lower-level pedestrian area,
lighted by small courtyards, and a group of
office buildings organized along a street-
level pedestrian mall.

Penn Center was significant not for the
design of the individual buildings but for
the project as a whole. The concept of a
separate pedestrian concourse linking transportation, retail and office facilities was
innovative at the time and influenced downtown development in many other cities. In
Philadelphia, Penn Center created a huge
parcel of developable land in the heart of
the city. Since the 1950s, nearly all major
office development has occurred in or
around this complex.

---

342 G

Schuylkill Falls Public Housing, 1954–55
Ridge Ave. and Merrick St.
Oscar Stonorov

Of the many public housing projects built in
the city in the 1950s, Schuylkill Falls most
clearly reflected the housing concepts developed by European architects of the International style.

Schuylkill Falls is located on a hilly, 27-
acre site overlooking the Schuylkill River.
The carefully organized plan consists of
two large elevator apartment buildings and
a series of two-story row house units arranged to leave a significant amount of open
space for community use. The large apartment buildings were considered to be archi-
tecturally and socially innovative when they
were built. Both buildings have long, common balconies on each floor, similar to the
"streets in the sky" concept developed by
the noted French architect Le Corbusier.
These balconies were intended to provide
places for children to play, easily visible
from each apartment. One of the other innovative features was the use of many individual elevators to provide access to three
or four apartments on each floor, thereby
eliminating long internal corridors.

Although the row houses remain occupied, the apartment buildings were vacated
in 1976 as a result of crime and vandalism,
which could not be controlled due to the
inability to secure the many elevator entrances and the open, unsupervised
balconies.

343

343   E,J
Richards Medical Research Laboratory,
1957–61
37th St. and Hamilton Walk
Louis I. Kahn

The Richards Medical Research Laboratory is considered one of the most significant buildings in modern American architecture. It was the pivotal project in the career of Louis Kahn and transformed him from an influential theoretical architect to one of international importance. Beginning with the Richards Laboratory, Kahn evolved a style of design that emphasized the use of heavy masonry construction, structural innovation and building volume, in contrast to the thin, steel-and-glass image of the International style. In the 1960s this approach, used by many locally based and trained architects, was referred to as the Philadelphia School.

At the Richards Laboratory, Kahn brought together in a unified design several concepts developed previously in other projects. He divided the building into served and servant spaces, giving each its own form and expression. The core tower of the building is poured-in-place concrete; it contains such services as elevators, animal quarters and utilities. The laboratories are located in three eight-story towers, connected to the core. Each of these towers in turn is served by smaller brick shafts containing additional services. The laboratories are open spaces made possible by placing both services and the structural system on the periphery of the building. Within the laboratories, the interlocking grid of supporting precast beams is exposed to allow for easy connection of utility systems to the surrounding towers.

Kahn felt that a building should reflect the way it was built. The innovative precast and poured-in-place concrete system, designed by August E. Komandant, articulates the structural principles of the cantilevered construction while providing visual interest to the facade.

The Biological Research Laboratory, added later, follows the same design principles, with some simplification of the structural system and the addition of projecting study carrels on the upper floors.

●
1947
*Better Philadelphia
Exhibit at Gimbels
department store*

●
1948
*Democratic and
Republican national
conventions held in
Philadelphia*

344

344 K
Beth Sholom Synagogue, 1959–60
York and Foxcroft Rds.
Elkins Park, PA
Frank Lloyd Wright

Beth Sholom Synagogue is the only major
building by Frank Lloyd Wright in the Philadelphia area. Wright designed many religious buildings in his career, dating back to
his 1906 Unity Temple in Chicago. His designs always incorporated the use of natural
light to illuminate the sanctuary. In the
1930s he envisioned a church in the shape
of a gigantic glass pyramid. Like many of
his other early conceptual projects, this did
not become an actual building until late in
his career.

Wright found a sympathetic client in
Rabbi Mortimer J. Cohen, who wanted a
building that would make people feel "as if
they were resting in the very hands of God."
The pyramid form also had symbolic associations with Mt. Sinai. The synagogue consists of a temple seating 1,000 persons and
a chapel below. The temple has a hexagonal
plan with an inwardly sloping floor. It is
brilliantly illuminated by the translucent
roof, from the center of which hangs a col-
ored-glass chandelier trimmed in incandescent lights. It is a spectacular and inspiring
religious space. The pyramid structure, supported by a giant steel tripod, has double
walls of plastic sheathed in glass. Along the
spines of the pyramid are symbols of the
menorah.

Wright's other significant project in this
area is the Suntop Homes, on Sutton Road
in Ardmore. Built in 1939, this complex is
an early example of Wright's Usonian
houses. Four houses are grouped together
under a single roof, similar to the quadruple
houses on Benezet Street. They were built
as prototypes of moderate-income housing
and used such innovative features as radiant
heating in the floor slabs. Although several
have been altered, they still retain Wright's
distinctive style.

●
1950
Phillies "Whiz Kids" win National League pennant

●
1951
New city charter approved; Independence National Park established

●
1952
Camden/Philadelphia ferry service ends

346

345 E,J
Hill Hall, 1960
34th and Walnut Sts.
Eero Saarinen and Associates

Hill Hall, originally a women's dormitory, was planned during the university's expansion in the 1950s. It is the only building in the city designed by Saarinen, one of the country's most influential modern architects.

From the outside the building is a simple, rectangular form. It is made of irregular brick, with recessed windows alternating in a horizontal and vertical pattern, behind which are the bedroom cubicles. This simple, austere exterior gives no indication that the interior focuses on a bright, spacious atrium that extends the full height of the building. Clerestory windows and glass walls above the dormitory floors light the atrium, which has private lounges and balconies opening onto it. The first floor contains a dining area for the dormitory, which is open to other university members and the public.

346 H PR
Margaret Esherick House, 1960
204 Sunrise Lane
Louis I. Kahn

Kahn designed a number of residences in the course of his career, only a few of which were built. The Esherick house is an outstanding example of a modest building transformed by the use of natural light to define interior spaces. It is built of concrete block covered with stucco. The walls of the street facade are pierced by two T-shaped windows, which provide light to the interior but ensure privacy. By contrast, the rear wall, which faces onto a wooded area and public park, is almost entirely glazed and open to the view. Additional light is bought in by a window placed behind a freestanding fireplace chimney on the side of the house. The interior rooms, though modest in size, are extremely handsome because of the thoughtful use of natural light.

347 K
Guild House, 1960–63

See page 117.

348 A PR
Society Hill Townhouses, 1962
3rd and Locust Sts.
I. M. Pei and Associates

When the Dock Street wholesale food markets were relocated to assist the redevelopment of Society Hill, a competition was held to select a housing project to be built on the site. Pei's winning design included three towers and 25 townhouses.

The townhouses were designed to provide a transition between the scale of the apartment towers and the 18th- and 19th-century rowhouses on Third Street. The new three-story houses are clustered around an attractively landscaped parking court in the center of which is the bronze sculpture "Floating Figure," by Gaston Lachaise. The more formal street facades are dark brick, with modest window openings similar to their predecessors and round-arch recessed doorways. But these unornamented, handsome houses do not imitate the Georgian style. The houses were regarded as distinguished contemporary design that respected the historic character of Society Hill. They influenced other groups of new houses in the area, including Bingham Court, on 4th Street, also designed by Pei in 1968.

1952
FCC approves four TV
stations for Philadelphia

1953
Broad Street Station
demolished to make way
for Penn Center

1953
Protests in Montgomery,
Alabama, begin Civil
Rights movement

347

347   K
Guild House, 1960–63
7th and Spring Garden Sts.
Venturi and Rauch with Cope and Lippincott

Venturi and Rauch have transformed contemporary architecture through their imaginative use of standard building materials, popular imagery and historical references. The Guild House, an apartment building for low-income elderly persons designed for the Friends Neighborhood Guild, is an outstanding example of their ability to create a distinctive building from ordinary materials and forms.

The building is dominated by a six-story entrance facade, designed as a single unit in the classical tradition. The first-floor base is faced in white glazed brick; the upper floors have balconies puncturing the flat facade and the top floor terminates the composition with the flat arch of the common room window. From this facade, the building steps back on either side, permitting most apartments an east, west or south exposure onto the small landscaped areas.

The composition of the elevation is particularly skillful in the placement, size and shape of standard metal windows. A decorative stripe of white brick appears to be a string course but is broken by windows rather than defining a floor level. By contrast with the articulated form and varied windows of the front elevation, the rear of the building is a flat surface with uniform windows, in keeping with the ordinary character of the surrounding housing. On the interior, apartments are arranged along a corridor that bends and turns, giving a more intimate scale and informal organization.

Guild House is a masterpiece of siting, interior planning and the use of standard materials to create a building that both fits its context and is strikingly new.

116

● *1956*
Grace Kelly marries
Prince Rainier

● *1957*
Walt Whitman Bridge
opens

349

350

349   H   *PR*
Vanna Venturi House, 1962
8330 Millman St.
Venturi and Rauch

Venturi's house for his mother is now considered a classic of contemporary architecture and one of the earliest expressions of post-Modern design concepts. The house reflects the firm's interest in applied decoration, historical references and the use of traditional elements in a nontraditional manner.

At first glance the house seems very simple. It has a large, sloping, gabled roof, deliberately reminiscent of 19th-century Shingle style. The smooth, flat stucco facade is nearly symmetrical, but the symmetry is broken by the placement of windows, and the roof is split by a deep recess, similar to the incomplete pediments of Baroque buildings. Other motifs used in a novel manner include the applied arch over the entranceway and the overscaled molding.

On the interior, complexity is achieved through the use of a few simple devices. Diagonal walls, to accommodate circulation, break the simple spaces of the rooms, and the stair to the second floor is distorted by the dominant chimney of the central fireplace.

Traditional elements used in a new way give the house a liveliness that is unified by its overall form and plain stucco exterior. Even today, the house seems remarkably innovative.

350   C
Municipal Services Building, 1962–65
15th St. and John F. Kennedy Blvd.
Vincent G. Kling and Associates

Plans for a new city office building on Reyburn Plaza were put forward before the Depression, but the proposal was not implemented until after new private office buildings were completed in Penn Center.

The new building was part of a larger redevelopment effort that included an underground parking garage and public plaza to the west.

The Municipal Services Building forms a backdrop for a new plaza on the west side of City Hall. The design extends the lower-level pedestrian concourse created in Penn Center, with connections to City Hall, the parking garage and subway stations. Within the building this lower level contains the offices of city agencies with the greatest public use. Two-story light wells in the building lobby and a sunken garden to the east allow natural light to reach the lower level.

The office tower has a cruciform plan created by cantilevering the floors above the lobby. Carefully detailed panels give the facade a rich masonry character, which complements City Hall. Advanced energy-saving features included double glazing in the windows and the separate heating and cooling zones for each face of the building. The Municipal Services Building is typical of the many carefully designed buildings by the Kling firm in the Penn Center area.

351   H   *PR*
Dorothy Shipley White House, 1963
717 Glen Gary Dr.
Mitchell/Giurgola Associates

Mrs. White, an artist and author, wanted a house that would accommodate a private studio for painting and writing, a place for entertaining and ample space for her large collection of antiques, art objects and books.

The house is located on a high knoll overlooking the Wissahickon Valley. From the street it appears to be a modest group of plain rectangular volumes, with relatively few visible windows. This reflects the asymmetrical plan, which consists of separate rooms linked by an entrance hall with a

●
1959
*Dock Street markets
relocated: Society
Hill renewal begins*

●
1960
*John F. Kennedy
elected President*

353

studio above. Each room is designed to
meet the specific requirements of the client's
work and collections. The principal rooms
have high ceilings and are lit by square
clerestory windows, which ensure privacy
and allow ample wall space for storage and
display. As in Kahn's Esherick house, the
private side of the house away from the
street is more open to the light and view.
The White house is an excellent example of
Mitchell/Giurgola's fine sense of proportion
and scale.

352 C
1500 Walnut Street Addition, 1963
15th St. below Walnut St.
Bower and Fradley

The office building at 1500 Walnut Street,
designed in 1928 by Ritter and Shay, is a
good example of the firm's restrained Art
Deco style. Bower and Fradley's addition
respects the basic form of the older building
in spite of its distinctively contemporary
glass curtain wall. This is one of the city's
best examples of the type of finely detailed
curtain wall made popular by Mies van der
Rohe. It is used in a very sophisticated manner. The height and certain indentations on
the new facade respond to cornice lines of
the older building. Inset panels beneath the
windows and larger windows at the corners
create a richer expression than the normally
flat, uniform curtain wall of most commercial buildings.

This was Bower and Fradley's first commission, and it established the firm's reputation for thoughtful and distinctive design.

353 K
Police Administration Building, 1963
Race St. between 7th and 8th Sts.
Geddes Brecher Qualls Cunningham

The Police Administration Building is one
of the most unusually shaped structures in
the city. It was built as part of the Independence Mall urban renewal project to provide
offices and facilities for the Philadelphia
Police Department, replacing those in City
Hall. The unusual form, which consists of
two circular units linked by a curved center
section, was selected for its efficient use of
floor space.

The building is notable for its innovative,
precast concrete structural system, designed
by August Komendant. The building is
made of over 2,000 pieces of precast white
concrete. The panels that make up the
facade are structural units and also carry
mechanical systems for heating and air
conditioning.

354 E
University Parking Garage, 1963
3201 Walnut St.
Mitchell/Giurgola Associates

In the 1960s, the University of Pennsylvania
planned a decentralized system of parking
garages to serve the campus. This first garage demonstrates Mitchell/Giurgola's use
of creative structural systems as a source of
architectural form and expression. The form
of the garage is determined by the two-level
site and by the system of ramps, which
creates a continuous spiral within the building. The main elevations consist of deep,
heavy, diagonal concrete trusses that support
beams spanning 60 feet over the parking
areas to a row of central columns. The light-
colored concrete shows the patterns of its
formwork.

High end walls, shaped by the ramps and
exit stairs, rise above the garage to accommodate a planned (but never constructed)
addition. The walls are clad in purple brick

●
1963
President Kennedy
assassinated

●
1965
Community College of
Philadelphia opens

354

356

and provide a counterfoil to the heavy, colorless concrete of the main structure.

In 1968 the architects designed a second garage, on South Street. This building, with its thin, precast components and massive brick end walls, is an interesting contrast to the Walnut Street garage.

---

355 K
Ukrainian Cathedral, 1963–66
816 North Franklin St.
Julian K. Jastemsky

East Poplar was one of the city's early urban renewal areas designed to remove deteriorated housing and provide new housing and community facilities. To keep the stabilizing Ukrainian population in the area, the city made land available for construction of a Ukrainian cathedral. It is the largest in the country and serves 300,000 Catholic Ukrainians of the Byzantine Rite.

The cathedral is a contemporary interpretation of Byzantine architecture, with a central domed space for worship. The exterior of the dome is covered with Venetian tile of glass fused with gold, making it a very visible landmark in the area. The concrete walls supporting the dome are shaped in graceful arches, within which are stained-glass windows. The interior is richly decorated and includes a figure of Christ worked in mosaic on the dome.

---

356 A,J
Society Hill Towers, 1964
2nd and Locust Sts.
I. M. Pei and Associates

By the 1940s, Society Hill was one of the city's worst slums. Most of the 18th-century houses were in dilapidated condition, and the area was dominated by the wholesale food market. As part of a comprehensive plan to redevelop the area, the food markets were relocated to a new food distribution center, in South Philadelphia.

A competition was held to select a housing design for the site that would symbolize the renewal of the area. Pei's winning entry included the townhouses on Third Street and three tall apartment buildings located on the axis of Second Street. The buildings are constructed of poured-in-place concrete, divided into meticulous rectilinear units that are both the structural frame and the facade. Each apartment has floor-to-ceiling glass windows, which provide dramatic views of the river and the city. The entrance court contains the sculptural group "Old Man, Young Man, The Future," by Leonard Baskin.

---

357 B
Rohm and Haas Building, 1964
6th and Market Sts.
Pietro Belluschi with George M. Ewing Company

Rohm and Haas, founded in 1909, is one of the country's leading chemical processors and the producer of plexiglass. When the company outgrew its headquarters on Washington Square, it became the first private investor to build on Independence Mall. The mall and facing blocks on either side were cleared of older buildings as part of the city's urban renewal program. New buildings were expected to be of contemporary design to contrast deliberately with the Georgian style of Independence Hall.

The Rohm and Haas Building was designed by Belluschi, then dean of the School of Architecture at M.I.T. He advocated the use of subdued color tones, resulting in a handsome, restrained, nine-story structure of concrete faced with dark bronze sunscreens and spandrel panels. Belluschi used plexiglass, manufactured by the company, for the sunscreens and spandrels and for the prominent lighting fixtures, designed by the Bauhaus artist Gyory Kepes, in the ground floor lobby and bank.

● **1967**
Martin Luther King
assassinated

● **1967**
Venturi's Complexity
and Contradiction in
Architecture *published*

358

360

---

358 C,J

United Fund Headquarters, 1969
Benjamin Franklin Pkwy. between 17th
and 18th Sts.
Mitchell/Giurgola Associates

When the Benjamin Franklin Parkway was
built, the city adopted elaborate design controls, in part to ensure that buildings east of
18th Street would create a narrow urban
space. Mitchell/Giurgola's United Fund
building is faithful to the intent of the parkway controls and illustrates the firm's
sophisticated response to the urban context.

The small, seven-story structure conforms
to its trapezoidal site. Each elevation responds to the unique conditions of its orientation. The north side is a curtain wall of
gray-tinted glass, which allows maximum
light for the office floors. The west wall is
shielded from the sun by horizontal concrete
sunscreens. The south wall, of structural
concrete, has deeply recessed windows that
block the south sunlight but afford views of
Logan Circle.

The different character of each elevation
was a dramatic contrast to the uniform
exterior design of most contemporary buildings and reflected a concern for environmental conditions that would not become
prevalent in architecture until the late 1970s.

---

359 A *PR*

Franklin Roberts House, 1969
228 Delancey St.
Mitchell/Giurgola Associates with
Roy Vollmer

As part of the Society Hill urban renewal
program, many 19th-century buildings were
demolished and vacant land made available
for new construction. The Roberts house is
one of the better examples of a new house
designed in a contemporary style sympathetic to its historic neighbors.

The austere brick facade is similar in
scale and material to the adjacent 18th-
century houses. It has fewer windows, however, and these are highly placed to ensure
privacy in a manner that is reminiscent of
Mitchell/Giurgola's White house. Behind
the modest facade, the L-shaped plan focuses on a two-storied, skylit living room.
A cantilevered library and balcony overlook
the living area, which opens onto a large
courtyard visible through the rear glass wall.

Mitchell/Giurgola also designed the
Zebooker house, at 110–12 Delancey Street,
which has a brick facade similar to its neighbors but uses large windows to create a contemporary contrast.

---

360 E *OP*

International House, 1970
3701 Chestnut St.
Bower and Fradley; Renovated 1983, 1992,
Dagit/Saylor Architects

In 1908, Dr. A. Waldo Stevenson began
informal meetings with foreign students in
his West Philadelphia home. These led to
the establishment of the International Students House in 1918, the first such organization in the country.

When expanded facilities were required
in 1965, a competition was held to select
the design for the new building. Bower and
Fradley's winning design was considerably
modified. The final design is composed of
two major elements. The eight upper floors
contain single rooms arranged in suites of
10, an organization that is articulated on the
facade. The stepped floors of the lower
levels are shaped by a dramatic interior arcade that runs the length of the building.
Restaurants and shops are located on the
first floor, with social and educational facilities and apartments on the upper five levels
that overlook and form the roof of the
arcade.

The building is an excellent example of
poured-in-place concrete construction with
exposed formwork patterns.

1968
Black students
admitted to Girard
College

1968
U.S. Mint, fourth in
Philadelphia history,
dedicated on
Independence Mall

1969
First landing on the
moon

364

361 J
Philadelphia Electric Company, 1970
2301 Market St.
Harbeson, Hough, Livingston, Larson

Electricity was introduced to most Philadelphia homes after World War I but did not
increase in use dramatically until the 1920s,
when the electrification of trolleys, suburban
railroads and subways added to normal de-
mands. Philadelphia Electric built new stations and expanded old ones. One of these
later provided the location for its headquarters building.

A three-story building on the site was
renovated to adjoin a new 23-story office
tower. The tower is one of the few excellent
examples in the city of buildings designed
in the style of internationally famous contemporary architect Ludwig Mies van der
Rohe. Structural steel columns, placed on
the two long sides of the rectangular floor
plan, are expressed on the facade and emphasize the height of the building. They are
sheathed in black aluminum, matching the
spandrel panels and windows, which are
carefully divided into individual units to
give scale to the tall facade.

A dramatic, illuminated billboard surrounding the top four floors carries mes-
sages appropriate to the season or current
events. Because of its location on the western edge of downtown, it is a highly visible
and handsome landmark on the city skyline.

362 A
**Penn Mutual Life Insurance Company
Addition,** 1969–70

See page 122.

363 K
Federal Reserve Bank, 1973–76
6th and Arch Sts.
Ewing, Cole, Cherry, Parsky

When the Federal Reserve Bank outgrew
Cret's neoclassical building on Chestnut
Street, a site on Independence Mall was
selected for its new headquarters. The new
building contains the offices of the Federal
Reserve and other government agencies, as
well as specialized banking facilities for the
storage and disposal of currency. One of the
vaults is as long as a football field and holds
millions of dollars.

Fine materials were used for interior and
exterior finishes, conveying a monumental
dignity and elegance that is unique in recent
government buildings in the city. The
meticulously detailed exterior is covered in
polished pink granite panels set flush with
horizontal banks of windows of varying
sizes. A large vertical window divides the
facade in half, reflecting the large entrance
court within the building.

The spacious court is eight stories high,
sheathed in travertine and covered with a
skylight. Suspended in the court is a 10-ton
mobile, the largest in the world, designed
by Alexander Calder.

364 B OP
Franklin Court, 1973–76
312–22 Market St.
Venturi and Rauch with John Milner
Associates

Benjamin Franklin built his own house and
print shop in the courtyard behind a row of
tenant buildings on Market Street. Although
the tenant buildings survived, Franklin's
house, except for sections of the foun-
dations, was destroyed. Lacking sufficient
evidence to reconstruct the house faithfully,
the National Park Service commissioned
the architects to design an interpretive complex. The resulting project is one of the
most imaginative historic restorations in
the country.

continued on page 123

362

Penn Mutual Life Insurance Company Addition, 1969–70
Walnut St. between 5th and 6th Sts.
Mitchell/Giurgola Associates

Penn Mutual's headquarters have been located on this site since the 19th century. The original, cast-iron structure was replaced by the current headquarters building in 1913, which was added to in 1931. When the company decided to expand again, they wanted a new addition that would connect to each floor level of the existing building.

Mitchell/Giurgola's design again demonstrates the firm's responsiveness to the urban context. In addition to the constraints of a small site, the design had to incorporate the 1838 Egyptian Revival facade of John Haviland's Pennsylvania Fire Insurance Co. The north facade, facing Independence Hall, is a continuous plane of dark glass rising to a concrete roof structure. An observation deck on the roof, no longer in use, is reached by an exterior elevator expressed by concrete piers. At the ground level the glass facade steps back to allow Haviland's facade to stand in its original location, serving as a screen to the entrance courtyard.

In keeping with the firm's earlier work, each facade responds uniquely to its environment. The east wall has cantilevered concrete sunscreens and large recessed windows, the south wall is tinted reflecting glass and the west wall has indentations responding to the older building. Because of the small site, a special structural system was designed to simplify construction. Steel columns on the east wall support paired steel trusses, which span the full width of the building and support steel decks for the floors. The steel is covered with concrete. This system takes advantage of the high ceiling heights, resulting from the requirement to connect with floor levels of the existing building, and provides column-free office floors in the addition.

The overall composition provides a beautiful backdrop for Independence Hall.

●
1970
Penn Central Railroad
goes bankrupt

●
1974
Episcopal diocese
ordains first women
priests

365

366

The complex consists of four elements: the restored Market Street buildings, a garden, the "ghost structures" representing the house and print shop, and an underground museum. The most original aspect of the design is the white tubular-steel frames outlining Franklin's original buildings. The plans of the house and print shop are inlaid in the paving beneath the frames, supplemented by quotes from Franklin and his wife cut into the slate paving. Beneath the ghost structure and 18th-century garden is a museum, reached by a long, sloping ramp. The museum contains imaginative exhibits about Franklin's life and accomplishments. The restored Market Street buildings also interpret Franklin's activitites; one contains a post office and another a print shop. Of particular interest is the building west of the entrance archway, which has been left unfinished on the inside so that it is possible to see the original construction details.

365   A
Old Pine Community Center, 1974–77
4th and Lombard Sts.
Friday Architects

The Third Presbyterian Church, informally known as the Old Pine Street Church, was built in 1766 and extensively remodeled during the 19th century. The community center to the south was built to serve a number of local organizations, including two churches, a historical society, an elementary school and the community at large. It contains a nursery school, community room, gym and historic archives.

The design incorporates historical elements of different periods into a wholly original composition. Flemish bond brick and white trim, typical of the colonial neighborhood, are combined with glass block and ziggurat ornamentation derived from the Art Deco style. A portion of the site is developed as a small park, with a miniature amphitheater surrounded by a

terrace decorated with mosaics created by community organizations in the area. The interior shows the architects' fondness for decorative patterns and imaginative details in the tile work of the lobby and the common room, which has a trompe l'oeil Persian rug with fringe set in tile.

366   C,J
The Gallery, 1974–77/1982–83
Market St. between 9th and 11th Sts.
Bower and Fradley/Bower Lewis Thrower and Cope Linder Associates

In the late 1950s, the City Planning Commission proposed the construction of a new retail and office complex east of City Hall over a rail tunnel connecting the Pennsylvania and Reading railroad lines. In 1964 the city and business community adopted a plan for a six-block-long skylit pedestrian mall, one level below the street, with retail shops connecting existing department stores at either end.

This ambitious proposal was eventually carried out by the city and the Rouse Company, one of the most innovative retail developers in the country. It is one of the first downtown enclosed shopping malls in an American city. A dramatic skylit pedestrian mall connects four levels of retail stores and a new Gimbels department store to the existing Strawbridge and Clothier store. The entrance at 9th Street has a stepped, glass-covered atrium leading to the multilevel mall. Fountains, special displays and glass-enclosed elevators enliven the public areas. The second phase of the mall opened in 1983 and includes a new J. C. Penney store, a major office building and a new underground rail station with a magnificent wall mural designed by the architect David Beck. The total complex, running from 8th to 11th streets, combines the excitement of the city with the successful marketing techniques of suburban shopping centers.

•
1975
*Southeast Asian
refugees begin to
arrive in city*

•
1976
*Bicentennial celebration;
Flyers win Stanley
Cup*

368

367 K
American Postal Workers Housing,
1977–79
801 Locust St.
Hassinger and Schwamm

In the 1970s the federal government encouraged private developers and nonprofit organizations to create low-income housing by providing subsidies to make up the difference between what tenants could afford to pay and the prevailing fair-market rents. This expensive but successful program resulted in the construction of many new housing complexes for the elderly and for low-income families.

The Postal Workers Housing is one of this program's more imaginatively designed elderly housing developments. It was created jointly by the union and Berger Brothers, a private housing developer. The building contains 300 apartments, organized in a long, horizontal form. The south-facing main facade is given a special character by the use of projecting window bays, which provide a vertical contrast to the horizontal building mass, and by the glass-enclosed solarium on the southeast corner. These elements, and the use of a richly colored traditional brick over the structural frame, give the building a conventional appearance rather than the stereotyped image of a subsidized housing project.

368 E,F,J
ISI Building, 1978–79
3501 Market St.
Venturi Rauch and Scott Brown

The four-story office building of the Institute for Scientific Information is part of the University City Science Center, a research complex sponsored by most of the colleges and universities in the Philadelphia area. The ISI Building is a straightforward, inexpensive structure with a typical office layout. It is noteworthy because it is a literal expression of Venturi Rauch and Scott Brown's concept that buildings should be viewed as "decorated sheds." In this instance, the decoration consists of a symmetrical pattern of brightly colored tiles set in long horizontal bands on the main facade. The entrance is marked by porcelain enamel panels decorated with a bold floral design similar to that used by the firm for the facade of a Best store in suburban Philadelphia.

369 K
The Eye Institute, Pennsylvania College of Optometry, 1978
1201 West Spencer St.
Hardy Holzman Pfeiffer Associates

The Eye Institute provides patient services and is also an educational facility. The Institute's building is the only work in Philadelphia by the distinguished New York firm Hardy Holzman Pfeiffer. Its form is partially determined by the siting of the two-story structure on a gentle slope and in a diagonal relationship to adjacent buildings. The irregularly shaped structure has large-frame glass walls along the main facade, allowing light to pour into the lobby areas. Within the building, the irregular floor plan is subdivided by low walls and enclosed rooms, placed at an angle to the building walls. As is characteristic of the firm's work, the interiors are brightly painted, including the exposed ducts and pipes of the mechanical systems.

The distinctive character of the building results from its imaginative siting and surrounding landscape plan, and from the colorful and spacious interior design.

370

372

---

370 C
**Insurance Company of North America
Annex,** 1979
17th and Arch Sts.
Mitchell/Giurgola Associates

The Insurance Company of North America, organized in Independence Hall in 1792, is the oldest stock and marine insurance company in the country. In 1925 the company built its new home office at 16th and Arch streets. The Georgian Revival building was designed by Stewardson and Page. Mitchell/Giurgola's addition is designed with the firm's usual sensitivity to adjacent buildings. But the use of a sleek, pale-green aluminum and the strong horizontal character of three sides of the building give it a different and a more sophisticated appearance than the firm's earlier buildings.

The design incorporates many of the firm's standard devices. The north wall is essentially glass, with a clear expression of structural columns and beams. The south, east and west walls have long horizontal aluminum sunscreens protecting the deeply recessed glass windows. The mechanical equipment floor at the 15th level is clearly expressed by a wide aluminum band on the facade, which corresponds to the cornice height of the 1925 building, visually connecting the two structures. Portions of the facade are set back to mark the corner entrance and allow the structural grid to stand free. The complex, multistory lobby space is decorated with a 35-foot-high painting and is given added interest by the prominent display of antique fire apparatus from the company's collections. Although crowded into the urban fabric and difficult to view, the building is one of the most handsome office structures in the area.

371 C
**Franklin Plaza Hotel and SmithKline
Office Building,** 1978−82
Vine St. between 15th and 16th Sts.
Geddes Brecher Qualls Cunningham

Philadelphia had many elegant hotels in the early 20th century. But by the time the Bellevue Stratford closed in 1977, as a result of the publicity over Legionnaires' Disease, the city was left with no significant downtown convention hotel. The Franklin Plaza was built by Pattison Partners and the Franklintown Corporation, a coalition of private companies. This organization, led by SmithKline Beckman, was created to develop a new residential and commercial community north of Logan Circle.

The hotel and office building are designed as a single composition. The towers are linked by a lower skylit atrium structure containing the lobby and meeting rooms. This dramatic space contains escalators rising to a series of balconies, which provide access to the ballroom and meeting facilities. On the exterior, each of the towers is sheathed in buff-colored precast concrete panels. But the fenestration of each building is different to reflect the different functions, and the office building panels are accented with bands of red clay tile.

372 J
The Atrium, 1982
Market St. between 19th and 20th Sts.
Cope Linder Associates

Most recent office buildings have been built to the maximum height allowed by the city's zoning ordinances. Rouse and Associates created a prestigious office setting by constructing a low, eight-story structure around a skylit atrium extending the full height of the building. This atrium is designed as if it were a gigantic interior greenhouse. Hanging plants on the end walls complement the lush tropical landscape of the main floor. The predominantly glass walls facing the atrium have balconies and small terraces

● **1980**
Phillies win World
Series

● **1983**
Sixers win NBA
championship

373

374

projecting into the space. Terraced, land-scaped courts step down to the lower-level offices of the Philadelphia Stock Exchange, the building's principal tenant. Large windows allow visitors to watch the activities on the exchange floor.

On the exterior, the curtain wall has horizontal windows and spandrels, which change dimension to accent the center. Corner entrances are created by simple set-backs within the building volume.

The Post-Modern Style

In recent years many American architects have expressed dissatisfaction with Modern architecture. References to historic styles have become more acceptable, often interpreted in an abstract manner or used in a way that reflects their borrowed nature. One of the principal sources of this post-Modern movement is the work and writings of the Philadelphia architectural firm Venturi Rauch and Scott Brown.

Post-Modern buildings are characterized by a greater use of ornamentation and color, richer materials and an eclectic combination of elements from previous architectural styles.

373   C
Alfred J. D'Angelo Pavilion, Magee Rehabilitation Hospital, 1982–83
15th and Race Sts.
Dagit/Saylor Architects

In 1958 the Magee Hospital constructed a modest facility to serve physically handicapped patients. The recent six-story addition, which more than doubled the hospital's size, is one of the earliest buildings in the city designed in a post-Modern manner.

Although modest in scale, the hospital addition skillfully unites the old and new buildings into a single composition. This is achieved by a continuous rusticated granite base, and by the horizontal bands of molded brick and projecting second-level terrace, which extend over both facades. The overall appearance of the building is reminiscent of designs of the 1930s, a feeling that is enhanced by the use of glass block, horizontal bands of brick and square windows.

374   C,J
Four Seasons Hotel and One Logan Square, 1982–83
Race St. between 18th and 19th Sts.
Kohn Pedersen Fox

The strict controls for the Benjamin Franklin Parkway limit the height of any building on Logan Circle to 80 feet. In the early 20th century, new buildings in the neoclassical style for the Free Library, the Family Court and the Franklin Institute all adhered to the height limitation. One parcel remained undeveloped until the Insurance Company of North America commissioned this exceptional design for a hotel and office complex.

To follow the parkway controls, the architects placed the seven-story hotel on Logan Circle and the 30-story office tower to the rear, with a courtyard between the two buildings. Both buildings are faced with polished granite, giving the complex an elegant character. Light-colored granite is used on the hotel to match the color of the Franklin Institute; the office building is a darker tone. Fine materials, equally well detailed, are used in the public spaces on the interior of both buildings.

375

376

---

375 F,J
University City Family Housing, 1982–83
Market St. between 39th and 40th Sts.
Friday Architects

In the late 1970's, the federal government
required some new low income housing be
built in locations that would promote racial
and economic integration. Neighborhood
opposition to this policy often led to the
selection of sites in unusual locations.

This imaginatively designed low income
housing complex creates a sense of place
for residents to overcome its predominantly
institutional and commercial surroundings.
The strikingly simple yet original design
shows an appreciation for vernacular architecture while also incorporating Victorian
motifs from West Philadelphia houses. Most
of the houses are arranged in rows perpendicular to Market Street, with small back-
yards and common entrance courts. The
courts are framed by entrance arches and by
a long row of houses on the southern edge
of the site, giving privacy to the common
open space. Brick is used for the facades
facing the entrance courts, which also have
Queen Anne–style wood porches with decorated gables and bay windows. On the back
the houses are covered in green aluminum
siding, symbolizing the garden side of the
building.

In 1992, this project was selected by the
Foundation for Architecture as the best designed low income housing complex of the
previous ten years.

376 K
Shelly Ridge Girl Scout Center, 1984
330 Manor Road
Bohlin Powell Larkin Cywinski

As late as the 1990's, Upper Roxborough
retained a largely rural character made possible by the dedication of large tracts of land
as a nature center and the preservation of
previous farmland. The 88 acres of woods
and deep ravines of Shelly Ridge provided
the Girl Scouts with a wilderness setting
for a summer camp virtually within the
city limits.

To preserve the one large open space on
the site, five new buildings were grouped
around its edge in an informal composition
with an existing barn. The buildings derive
their form from the barn, traditional wood-
frame cabins of summer camps playfully
interpreted, and an innovative use of passive
solar energy. Gray clapboard, green gables,
bright red trim, and red columns with un-
dulating gray capitals marking the entrances
to buildings, provide a unifying vocabulary.

The main building, triangular in plan,
has a twenty-five foot high timber-framed
Trombe wall with brick in-fill panels that
store heat in the early part of the day for
release in late afternoon. Exposed structural
timber trusses cover a spacious interior with
a prominent free-standing Rumford fireplace
and adjacent stepped seating and perfor-
mance area. A semi-circular wall facing
south creates a warming area and also serves
as a sun dial. The caretaker's house has a
central two-story space allowing heat from
a wood burning stove with exposed pipes to
rise to the second floor. Exaggerated south
facing dormer windows allow deep penetra-
tion of natural light.

378

379

377 K
Cecil B. Moore Avenue Subway Station,
1984
Cecil B. Moore Ave. and Broad St.
Mitchell/Giurgola Associates

Almost 100 years after its founding, Temple University had grown from a small college to a state-supported institution with over 19,000 students. Many commuted to the main campus by public transportation, making the Cecil B. Moore Avenue station of the Broad Street subway a main entrance to the campus.

Following concepts initiated in Center City subway station design, a lower level courtyard opens the east side of the station allowing natural light to reach the platform level. The courtyard extends into a terraced, landscaped plaza connecting to exit stairs from the station at three different levels. The main plaza, set three feet below street level, is paved in brick and cast concrete with ornamental railings and patterned concrete retaining walls. A grid of 20 trees in the center provides shade and color. The plaza is shielded from Broad Street traffic by a linear brick structure with a continuous skylight covering stairs and an escalator.

378 D,J
George D. Widener Memorial Tree House, 1985
The Philadelphia Zoological Gardens
34th St. and Girard Ave.
Venturi, Rauch and Scott Brown

The 42 acre Philadelphia Zoo contains an interesting collection of buildings by some of the city's most distinguished architects. (See page 181.) One of the most interesting areas is the Children's Zoo where animals are free to be touched and fed. When the Children's Zoo was redesigned in the 1980's to foster a greater understanding of the natural world, the 1876 Antelope House designed by George Hewitt was transformed into a central feature. Six separate environmental settings were created within the Victorian structure, each designed to enable participants to view these environments as their natural inhabitants would. A large cell honeycomb, for example, allows children to experience what it would be like to be a bee. Fiberglass, rubber, insulation and other artificial materials were used to create lifelike trees, vegetation and animal forms of exaggerated size. The building derives its name from a 24 foot high, 16 foot wide artificial ficus tree which projects through the roof of the existing building into an added cupola.

Not just for children, the Tree House is one of the city's most popular interior spaces and the site of many fundraising events.

379 K
Renfrew Center, 1986
475 Spring Lane
Atkins, Voith and Associates

The 27 acre Renfrew farm was originally the estate of Mrs. Samuel F. Houston for whom Robert McGoodwin designed an elegant manor house modeled after a late 17th century French chateau. When the farm was purchased for a clinic to treat bulimia and anorexia nervosa, the manor house was adapted to administrative and therapeutic offices and a new building added for dormitory and dining facilities.

The residential building is set into the hillside, providing a commanding view of the farmland as well as good views of the original house. The long, thin building has its narrow end toward the manor house to minimize impact. Its scale, roof silhouette, pattern of windows, arched central bay and exterior masonry details are all derived from the manor house, but used in non-imitative ways. On the interior, the building has a residential character while maintaining the standards required of a medical institution. A pair of spacious living rooms behind the

● *1985*
Police drop bomb on MOVE house;
11 children and adults killed,
62 homes destroyed

● *1985*
First U.S. Pro Championship Bicycle
Race climbs the "Manayunk wall"

380

381

large bay window and a wide grand stair provide a central focus. Rooms for 42 residents are provided on two floors. The exterior is stucco over concrete block. Cast stone is used for the water table, still course, cornice, quoins and entrance columns reflecting the details and character of the manor house.

380   C
The Graham Building/One Penn Square West, 1986
30 South 15th Street
Cope Linder Associates

The area immediately west of City Hall once contained a concentration of large and ornate movie theaters. After the development of Penn Center, the demand for office sites coupled with the decline in theater attendance led to the eventual demolition of these marvelous movie palaces.

This office building, on the site of the former Goldman Theater, turns a difficult location into a thoughtful example of urban design. Taking advantage of an adjacent small street, the main entrance is located at the corner and marked by a cylindrical tower of glass rising the full height of the building. The masonry walls appear to be a screen set in front of the glass facade. Window openings, cornice lines and floor levels of the main facade respond to the adjacent office building, providing continuity in scale without imitating the older forms. The lobby creates a gracious transition from the corner entrance to the central elevator core through an oval space with a small fountain.

381   K
Philadelphia Industrial Correction Center, 1986
8301 State Road
Jacobs/Wyper Architects and
The Ehrenkrantz Group

Prisons have been part of Philadelphia society since the first was built at 5th and Walnut Streets in 1778. Most have been located on the outskirts of the city at the time they were built and some, such as Eastern State Penitentiary, set innovative standards for prison reform for their times. This prison follows in that tradition. The site, in the far northeast section of the city, was a garbage dump close to other prison facilities.

The design is based on an innovative approach to improving the quality of prison life and reducing potential for conflict. This is achieved by reducing barriers between inmates and officers and by grouping inmates in small clusters. The basic unit of the prison is 50 cells organized on two floors around a double-height dayroom with access to outdoor recreation. Inmates spend their entire time within this unit, thereby minimizing contact and the potential for conflict among the 650 inmates. A generous use of natural light in the corridors and brightly painted common rooms adds to the non-threatening character. The lobby visiting area, with marble wainscotting and picture windows, was deliberately designed to provide an atmosphere that would not intimidate visitors.

A well equipped gymnasium, shops and classrooms are grouped behind a semi-circular rusticated stone and brick colonnade. The semi-circular motif also interrupts the stone and marble wall that masks the facility from its neighbors, providing an entrance courtyard for the complex.

382

384

382 J
Commerce Square, 1987, 1992
Market St. between 20th and 21st Sts.
Pei Cobb Freed & Partners

As office sites close to City Hall became more difficult to acquire, developers began to look farther west along Market Street and Kennedy Boulevard. Commerce Square, the most distinctive of the new office buildings in this area, created a civic setting as well as office center in an area with few surrounding amenities. The heart of the project is a handsome landscaped public plaza designed by Hanna-Olin Ltd. The plaza contains a circular fountain surrounded by tree-shaded outdoor cafes and retail shops. The granite paving inset with red pavers and black squares extends the materials and patterns of the towers.

The twin 40-story office towers, built in two phases, are set back in a series of slabs to reduce their scale and allow natural light to reach the courtyard most of the day. The 45 foot height line of the lower slab and ground floor arcade create a pedestrian scale. Each slab is topped by a parapet with geometric openings lightening the edge of the building at the skyline. Horizontal bands of gray glass and gray Caledonia granite inset with squares of darker granite also help to reduce the scale, except along the short sides of the towers where paired square windows form a vertical seam emphasizing the height.

383 C,J
One Liberty Place, 1987
See page 132.

384 K
Frankford Post Office, 1988
4410 Paul St.
Agoos/Lovera Architects

Early growth in Philadelphia expanded north and south along the Delaware River, rather than westward as William Penn intended. Frankford, one of the earliest settlements outside the official city-limits, still retains buildings from the 18th century. In the 19th century, Frankford, like much of area north of downtown, was the site of many manufacturing plants. The neighborhood post office draws inspiration from this mixed architectural heritage.

The building consists of two simple parts: a service area for customers and a work area to sort and distribute mail. The clerestory monitor over the work area is a form common to industrial buildings in the area while the small gable roof over the entrance to the public spaces reflects a nearby church. The main facade and exterior walls of traditional red brick are residential in scale and use glazed headers, typical of colonial houses, to create a decorative pattern. Exposed, brightly painted duct work in the public areas gives the interior a simple but playful character.

385 F PR
Gaither House, 1988
3601 Baring St.
Atkins, Voith and Associates

Powelton Village developed in the 1850s when horse drawn carriage lines were extended to West Philadelphia. Most of its housing took the form of suburban villas in the Italianate style, influenced by the work of Samuel Sloan, with later 19th century houses influenced by such architects as Wilson Eyre. This three story house, on a tight corner site, reflects these local influences but interprets them in an original manner.

385

387

The main living areas are located on the second floor. This provides room on the first floor for a two car garage while giving the living areas a greater amount of natural light and better views. The double-height living room, with a large fireplace, is brightly lit by a south-facing bay window. Bay windows also provide light to the dining room and master bedroom. Like many of the older houses in the area, the exterior is a combination of two materials, brick on the first floor and stucco above with a sloping slate roof. The house is a sophisticated contemporary interpretation of the suburban villa.

---

386   C
Two Logan Square, 1988
100 North 18th St.
Kohn Pederson Fox

When Kohn Pederson Fox designed One Logan Square and the Four Seasons Hotel, the Benjamin Franklin Parkway design controls encouraged a simple and understated architectural expression. Freed from these controls for an expansion of the office space on an adjacent site, the architects produced an exuberant example of post-Modern design.

The 34-story office tower is set on a heavily masonry base of pink and gray granite corresponding in materials and character to the adjacent office building and hotel. However, doorways and windows are surrounded by an almost Mannerist interpretation of such classical details as quoins, keystones and cornices. This effect continues in the ornate lobby of gleaming white, gray and green striped marble. In contrast to the masonry base, the tower consists of vertical strips of gray and silver glass emphasizing the height of the building. The top five floors are set back and terminate on the skyline in a pedimented roof giving these floors the appearance of a separate structure.

387   A
Center for Judaic Studies, University of Pennsylvania, 1988
420 Walnut St.
Geddes Brecher Qualls Cunningham

Dropsie College, founded in 1911 and originally located in North Philadelphia, was the only center for Judaic studies in the country. A generous gift from Walter F. Annenberg resulted in the move to a new location on a prominent site near Independence Hall and a subsequent affiliation with the University of Pennsylvania. The center is a postdoctoral research institution for the scientific study of the history, culture, literature and religion of Judaism, and of Christianity and Islam in the Middle East. It is primarily a research library with offices for staff and resident scholars.

The building is shaped by its simple program. The window pattern of the main facade reflects the individual offices behind; the west side, overlooking one of the pedestrian walkways through Society Hill, has a large bay window providing light to the reading room, the principal room of the building. Large dormers on the roof let light into the conference facilities.

The building incorporates references to traditional elements and materials in the surrounding area, interpreting them in a new manner. The dormers are typical of colonial row houses, though here much larger in size. The brick and limestone facades are consistent with other institutional buildings in the area and the limestone-topped walls of the adjacent garden.

388, 383, 390, 392

---

383 C,J
One Liberty Place, 1987
1650 Market St.
Murphy/Jahn

---

388 C,J
Two Liberty Place, 1990
Murphy/Jahn with Zeidler Roberts
Partnership

---

389 C,J
**The Shops at Liberty Place and
Ritz-Carlton Hotel,** 1990
Zeidler Roberts Partnership
16th to 17th Sts., Market to Chestnut Sts.

When new office buildings were developed
west of City Hall in the 1950s, an informal
"gentleman's agreement" limited new buildings to a height no greater than the 491 foot
City Hall tower, thereby enabling the statue
of William Penn atop the tower to preside
symbolically over the city. Willard G.
Rouse's proposal to build a higher office
building sparked controversy and extensive
public debate before receiving City Council
approval.

Initially intending only to build a single
building, Rouse commissioned Wallace,
Roberts and Todd to develop an approach
to the entire block. Their master plan envisioned two tall office buildings, retail
shops, a hotel and underground parking all
of which were completed by 1990.

One Liberty Place, at a height of 960 feet
to the top of its spire, is the tallest building
in the city and the most striking landmark
day or night. The 61 story tower is set on a
three story podium which creates a pedestrian scale at the ground level. This podium
is sheathed in blue-gray polished granite
interrupted by bay windows for retail uses
and a four story entrance portico. The tower
has a silver-blue aluminum grid which holds
horizontal bands of blue glass and gray granite at the corners. The central portion of the
facade is silver metallic glass interrupted by
bands of gray granite at every fourth floor,
giving scale and decoration to the facade.
This combination of silver and blue glass
gives the building a delicate, shimmering
quality in spite of its massive size.

The top of the building, sheathed entirely
in glass, is formed by the repetitive use of a
gable form, resulting in a silhouette reminiscent of the Chrysler building. Linear bands
of light along the gable edges give the building a striking presence on the skyline of the
city at night.

Due to the height of the building, special
consideration had to be given to the structural system. The elevator shafts and emer-
gency stairs create a central vertical core
which is connected to four major columns
and eight super-columns, located in pairs
at the corners of the building. The super-
columns are tied back to the core by four
story high trusses at three different intervals
in the height of the tower. This system acts

389

much like the riggings on a sailboat, adapting to changing directions and velocity of winds.

Two Liberty Place uses the same architectural vocabulary but in a more subdued fashion. It also has a three-story podium sheathed in the dark blue-gray polished granite, with generous windows for the lobby. The rectilinear tower plan is less elegant than One Liberty Place, due to the need to expand floor areas to suit the requirements of the building's tenant. The facade continues the pattern of silver metallic glass in the center with bands of masonry and blue-tinted glass at the corners, but use darker masonry. A single gable roof, also illuminated on its edges, crowns the tower.

One and Two Liberty Place are connected by an elegant two-story arcade of retail stores. Corner entrances lead to a glass enclosed rotunda surrounded by two levels of shops and a large food court. Along Chestnut Street, the facade is divided into bays similar in width to the older stores along the street. Elements and materials from the towers are repeated, giving continuity to the entire design; silver-blue aluminum window mullions incorporate the gable form. The 290-room Ritz-Carlton Hotel is located above the retail arcade. The hotel's simple, masonry wall surface and uniform window pattern are a neutral foil to the office towers.

Liberty Place is an outstanding achievement of both urban design and architecture. Its dramatic break with the past, carried out at such a high standard of excellence, offered Philadelphia a symbol of new possibilities and civic pride.

390   C,J
Mellon Bank Center, 1990
1735 Market St.
Kohn Pederson Fox

City Council approval of One Liberty Place paved the way for other office buildings exceeding the height of City Hall tower. However, dense development west of City Hall made finding suitable sites difficult. The site for Mellon Center was created by relocating a bus terminal and demolishing a parking garage built in the 1950s for Penn Center.

The large site allows the 53-story office tower to take the form of a gigantic, free standing obelisk on axis with the City Hall tower. The five-story base is sheathed in granite, with modestly articulated ornamentation, somewhat similar to the Four Seasons Hotel. The tapering tower has central bays of vertical columns expressing the structural system of the building, rising to a projecting cornice. A lattice, pyramidal structure, housing the building's cooling system, tops the tower and completes the obelisk analogy. Lobbies with walls and floors of polished marble open to both Mar-

391

ket Street and Kennedy Boulevard. The lower level contains retail shops and connects to the underground concourse leading to the subway and commuter rail stations. A public winter garden for exhibits and displays, accessed from this lower level, is housed in a small glass structure between the tower and an older office building.

391 K
Mandell Futures Center, 1990

Follows 392

392 C,J
Bell Atlantic Tower, 1991
17th and Arch Sts.
The Kling-Lindquist Partnership

The Bell Atlantic Tower, the last of the four very tall office buildings to be designed, is a contrast to its predecessors in almost every way. The form and location of the building were influenced by the special design controls along the Benjamin Franklin Parkway which limit the height of buildings within 200 feet of the Parkway. To avoid the line of controls, the office tower was located on the southern edge of the site and designed with stepped back corners. This left the northern portion of the site for a large landscaped park and fountain.

The 53 story building is easily distinguished by its rectangular shape, flat roof and warm red color. The facades are formed by projecting the stepped back corners into a series of stepped slabs creating terraces at the top of the building and culminating in the flat roof. This breaks down the scale of the broad facades while giving the ends a narrow, graceful silhouette. The stepped

back corners and narrow floor plan create 16 corner offices per floor and allow an unusual amount of natural light to reach all interior spaces.

One of the most appealing qualities of the building is its color. Factory-built red granite panels with gray-tinted glass reflect the brick color of traditional Philadelphia architecture. Honed granite spandrels accent the facade and polished granite surrounds the entrance porticos. The top of the building is more glass than masonry and is the source of the cascade of light that gives the building its distinctive appearance at night.

The building's structural system consists of a central structural core connected to four major columns and four super-columns. Five story high vierendeel trusses give stability to the broad facades and two story vierendeel girders tie the super-columns back to the central core.

Although the tower lacks the dramatic impact of its predecessors, the choice of materials and simplicity of form give the building a refined elegance and lasting presence on the Philadelphia skyline.

391 K
Mandell Futures Center at the Franklin Institute, 1990
20th St. and Benjamin Franklin Parkway
Geddes Brecher Qualls Cunningham

The Franklin Institute, founded in 1842, was the country's first science museum and an important center of scientific research in the 19th century. When the Institute's original building on South 7th Street became too small, it moved to the newly completed Benjamin Franklin Parkway and erected a sprawling neoclassical structure designed by John T. Windram. Only a portion of Windram's design was completed before the Depression halted construction, leaving the Memorial Hall, with its enormous marble statue of Benjamin Franklin, isolated from the museum galleries. The addition

1991
Robert Venturi named laureate of the Pritzker Architecture Prize

1991
Gulf War with Iraq

1991
Soviet Union dissolves; Commonwealth of Independent States established

393

394

completes the circulation scheme and connects the Memorial Hall and old galleries to a new exhibit area.

The new structure is set behind the wings of the original building so that it is not visible from Logan Circle or the Parkway. New exhibit areas are reached through a central atrium which also contains a cafe and museum shop. The atrium has steps that can be used as seating for special events, a gray terrazzo floor and bright red metal ramps along the sides. In the center, on the central axis of the original building, a bright yellow column with skylight above symbolizes the difference between neoclassical and Modern design. Glass windows provide views of the exhibit areas, each of which contains an interactive computer system permitting visitors to obtain additional information on the subject of each exhibit. The atrium also provides access to the Tuttleman Omniverse Theater with its huge, multi-screen Imax theater.

The exterior of the building is a deliberate contrast to the classicism of Windram's design. Geometric volumes, handled in a straight forward Modern style, are shaped to reflect the different interior functions. A large projecting window gives a preview of the high-tech character within.

393 E
Clinical Research Building, University of Pennsylvania, 1991
36th St. below Hamilton Walk
Payette Associates and Venturi, Scott Brown and Associates

The closing and demolition of the Philadelphia General Hospital provided a large site for the creation of new health care facilities and expansion of the University of Pennsylvania Hospital. This building contains state-of-the-art wet laboratory and research space for Penn's School of Medicine. The plan of the building places human activities at the edges to take advantage of natural light and

views. Offices along the long sides of the building and lounges and seminar rooms at the end of each floor surround the interior laboratory spaces. The exterior treatment of patterned brick and cast-stone window surrounds is similar to older buildings on the Penn campus. However, both the bricks and windows are larger than usual to reduce the sense of the building's size. The top story, housing massive mechanical equipment, is differentiated by great louvers of porcelain enamelled steel. It also carries a giant rendering of Penn's shield giving visual identity at great distance.

The design is a sophisticated expression of Venturi and Scott Brown's early architectural concepts of buildings as decorated sheds and large scale signage as symbol, articulated in their studies of Las Vegas.

394 E
LeBow Engineering Center and Center for Automation Technlogy, Drexel University, 1992
Market Street between 31st and 32nd Sts.
The King-Lindquist Partnership

Since its founding in 1890, Drexel University has grown from a single building to a campus covering many city blocks and serving over 8,000 students. This building complex marks the eastern edge of the campus and provides a gateway from public transportation at 30th Street used by many commuting students.

The complex consists of two buildings organized as a single composition. The LeBow building houses several engineering departments and laboratories; the CAT building features labs for computer-driven manufacturing technology as well as facilities for chemical and architectural engineering. Within each building most labs face outward with views of the city, while offices and public areas face inward on a landscaped courtyard. The courtyard is part of

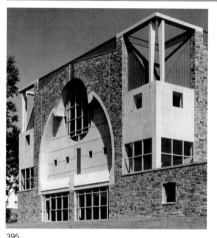

395

396

a pedestrian path that passes through the LeBow building from Market Street to a future pedestrian street connecting west to the main part of the campus.

On the Market Street facade, large windows set behind a ground floor arcade allow the computer lab to be visible to passers-by. Two story high windows add scale to the building while providing north light for third and fourth floor labs. Round windows mark the mechanical systems floor. On the courtyard side, both buildings have a mixture of materials and fenestration. Orange brick, traditional for Drexel buildings, and strip windows enclose lab spaces, classrooms and offices. Curved glass and metal curtain walls bring light into stairwells, lounges and lobbies as well as a demonstration room and computer lab in the CAT building.

The two buildings provide a sense of place on the edge of the campus while also giving visual expression to the high-tech facilities within.

395 K
St. Joseph's University Chapel, 1992
City Line Ave.
Francis Caufman Foley Hoffman Architects

St. Joseph's College was founded in 1851 to serve the expanding middle class neighborhoods of North Philadelphia. When the college moved to its present location in 1927, the small population of commuting students and the lack of residential development in the surrounding area did not justify the construction of a chapel. However, by the 1990s an expanded student body, resident dormitories and established residential neighborhoods prompted the addition of a chapel.

The university administration wanted a building with sacred spaces and traditional references to Catholic symbolism. It also wanted a building that would be central to student life in the 1990s and sufficiently prominent to be inviting to surrounding residents.

The chapel is sited between the playing fields and the student union. The exterior is boldly contemporary in design, with relatively little religious symbolism. Traditional stone is offset with concrete frames and panels. Large circular windows on all four sides and concrete arches suggest the main sanctuary space within. A curved, glass-enclosed arcade distinguishes the entrance facade.

The spacious main worship space is framed with three-story Gothic arches supporting a vaulted ceiling that culminates in a sky-lit Greek cross. Stained glass depictions of religious themes, set in the large circular windows, provide an element of traditional symbolism.

The handsome chapel is enriched by a pipe organ built by the Hook Co. in 1868, which was rescued from a deteriorating North Philadelphia church.

396 E
Institute of Contemporary Art, 1992
36th and Sansom Sts.
Adele Naude Santos and Associates with Jacobs/Wyper Architects

When the ICA decided to move from its location in the Graduate School of Fine Arts building, a difficult site for a new building was selected on the edge of Richard Neutra's dormitory complex, adjacent to a ramp for the handicapped. The building contains two floors of gallery spaces linked by a ramp which is visible on the main facade. The galleries are windowless, with exposed beams and ductwork, providing simple, flexible space for exhibits. The second floor gallery is divided into four quad-

●
1992
*Old-fashioned trolley service ended
on all SEPTA routes*

●
1992
*Former Mayor Frank L. Rizzo dies
after winning Republican nomination
for mayor*

397

rants by cruciform shaped girders supported by a massive column. One quadrant has a 30 foot high ceiling and skylight. In contrast to the galleries, the lobby is entirely enclosed in glass to be open and inviting to visitors. Stairs rise to a mezzanine level with access to a sculpture garden.

The sleek exterior harks back to the tradition of the International style. Ribbon windows and aluminum cladding are treated as simple flat surfaces; the free standing column at the corner is a clear historic reference, but in this case to the work of Le Corbuiser and the International movement.

---

397 K
The Caring Center, 1992
3101 Spring Garden St.
Friday Architects

When the ISI Caring Center's initial sponsor decided to close its day care business, concerned parents formed a non-profit corporation to carry on what had become a tradition of excellent child care. A prominent site was selected, with views of the Art Museum and Center City skyline, and a building designed from a child's perspective.

The exterior of the building is an immediate indication of the parents' and architects' commitment to make the center fun for children, without making it uncomfortable for adults. A colorful orange corrugated aluminum facade is decorated on two sides with green tadpoles growing into frogs, symbolizing the different stages of a child's growth while at the same time moving in the direction of the Zoo. The motif is carried through into the lobby which has a floor pattern in the design of a lily pond. Small

details throughout the building reflect similar thoughtfulness about children's interests: child-height bubble windows provide great views to the world outside, cloud fixtures hang from high ceilings and a window in the stairwell allows children to observe the workings of an institutional kitchen. An outside playground provides off-hours recreation for neighborhood children.

---

398 K
Thomas H. Kean New Jersey State Aquarium, 1993
One Riverside Drive
Camden, New Jersey
The Hillier Group

In the 18th century, ferries brought agricultural products from southern New Jersey to markets in Philadelphia. Ferry service continued until completion of the Benjamin Franklin bridge in 1928. Camden, directly across the river from Philadelphia, grew as an independent city famous as the last home of Walt Whitman and as the headquarters of the Campbell Soup Company. However, after 1950 Camden declined in much the same manner inner-city Philadelphia neighborhoods declined. To rejuvenate the city, plans were developed for a waterfront park and office complex, of which the aquarium is the center-piece.

The aquarium features aquatic and wildlife native to the waters and wetlands of New Jersey and the north Atlantic Ocean. Exhibits on two floors surround the 760,000 gallon open ocean tank, second largest in the country, which has enormous windows through which to view sharks, fish and other forms of sea life. Outside exhibits include a seal pool and rushing trout stream.

The building was designed to be viewed both from Philadelphia and Camden. The river facade achieves a grand scale through the use of large window openings and sim-

398

ple geometric volumes such as the domed roof and projecting corner pavilions. Large, brightly painted wall surfaces relieve the cast-in-place and pre-cast concrete structure. Observation decks and an outdoor cafe overlook the river and provide wonderful views of the Philadelphia skyline. The Camden side is more informal. Fabric roofs over the lobby, garden pavilions and shark tank give a playful character to the building and allow filtered light to enter public spaces.

The Riverbus provides ferry service to the aquarium from Penn's Landing and a view of shipping activity along the Delaware River.

---

399 K *PR*
Latimer Street House, 1993–94
1200 Latimer Street
David Slovic Associates

The restoration of Society Hill in the 1960s provided opportunities for construction of new houses on small row-house lots where older buildings had been demolished. This led to similar new construction in other sections of Center City. Most new houses respected the scale, materials, color and patterns of fenestration of traditional brick row-houses, while interpreting these elements in a contemporary manner. This house is a startling and deliberate departure from that tradition in virtually every respect.

The house was designed by the husband and wife principals of the firm for themselves and reflects their personal philosophy of architecture and urbanism. It attempts to bring amenities of suburban living to an urban setting and to recognize that the declining city population presents an opportunity to build at lower densities without sacrificing urban character.

The site was previously occupied by three row houses demolished in the 1940s. It is unusually large for a single family house and has frontage on three streets. The house is organized around a courtyard reached by a large porte cochere which also provides an off-street parking space. The courtyard divides the building into two sections. The larger section contains living areas on the first floor with a bedroom mezzanine above, connected to a roof terrace by a suspended stair. Interior spaces reflect the simplicity of industrial lofts, opening to the courtyard through a wall of glass and steel. The smaller part of the house on the other side of the courtyard contains a guest suite and studio for the owners.

Every aspect of the exterior exaggerates its difference from its neighbors. The low, two story building is a contrast to the taller, narrow row-houses on the block. This horizontal character is emphasized by the use of dark green slate panels covering the first floor and a white stucco band covering the upper floor. The inward focus of the plan reduces the need for exterior windows resulting in facades of large, blank wall surfaces interrupted by only a few windows asymmetrically placed and by protruding structural steel elements.

Not only is the house different from the traditional row-house but it also abandons the post-Modern interest in ornamentation and reinterpretation of elements from previous architectural styles in favor of a style that combines elegant materials and details with stark industrial simplicity.

399

400

400   C,J
Pennsylvania Convention Center,
1993–94

Arch to Race Sts., 11th to 13th Sts.
Thompson, Ventulett, Stainback &
Associates with the Vitetta Group,
Kelly/Maiello Architects and Planners,
and Livingston/Rosenwinkel P.C.

As the convention industry in the United
States grew in economic importance, Philadelphia's political and business leaders recognized that the convention center in West
Philadelphia was too small to compete with
other cities and poorly located. A site for a
new center was selected in the heart of
downtown immediately adjacent to the Market East Station of the regional rail and subway lines. To accommodate the 440,000
square feet of exhibit space, the main building required the demolition of four city
blocks.

The center is located in two separate
structures: the main meeting and exhibition
area is in a new building north of Arch
Street, while the Grand Hall, Ballroom and
other meeting rooms are located in the historic Reading Terminal train shed. The
major convention spaces are on the second
level of the new building spanning 12th
Street to provide a continuous floor area.
Since all the functions are interior ones, the
building is a simple box, relieved on the
east and west facades by curved bay windows that reduce the building's scale.
Folded roofs, large entryways and sculptural
features for flags and lighting, mark the
limestone and granite-faced main facade
along Arch Street. Within the building, a
three-story high pedestrian spine with large
windows and skylights provides access to
the main exhibit hall and to a pedestrian
bridge over Arch Street leading to the train
shed.

The train shed contains a spectacular
Grand Hall, ballroom and meeting spaces.
These new facilities take the form of a
building within a building to preserve the
visual continuity of the original shed roof.

Long skylights between the iron trusses
allow natural light to flood the space, consistent with the original roof design. From
the main floor a three-tiered staircase,
flanked by escalators and waterfall fountains, leads to the ballroom. Terraced balconies provide dramatic views back into the
vast spaciousness of the shed. A few features recall the past functions of the train
terminal; the dispatcher's box overhead has
been retained and pairs of stainless steel
bands imbedded in the terrazzo floor symbolize train tracks. Building in the shed was
completed without halting operation of the
Reading Terminal Farmers Market below.
When completed, the main entrance to the
train shed will be from Market Street
through the historic Head House building.

The center is supported by an adjacent
1,200 room hotel designed by Bower Lewis
Thrower. Philadelphia's political and business leadership hope the convention/hotel
complex will be an important economic
catalyst, leading to a growth in tourism and
the creation of new jobs for city residents.

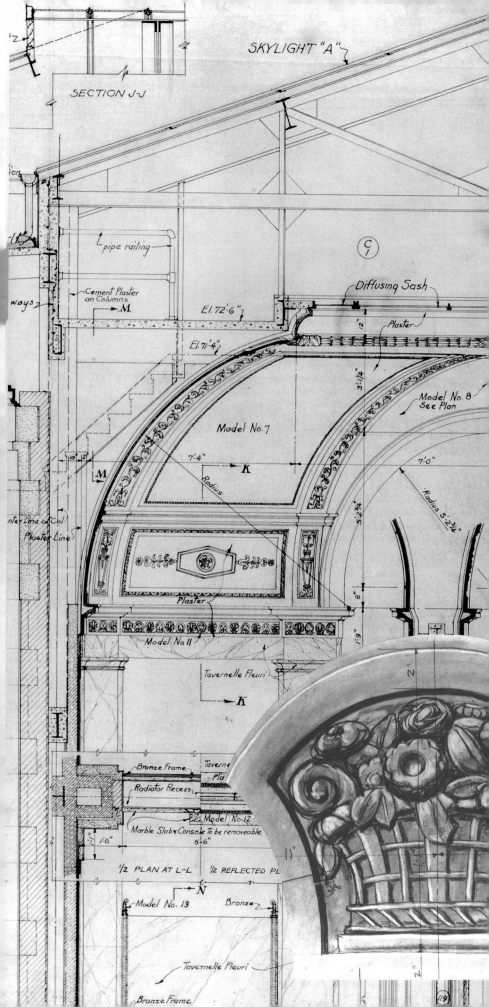

SECTION J-J

SKYLIGHT "A"

ⓒ
1

pipe railing

Diffusing Sash

Cement Plaster
on Columns

M

Plaster

El. 72'-6"

12"

ways

El. 71'-4"

3-1¼"

Model No. 8
See Plan

Model No. 7

7'-4"

K

Radius

5-2¾"

7'-0"

Radius 5'-2¾"

M

10" 2"

Inter Line of Col
Plaster Line

8"

Plaster

1'-9"

2"

Model No. 11

Tavernelle Fleuri

K

Bronze Frame

Taverne

Pla

Radiator Recess

Model No. 12

Marble Slab Console to be removeable
5'-6"

1-0"

1-6"

1"

½ PLAN AT L-L   ½ REFLECTED PL

N

Model No. 13   Bronze

2"

2"

Tavernelle Fleuri

2"

Bronze Frame

19

Philadelphia Architects

Philadelphia architects have had national impact on the evolution of architectural styles since the late 18th century. The eleven individuals and firms described here have made unique contributions to American architecture well beyond the importance of their work in Philadelphia. Many other architects have contributed to the development of the city, however, and deserve mention.

Benjamin Latrobe, Robert Mills and John Haviland introduced classical details in the early 19th century and helped popularize the Greek Revival style. Samuel Sloan, working in the Gothic and Italianate styles, was one of the finest residential architects of his time and an important hospital designer. In the late 19th century The Wilson Brothers, one of the largest firms in the city, designed some of the most important railroad stations in the world. George and William Hewitt and Willis Hale created many outstanding houses in the High Victorian and Queen Anne styles.

There were also a number of fine residential architects in the early 20th century. Horace Trumbauer created fashionable mansions in addition to important civic buildings; outstanding suburban houses were built by Frank Miles Day, Edmund Gilchrist, Robert McGoodwin, Mellor and Meigs, and Duhring Okie and Zeigler. Ralph Bencker and Ritter and Shay were proponents of the Art Deco style of the 1930s. Oscar Stonorov introduced European housing concepts of the 1920s and 30s to the city.

Contemporary architecture in the 1950s and 60s was strongly influenced by Edmund Bacon, director of the City Planning Commission, and G. Holmes Perkins, dean of the School of Fine Arts at the University of Pennsylvania. They created a climate that encouraged many young architects in the city. Among the most influential firms were Vincent G. Kling, Bower and Fradley and Geddes Brecher Qualls Cunningham. These firms, the strength of Penn's architecture school and the presence of Louis I. Kahn, Robert Venturi and Romaldo Giurgola produced a subsequent generation of talented architects whose work has come to prominence in the past decade.

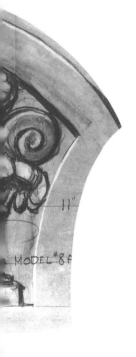

From the office of Paul Philippe Cret and Jacques Greber Associated Architects, 1928

Robert Smith
1722–1777

Robert Smith was born in Scotland into a family that included many masons. After an early apprenticeship in the building trades, he emigrated to America sometime before 1749, for in that year he was married in Philadelphia.

Most scholars consider Smith the foremost carpenter-architect of the colonial period. The carpenter-architect was primarily a builder. It was his responsibility to imitate the models of the past and adapt those to the modest building needs of the colonial city. Smith worked closely with his clients to determine the building design and to select details from the numerous architectural handbooks in the city and in his own collection. Once the design was agreed upon, Smith hired a team of men and acted as general contractor.

Smith's principal buildings in Philadelphia are the Christ Church steeple, St. Peter's Church and Carpenters' Hall. He designed the first building for the institution that would later become the University of Pennsylvania. His design for the Walnut Street Prison attracted attention for its use of fireproof vaults. Because of his fine reputation, Smith obtained commissions outside the city for Nassau Hall at Princeton University and for the first insane asylum in the colonies, at Williamsburg. His most prestigious patron was Benjamin Franklin, for whom he built a residence on Market Street while Franklin was in England.

Smith was active in cultural and political affairs. He was a member of the American Philosophical Society and the Carpenters' Company, serving on its Rule Book committee. He died a wealthy man; his estate included a country home, a tavern and at least thirteen rental properties.

Nassau Hall, Princeton University

William Strickland
1788–1854

William Strickland was born on a New Jersey farm. His family moved to Philadelphia, where his father worked as a carpenter for Benjamin Latrobe on the Bank of Pennsylvania. Strickland was apprenticed to Latrobe for two years before deciding to pursue a career as a painter. In 1815, however, he was catapulted to the front ranks of the architectural profession when he won the design competition for the Second Bank of the U.S. This design established the Greek Revival style in the United States.

Strickland was one of the foremost Greek Revival architects in the country. He relied completely on the illustrations in Stuart and Revett's *Antiquities of Athens* as the basis of his work, which combined the elegance and grace of Greek architecture with the practical requirements of new public buildings. In addition to the Second Bank, his outstanding work in Philadelphia includes the Merchants' Exchange and the U.S. Naval Home. Strickland worked in other styles, including Egyptian and Gothic Revival, and even used Georgian for his reconstruction of the Independence Hall steeple. Strickland was also a gifted engineer and one of the first to recognize the importance of the railroad. He predicted that railroads would supersede canals as a principal means of travel.

When the financial crisis of 1837 left a dearth of commissions in Philadelphia, Strickland was asked to design the new Tennessee State House in Nashville. It was his last major work and one of his most impressive. Strickland remained in Nashville until his death and is buried in a tomb beneath the State House.

Tennessee State Capitol Building, Nashville, Tennessee

Thomas Ustick Walter
1804–1887

As a young man, Thomas Walter followed his father's professional calling as a mason. He was twice apprenticed to William Strickland, from whom he received a sound training in architecture and engineering.

Walter established his own architectural practice in 1830. His first important commission was the Philadelphia County Prison, also known as Moyamensing, an early example of Gothic style. His national reputation was established when he won the competition for the design of Girard College in 1833, a project that occupied him for fourteen years.

Girard College was the high point of Walter's Philadelphia career. Soon after its completion he left the city to design the expansion of the U.S. Capitol Building in Washington, D.C. Walter was responsible for the extension of the Senate and House wings and the addition of the Capitol dome. Ill health forced his return to Philadelphia in 1865, where he worked as a consultant to John McArthur on the design of City Hall.

Walter taught at the Franklin Institute and was one of the founders of the first professional organization of architects; he was later a founding member of the American Institute of Architects and second president of the organization.

U.S. Capitol Building,
Washington, D.C.

John Notman
1810–1865

John Notman was one of the most distinguished 19th-century American architects. Notman was born in Edinburgh, Scotland; it is believed members of his family were stonemasons. He probably was first apprenticed to a carpenter and then worked in an architectural office in Edinburgh before coming to the United States in 1831.

Although his first building for the Library Company was simple and ordinary, Notman's subsequent work introduced a succession of sophisticated English architectural styles to Philadelphia and to the United States. Notman's innovative design for Bishop George Washington Doane's house in Burlington, New Jersey, was the first Italianate house built in this country. It was highly publicized by Andrew Jackson Downing in his influential pattern books. Notman also designed the first Renaissance Revival building in America, the Philadelphia Athenaeum. He was also an important source of the Gothic Revival style. His patron, Bishop Doane, was the first American member of the Camden Ecclesiological Society, which advocated archaeologically correct Gothic design for church architecture. Notman used the Gothic style for Doane's Chapel in Burlington, but his finest Gothic building is St. Mark's Church in Philadelphia.

Notman had a national reputation, and his commissions ranged from churches in Delaware, Maryland and western Pennsylvania to cemeteries and garden designs in Cincinnati, Ohio, and Richmond, Virginia. He designed several picturesque villas still standing in Princeton, New Jersey. Notman was a founding member of the American Institute of Architects and the Pennsylvania Institute of Architects.

*Guernsey Hall,
Princeton, New Jersey*

The Wilson Brothers

Joseph M. Wilson
1838–1902

Joseph Wilson was born in Phoenixville, Pennsylvania, an iron and steel manufacturing center. After receiving a civil engineering degree from Rensselaer Polytechnic Institute in New York, he came to Philadelphia and worked for the Pennsylvania Railroad designing bridges, factories, depots and warehouses. In 1876 he founded an architectural and engineering firm with his older brother, John, who also graduated from Rensselaer and worked for the railroad.

Their first commission was the design of two major exhibition buildings at the 1876 Centennial Exposition. By the 1880s the firm had risen to a position of unquestioned authority in the architectural and engineering field. Although they are best known for their railroad terminals, the firm designed every type of building in Victorian society. The diversity of their commissions, the engineering accomplishments and extraordinary eclecticism of their designs rank them as one of the most important firms in the last quarter of the 19th century.

The Wilson Brothers undertook projects throughout the United States and in Mexico and Central America, but their best buildings were in Philadelphia. For Anthony J. Drexel, the prominent banker, they designed a house, his first bank and the main building of Drexel Institute. While completing the Reading Terminal, they also created the Pennsylvania Railroad's Broad Street station, one of the greatest train stations in the world, which featured a three-hinged, wrought-iron arched shed considerably larger than the Reading shed.

Joseph Wilson was a fellow of the AIA, a member of the American Philosophical Society and the British and American societies of Civil Engineers, and president of the Franklin Institute. After he died the firm continued, but it never achieved the prominence it had under his leadership.

Broad Street Station
(demolished)

Frank Furness
1839–1912

Frank Furness was born and raised in Philadelphia. He began his career as a draftsman for John Fraser, architect of the Union League. In 1859 he entered the New York atelier of Richard Morris Hunt, the first American architect to study at the École des Beaux-Arts. There Furness was exposed to John Ruskin's theories of architectural ornament and Viollet-le-Duc's structural concepts, the two principal influences on his own architectural style.

Furness joined the Union Cavalry in 1861 and earned the Congressional Medal of Honor. After the war, he established an office in Philadelphia, first with Fraser, then with George Hewitt. Furness and Hewitt became nationally prominent through their design for the Pennsylvania Academy of Fine Arts. Louis Sullivan worked briefly for Furness at this time.

After the firm dissolved in 1875, Furness practiced alone for the next six years. His personal style of Victorian Gothic design reached its pinnacle and most of his finest banks were completed during this time, including his masterpiece, the Provident Life and Trust Co.

In 1881, his assistant, Allen Evans, became his partner. During the next fourteen years they became one of Philadelphia's largest and most prominent firms. Much of Furness's residential work dates from this period as well as his great railroad stations. His remodeling of The Wilson Brothers' Broad Street Station made it the world's largest railroad passenger terminal.

Furness completed the widely acclaimed University of Pennsylvania Library in 1888. By the time it was finished, architectural tastes had turned to the Classical Revival. Furness's career declined, and his accomplishments were virtually ignored for fifty years; many of his most important buildings were demolished. Today Furness is recognized as one of Philadelphia's greatest architects.

Provident Life Trust Co., Philadelphia (demolished)

National Bank of the Republic, Philadelphia (demolished)

147

Wilson Eyre
1858–1944

Wilson Eyre was born in Florence, Italy. His family returned to the United States in 1869 and lived in a number of different places, including Newport, Rhode Island. Eyre's desire to be a painter was discouraged by his family. Instead, he chose a career in architecture, considered a more reputable profession. He studied at the Massachusetts Institute of Technology with Henry Van Brunt, and moved to Philadelphia around 1877 to work for James Peacock Sims. When Sims died, Eyre took over his practice.

Eyre maintained a small office, preferring to supervise the details of design himself. His only partner, John McIlvain, joined him in 1912. Most of their commissions came from Pennsylvania and New York.

Eyre traveled abroad, particularly in England, where he undoubtedly saw the work of Norman Shaw and C. F. A. Voysey, residential architects who designed in the Queen Anne and Arts and Crafts styles. Eyre's Philadelphia friends included Maxfield Parrish, Violet Oakley, Henry Mercer and the architects Frank Miles Day and Walter Cope. Eyre helped form the T-Square Club, which promoted Arts and Crafts principles through its annual exhibitions and catalogs. He was also a founder, with Frank Miles Day, of *House and Garden* magazine, and its editor from 1901 to 1905.

Eyre was one of the most imaginative residential architects of his generation. His work brought national attention to Philadelphia's fine suburban architecture. Eyre's playful, witty details made frequent use of sculptural ornament, enigmatic human figures and the reversal of traditional architectural motifs. Initially, Eyre was attracted to the complexities of the Queen Anne style, but as his practice evolved, his fondness for the Shingle style led him to simple yet sophisticated forms. By 1920, Eyre's career had virtually ended. When he died in 1944, his accomplishments were generally forgotten.

E. S. Sand Residence,
Southport, Connecticut

Paul Philippe Cret
1876–1945

Paul Philippe Cret was born in Lyons, France. He studied at the École des Beaux-Arts in Paris. Cret came to Philadelphia at the age of 27 to establish an École system at the University of Pennsylvania. He held his teaching position for 34 years, during which time he revolutionized the architectural program and established the most successful Beaux-Arts curriculum in the country.

Cret entered 23 competitions during his career, winning his first competition in 1907 for the design of the Pan American Building in Washington, D.C., which some judge to be his best work. Cret's interest in city planning involved him with groups devoted to improving Philadelphia's physical structure. He prepared the original plans for the Benjamin Franklin Parkway and redesigned Rittenhouse Square as part of a general improvement of the area.

Cret served in the French army during World War I. Afterwards he reestablished a thriving practice in Philadelphia and continued to devote himself to architectural education. Two of his major commissions of this period were the Federal Reserve Bank in Philadelphia and the Folger Shakespeare Library in Washington, D.C., which Cret considered to be his finest work.

Although Cret advocated an architecture which honored the past, he was strongly influenced by the International style. His 1933 design for the Hall of Science at the Century of Progress Exhibition in Chicago had International style elements and featured a 175-foot tower bristling with neoned fins and crowned by a Deco *torchère*. Cret also designed a series of streamlined trains in the 30s, including the Denver and Pioneer Zephyrs.

Cret continued to practice architecture despite failing health. He died of a heart attack during an air inspection of the site for a veteran's hospital.

Pan American Union Building, Washington, D.C.

George Howe
1886–1955

George Howe was born in Worcester, Massachusetts. He lived abroad with his mother and attended school in Switzerland. After further education at Groton and Harvard, Howe returned to Paris for architectural training at the École des Beaux-Arts.

Howe settled in Philadelphia in 1913, originally working for Furness, Evans and Co. Later he joined the fashionable firm of Mellor and Meigs in a partnership that lasted until 1926. The three partners often worked independently but shared a common regard for fine building materials and traditional English and French residential styles. Howe later referred to this style as Wall Street Pastoral because of the number of stockbrokers attracted to these houses.

The commission for the PSFS office building caused dissension over the firm's direction. Howe favored the International style. Mellor and Meigs preferred traditional architectural styles. Howe left the firm and entered into partnership with the Swiss architect William Lescaze. Together they designed a building for PSFS that is still one of the outstanding examples of modern architecture in this country.

PSFS was the pinnacle of Howe's career. During the Depression and Second World War, Howe formed brief partnerships with Norman Bel Geddes, the New York industrial designer, and with Philadelphia architects Oscar Stonorov and Louis Kahn. He also was supervising architect for the Public Buildings Administration in Washington and dean of the Architecture School at Yale from 1950–54.

As a sophisticated gentleman of aristocratic breeding, Howe was a unique advocate of the modern movement. He brought the International style to America, with a sense of its possibilities for richness despite its austerity. That he achieved this in conservative Philadelphia was astounding.

William Stix Wasserman House, Whitemarsh, Pennsylvania

Louis I. Kahn
1901–1974

Louis Kahn was born in Estonia and came to Philadelphia in 1906. His family, although poor, stressed the value of art, music and the Old Testament. Kahn studied architecture at the University of Pennsylvania, where Paul Philippe Cret was one of his teachers. His first job was for the city architect John Molitor, with whom he designed a Beaux-Arts plan for the 1926 Sesquicentennial Exposition.

Through most of the Depression and early 1940s Kahn was unemployed. He formed a research group with other architects to study city planning and housing. Here he met George Howe and Oscar Stonorov, with whom he later associated. From 1947 to 1957, Kahn taught at Yale. During this time he evolved a personal philosophy of design that was an almost Platonic search for fundamental principles, which he expressed in poetic, often obscure language. From 1957 on he taught at Penn, where he was influenced by two brilliant engineers: Robert le Ricolais and August E. Komendant. Kahn and Komendant worked together on the Richards Medical Building, the first unified expression of Kahn's structural and spatial concepts, and later on the Kimbell Museum in Fort Worth, Texas, which Kahn considered his finest work.

Kahn's use of heavy materials, elaborate structural solutions and natural light to form interior space offered dramatic contrast to the prevailing styles of modern architecture. Major projects outside Philadelphia include the Salk Institute in California, the Library at Phillips Exeter Academy in New Hampshire and the Yale Center for British Art in New Haven. After returning from a trip to one of his last projects, the new government complex in Dhaka, Bangladesh, Kahn died suddenly of a heart attack. His drawings and sketches are located in Architectural Archives of the University of Pennsylvania.

Kimbell Art Museum, Fort Worth, Texas

Phillips Exeter Academy Library, Exeter, New Hampshire

Mitchell/Giurgola

*Romaldo Giurgola
1920–*

*Ehrman B. Mitchell, Jr.
1924–*

Romaldo Giurgola was born in Italy and received his architectural education at the University of Rome. He came to the United States in 1950 to study at Columbia, then taught at Cornell. Giurgola worked initially as a cover designer and editor of *Interiors* magazine. Because of his exceptional drawing skills, many architectural firms hired him to prepare renderings, including the Philadelphia firm Bellante and Clauss. There he met Ehrman Mitchell. Mitchell studied architecture at the University of Pennsylvania and had headed the firm's offices in London and Arizona. In 1958, when Giurgola came to teach at Penn, they established a partnership to design the Wright Brothers Museum at Kitty Hawk, North Carolina.

Mitchell/Giurgola's national reputation was established by their competition entries. Their second-place entry in the Boston City Hall competition received considerable attention, and in 1968 they won the competition for the AIA headquarters in Washington, D.C. They also won competitions to renovate Louis Sullivan's Wainwright Building in St. Louis and the 1982 international competition to design the New Parliament House in Australia.

Mitchell/Giurgola's work is distinguished by a strong concern for urban context and for structural and design innovation. Many of the firm's best buildings are in Philadelphia. Other significant buildings include the Swarthmore College Music Building, the Volvo headquarters in Gothenburg, Sweden, and the Anchorage Historical and Fine Arts Museum in Alaska. Both partners have made important contributions to the architectural profession. Ehrman Mitchell was president of the AIA in 1979; Romaldo Giurgola was chairman of the architecture department at Columbia and recipient of the 1982 AIA Gold Medal. Giurgola moved to Australia in 1984 to supervise construction of the New Parliament House and Mitchell retired in 1985.

*Parliament House,
Canberra, Australia*

*Sherman Fairchild
Center for the Life
Sciences, Columbia
University*

Venturi, Scott Brown and Associates

Robert Venturi 1925–

*Denise Scott Brown
1931–*

Robert Venturi was born in Philadelphia, the son of a wholesale fruit grocer. He studied architecture at Princeton and then worked briefly for Eero Saarinen. As recipient of the 1954 Prix de Rome, Venturi traveled in Italy, developing an appreciation for historical styles that influenced his architectural theories.

Venturi worked briefly for Louis Kahn before establishing a small practice first in partnership with William Short (1960) and then with John Rauch (1964). Rauch, after graduating from the University of Pennsylvania, joined the firm of Cope and Lippincott, with whom Venturi associated on several projects, including the Guild House. He remained in partnership with Venturi until 1988.

Venturi also taught at the University of Pennsylvania, where he met his future wife and collaborator, Denise Scott Brown, who joined the firm in 1967. She was born in South Africa and studied architecture and planning in England and at Penn. Her interests in vernacular design, social planning and neighborhood organization reinforced Venturi's architectural theories.

The firm's publications and buildings were instrumental in turning attention away from the International style toward the current eclectic design attitudes referred to as "post modern" architecture. Venturi's *Complexity and Contradiction in Architecture* (1966) is considered one of the most important statements of contemporary architectural theory. *Learning from Las Vegas* (1972) drew attention to the popular use of ornamentation in the urban landscape and its application to architectural theory. In recent years the firm has completed some of its finest work, including the Allen Art Museum Extension at Oberlin College, several buildings for Princeton University, the Sainsbury Wing of the National Gallery in London and the Seattle Art Museum. In 1991, Venturi was named laureate of the Pritzker Architecture Prize.

*Wu Hall, Butler College,
Princeton University*

Building Chart

	Before 1700	1700 to 1740	1740 to 1780
Row House or Block		Letitia House Elfreth's Alley	109–25 Kenilworth St. Workman Place Abercrombie House Shippen-Wistar House Powel House
Freestanding House	Wynnestay Wyck	Bel Air Stenton Glen Fern	Grumblethorpe Mount Pleasant Cliveden Bartram Hall Deshler-Morris House
Apartments and Hotels			
Retail Stores and Banks			Head House and Market Sheds Green Tree Tavern Man Full of Trouble Tavern
Office Buildings			
Industrial Buildings			
Religious Buildings	Gloria Dei	Christ Church	St. Peter's Church St. George's Methodist Church
Other Institutional Buildings			
Civic Buildings		State House (Independence Hall)	Carpenter's Hall
Other			Fort Mifflin

1780 to 1800	1800 to 1835	1835 to 1850	1850 to 1870
Sansom's Row	Franklin Row Girard Row Portico Row	1600 Locust St.	1800 Delancey Place 1500–2300 Green St. 2000–2100 Spruce St.
Hill-Physick-Keith House Reynolds-Morris House Woodlands Loudoun Upsala Lemon Hill			Gaul-Forrest Mansion Piper-Price House Watson House Mitchell House Burholme Ebenezer Maxwell House Woodland Terrace William Montelius House
			St. Charles Hotel
First Bank of the U.S.	Second Bank of the U.S.	PSFS	Farmers and Mechanics Bank Bank of Pennsylvania Lit Brothers PSFS
	Merchants Exchange	Philadelphia Contributionship	
	Girard Warehouses Fairmount Waterworks		Elliot and Leland Buildings Leland Building Smythe Buildings
	Arch St. Friends Meeting St. Stephen's Protestant Episcopal Church	Church of St. James the Less Cathedral of SS. Peter and Paul St. Augustine's Church St. Mark's Church	Arch St. Presbyterian Church Tenth Presbyterian Church St. Clement's Episcopal Church Church of the Holy Trinity St. Timothy's Protestant Episcopal Church Masonic Temple Second Presbyterian Church
Pennsylvania Hospital	Pennsylvania Institution for the Deaf and Dumb U.S. Naval Hospital Founders Hall, Girard College		Pennsylvania Hospital for Mental and Nervous Diseases
Congress Hall U.S. Supreme Court	Franklin Institute	The Athenaeum	Union League
	Sparks Shot Tower Eastern State Penitentiary Walnut Street Theatre Frankford Arsenal	Laurel Hill Cemetery	Academy of Music

	1870 to 1890	1890 to 1905	1905 to 1930
Row House or Block	Houses for a Moravian Community 1500 North 17th St. 4206–18 Spruce St. Bedell House	Moore House Neil and Mauren House Joseph Leidy House 3500 Powelton Ave.	Benezet St. Houses
Freestanding House	Thomas Hockley House William Rhawn House Anglecot Houston-Sauveur House Druim Moir Brinkwood Poth Mansion Charles Lister Townsend House	Kemble-Bergdol House Cummings House Overbrook Farms Fell–van Rensselaer House	100–102 West Mermaid Lane Adelbert Fischer House High Hollow Lincoln Drive Development Pepper House French Village Abraham Malmed House
Apartments and Hotels	Wissahickon Inn	Men's Dormitories St. James Apartments Bellevue Stratford Hotel	Robert Morris Hotel Alden Park The Drake Hotel
Retail Stores and Banks	Pennsylvania Co. for Insurance on Lives and Granting Annuities Ridge Ave. Farmers Market Centennial Bank Kensington National Bank Keystone National Bank	John Wanamaker's Department Store Jacob Reed's Sons Store	Girard Trust Co. Packard Motor Car Co. Drexel and Co. Bldg.
Office Buildings	Victory Building	Reading Terminal The Bourse Crozer Bldg. Land Title Bldg. Corn Exchange	Public Ledger Bldg. Fidelity Mutual Life Ins. Co. N. W. Ayer Bldg. WCAU Bldg.
Industrial Buildings	Dobson Carpet Mills A. J. Holman Factory	Tutlemann Brothers and Faggen Bldg.	Reading Co. Grain Elevator Lasher Printing Co.
Religious Buildings	Church of the Gesu St. Vincents Parrish Hall Tabernacle Presbyterian Church First Unitarian Church Mother Bethel African Methodist Church Baptist Temple	Mount Sinai Cemetery Chapel Church of the Advocate	Church of St. Francis de Sales Philadelphia Divinity School Rodeph Shalom Synagogue
Other Institutional Buildings	College Hall, University of Pennsylvania Pennsylvania Academy of the Fine Arts Ridgeway Library Pennsylvania Institution for the Deaf and Dumb University of Pennsylvania Library Drexel Institute Main Bldg.	Germantown Cricket Club University Museum Overbrook School for the Blind	
Civic Buildings	City Hall Memorial Hall		Philadelphia Museum of Art Free Library of Philadelphia Rodin Museum
Other	Graver's Lane Station	Reading Terminal Franklin Field	30th Street Station

1930 to 1950	1950 to 1970	1970 to 1983	1983 to 1993
Midvale Ave. Houses	Society Hill Town Houses Franklin Roberts House	University City Family Housing	
Schofield Andrews House Charles Woodward House	Margaret Esherick House Vanna Venturi House Dorothy Shipley White House		Gaither House Latimer Street House

Carl Mackley Houses
Mill Creek Housing
	Parkway House
	Schuylkill Falls Public
	  Housing
	Hill Hall
	Guild House
	Society Hill Towers
		International House
		American Postal Workers
		  Housing
		Franklin Plaza Hotel and
		  SmithKline Bldg.
		Four Seasons Hotel	

Federal Reserve Bank White Tower		The Gallery	The Shops at Liberty Place

One East Penn Square Bldg.
PSFS
	Penn Center Complex
	Municipal Services Bldg.
	1500 Walnut St. Addition
	Police Administration Bldg.
	Rohm and Haas Bldg.
	United Fund Headquarters
		Philadelphia Electric Co.
		Penn Mutual Life Ins. Co.
		  Addition
		Federal Reserve Bank
		ISI Bldg.
		Insurance Co. of North
		  America Annex
		The Atrium
		One Logan Square
			Graham Building/One Penn
			  Square West
			Commerce Square
			One Liberty Place
			Two Logan Square
			Two Liberty Place
			Mellon Bank Center
			Bell Atlantic Tower

	Beth Sholom Synagogue Ukrainian Cathedral		St. Joseph's University Chapel

U.S. Naval Hospital
Philadelphia Psychiatric
  Center
	Richards Medical Research
	  Lab.
		Old Pine Community Center
		The Eye Institute
		D'Angelo Pavilion, Magee
		  Rehabilitation Hospital
			Shelly Ridge Girl Scout Center
			George D. Widener Memorial
			  Tree House
			Renfrew Center
			Center for Judaic Studies
			Mandell Futures Center
			Clinical Research Building
			LeBow Engineering Center
			Institute of Contemporary Art
			The Caring Center

		Franklin Court	Frankford Post Office New Jersey State Aquarium Pennsylvania Convention Center

Mayfair Theater	University Parking Garage		Cecil B. Moore Ave. Subway
			  Station
			Philadelphia Industrial
			  Correction Center

The Tours

Philadelphia is a very easy and pleasant city to see. Center City, the area covered by Penn's original city plan, contains many interesting neighborhoods and significant buildings within close walking distance of one another. Other areas can be reached easily by public transportation or by beautiful drives along the Schuylkill River.

The nine tours that follow were selected to represent both significant concentrations of buildings described in the catalog and neighborhoods of different historic periods. Each tour follows a specific route that passes all buildings in the area that are listed in the catalog. In addition, other interesting buildings or special places of interest are noted on the maps. Every area contains many other distinctive buildings and handsome blocks of row houses that are worth wandering off the tour route to see.

The tours assume that most people are starting from City Hall. Directions are given for public transportation or driving routes from that point. Tours A, B, C and E are walking tours; tours D, F, G, H and J are intended to be driven. The map below shows rapid transit and bus routes connecting Center City and West Philadelphia tours; the map to the right shows road access to the Fairmount Park, Germantown and Chestnut Hill tours.

In addition to the tours of individual areas, tour J is a highlights driving tour, which provides an overview of the city and many important buildings.

All maps throughout the book are oriented north-up.

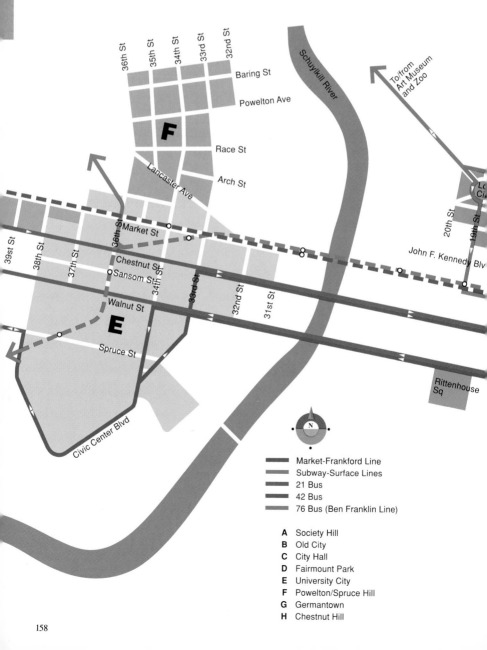

Market-Frankford Line
Subway-Surface Lines
21 Bus
42 Bus
76 Bus (Ben Franklin Line)

A Society Hill
B Old City
C City Hall
D Fairmount Park
E University City
F Powelton/Spruce Hill
G Germantown
H Chestnut Hill

Society Hill

Society Hill contains the largest concentration of original 18th-century architecture of any place in the United States. As one of the principal residential areas of colonial Philadelphia, the neighborhood included homes of the wealthy and poor, prominent churches, markets and taverns. Most of the important 18th-century civic buildings were adjacent to the neighborhood, including Independence Hall and other buildings associated with the founding of the country.

When the population of the city moved westward in the 19th century, Society Hill deteriorated and became an area of dilapidated houses and commercial buildings, dominated by the city's wholesale food market. Today, as a result of a major urban renewal program begun in the 1950s by the city, state and federal governments, it is one of the most attractive and affluent neighborhoods in the city. All 18th-century buildings in the area have been restored, and parks and landscaped walkways were created to replace demolished buildings. Where sites were available for new construction, the best modern design was encouraged to contrast with the original colonial buildings. The neighborhood was renamed Society Hill after the 18th-century Society of Free Traders, which had its offices on the hill above Dock Creek.

Society Hill is one of the most pleasant areas of the city to walk through. The easiest way to reach the area is to take a Market or Chestnut Street bus or the Market-Frankford subway to Fifth Street. The walking tour begins at Washington Square, proceeds along many of the landscaped walkways to Head House Square and ends at the Independence National Historical Park. The National Park Service conducts tours of the Independence Hall area, which start at the Visitor Center.

There are many outstanding contemporary buildings on this tour, including the Penn Mutual Office addition, which incorporates the facade of an earlier Egyptian Revival building. Many buildings are open to the public: St. Peter's Church, the Hill-Physick-Keith House, the Powel House and the Independence Hall complex should not be missed.

P Parking

1 **Independence Hall
(State House)**
Chestnut St. between 5th &
6th Sts. **109** *OP*

2 **Congress Hall**
Chestnut St. between 5th &
6th Sts. **130** *OP*

3 **U.S. Supreme Court**
Chestnut St. between 5th &
6th Sts. **132** *OP*

4 **American Philosophical
Society**
104 S. 5th St.
1785–89, Samuel Vaughan
OP

5 **Second Bank of the U.S.**
420 Chestnut St. **145** *OP*

6 **Carpenters' Hall**
320 Chestnut St. **125** *OP*

7 **First Bank of the U.S.**
120 S. 3rd St. **134** *OP*

8 **Independence National
Park Visitor Center**
125 S. 3rd St.
1976, Cambridge Seven
Assocs. *OP*

9 **Merchant's Exchange**
143 S. 3rd St. **154**

10 **Pennsylvania Company for
Insurances on Lives &
Granting Annuities**
304 Walnut St. 1859 *OP*

11 **PSFS Building**
306 Walnut St. **203**

12 **American Fire Insurance
Company**
308–10 Walnut St.
1840/1881, Furness & Evans

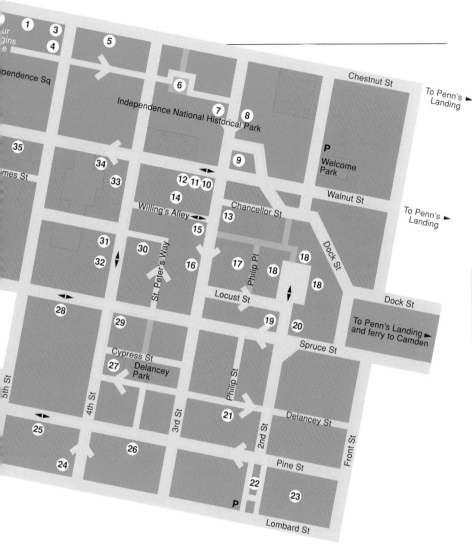

13 **St. Paul's Church**
225 S. 3rd St.
1761, William Dilworth;
1830, William Strickland

14 **St. Joseph's Church**
321 Willing's Alley, near
4th St. 1838

15 **Winder Houses**
232–34 S. 3rd St.
1843–44, possibly by
Thomas U. Walter *PR*

16 **Powel House**
244 S. 3rd St. **122** *OP*

17 **Society Hill Townhouses**
3rd & Locust Sts. **348** *PR*

18 **Society Hill Towers**
2nd & Locust Sts. **356** *PR*

19 **Abercrombie House**
268–70 S. 2nd St. **117** *PR*

20 **Man Full of Trouble Tavern**
127 Spruce St. **118** *OP*

21 **Franklin Roberts House**
230 Delancey St. **359** *PR*

22 **Head House & Market Shed**
2nd St. between Pine &
Lombard Sts. **113**

23 **New Market**
2nd St. between Pine &
Lombard Sts.
1973, Louis Sauer Assocs.

24 **Old Pine Community
Center**
4th & Lombard Sts. **365**

25 **Third Presbyterian Church**
Pine St. between 4th &
5th Sts.
1767, Robert Smith; 1857,
John Fraser

26 **St. Peter's Church**
Pine St. between 3rd &
4th Sts. **116** *OP*

27 **Hill-Physick-Keith House**
321 S. 4th St. **128** *OP*

28 **Society Hill Synagogue**
418 Spruce St.
1829–30/1851, Thomas U.
Walter

29 **Girard Row**
326–34 Spruce St. **152** *PR*

30 **Bingham Court**
4th & Locust Sts.
1967, I. M. Pei & Assocs.

31 **Shippen-Wistar House**
238 S. 4th St. **121**

32 **St. Mary's Church**
252 S. 4th St.
1763/1782/1810–11, Charles
Johnson, carpenter

33 **Philadelphia
Contributionship**
212 S. 4th St. **201**

34 **Center for Judaic Studies**
420 Walnut St. **387**

35 **Penn Mutual Life Insurance
Company Addition**
Walnut St. between 5th &
6th Sts. **362**

36 **The Athenaeum**
219 S. 6th St. **204** *OP*

37 **The Curtis Building**
6th and Walnut Sts.
1910, Edgar Seeler;
Renovated 1990, Oldham
and Seltz and John Milner
Associates

Old City

Old City, along with Society Hill, was one of the first residential areas in Philadelphia and contained some of the city's earliest houses and religious buildings. In the 18th century, the city's principal markets were located along Market Street from Front to Third, and there was a ferry terminal to New Jersey at the foot of Market Street. These activities encouraged commercial development in the blocks immediately north and south. By the 19th century, most of the houses had been displaced by commercial buildings. Now the area is noteworthy for its fine examples of 18th and 19th century commercial architecture of different styles and materials ranging from brick, terra cotta and marble to cast iron. Many of the buildings have recently been converted to apartments, as Old City has once again become a desirable residential neighborhood.

The Old City tour begins at Second Street, which can be reached by taking a Market Street bus or Market-Frankford subway to the Second Street station, a good example of contemporary subway station design. The tour first proceeds north past the three major colonial landmarks in the area: Christ Church; Arch Street Friends Meeting House; and Elfreth's Alley, the oldest continuously occupied street in the country. The route south of Market Street is along Chestnut Street, which was once the city's financial district.

The few remaining cast-iron fronted buildings are on Arch Street; commercial buildings of all eras may be seen on Third Street; and Chestnut Street has several outstanding examples of 19th-century Italianate banks as well as loft buildings, which were precursors of the late 19th- and 20th-century Commercial style.

Interspersed among the major streets are a number of small alleys with handsome commercial structures. It is worth wandering off the tour route to walk down Strawberry Street, Bank Street, Church Street or Letitia Street. There are also a number of unusual tourist attractions in the area, including the U.S. Mint, Betsy Ross's House and Benjamin Franklin's grave in Christ Church Cemetery.

P Parking

1 **Second Street Subway Station**
2nd & Market Sts.
1976–79, Murphy Levy Wurman

2 **Christ Church**
22–26 N. 2nd St. **107** *OP*

3 **Tutlemann Brothers & Faggen Building**
56–60 N. 2nd St. **292** *PR*

4 **Smythe Buildings**
101–11 Arch St. **219**

5 **Trotter Warehouses**
36–44 N. Front St. 1830s

6 **Girard Warehouses**
18–30 N. Front St. **143**

7 **Elfreth's Alley**
Between Front & 2nd, Arch & Race Sts. **106** *PR*

8 **Betsy Ross House**
239 Arch St. 1740 *OP*

9 **St. Charles Hotel**
60–66 N. 3rd St. **210** *PR*

10 **Hoop Skirt Factory**
309–313 Arch St.
1875; ren. 1980, David Beck, Architects *PR*

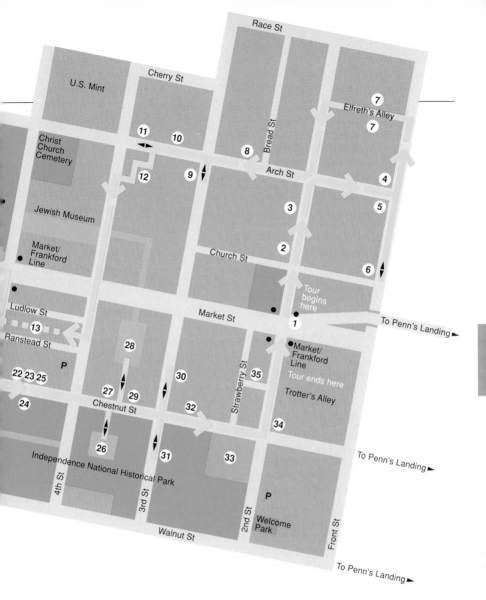

11 Loxley Court
Arch St. between 3rd & 4th Sts.
1741, Benjamin Loxley, carpenter *PR*

12 Arch Street Friends Meeting House
330 Arch St. **139** *OP*

13 The Bourse
11–21 S. 5th St. **284** *OP*

14 Liberty Bell Pavilion
Market St. between 5th & 6th Sts.
1976, Mitchell/Giurgola Assocs. *OP*

15 Rohm & Haas Building
6th & Market Sts. **357**

16 Atwater Kent Museum
15 S. 7th St. **149** *OP*

17 Philadelphia Life Insurance Company
Chestnut St. between 6th & 7th Sts.
1981, The Ballinger Co.

18 Public Ledger Building
6th & Chestnut Sts. **313**

19 Congress Hall
Chestnut St. at 6th St.
130 *OP*

20 Independence Hall (State House)
Chestnut St. between 5th & 6th Sts. **109** *OP*

21 U.S. Supreme Court Building
Chestnut St. at 5th St.
132 *OP*

22 Pennsylvania Company for Insurances on Lives & Granting Annuities
431 Chestnut St. **240**

23 Farmers' and Mechanics' Bank
427 Chestnut St. **217**

24 Second Bank of the U.S.
Chestnut St. between 4th & 5th Sts. **145** *OP*

25 Bank of Pennsylvania
421 Chestnut St. **226**

26 Carpenters' Hall
320 Chestnut St. **125** *OP*

27 Philadelphia National Bank
323 Chestnut St.
1898, Theophilus Chandler

28 Franklin Court
312–322 Market St. **364** *OP*

29 First National Bank
315 Chestnut St.
1865–67, John McArthur, Jr.

30 Leland Building
37–39 S. 3rd St. **218**

31 Independence National Park Visitor Center
125 S. 3rd St.
1976, Cambridge Seven Assocs. *OP*

32 Leland & Elliot Buildings
235–237 Chestnut St. **216**

33 Customs House
100 S. 2nd St.
1933, Ritter & Shay

34 Corn Exchange Bank
2nd & Chestnut Sts. **291** *OP*

35 Trotters Alley
32–34 S. 2nd St.
1889; ren. 1983, Adaptive Design *PR*

City Hall Area

c

When the decision was made to locate the new City Hall on Center Square in 1870, the surrounding area became the focus of commercial development. At the time, Center Square was on the edge of the developed area of the city. There were several civic institutions along Broad Street, and a few houses north and south built by prominent citizens drawn to the area because of its rural nature. All that changed as department stores, office buildings and banks surrounded City Hall. The central importance of the area was strengthened when the Pennsylvania and Reading railroads located their main stations west and east of City Hall.

In the past few decades, the railroad stations have provided a focus for even greater commercial and retail growth. During the 1950s, the Pennsylvania Railroad's Broad Street Station was demolished to create a new office complex west of City Hall known as Penn Center. Nearly all new office building construction has remained in this immediate area. The western portion of the City Hall area has been transformed during the past decade by the construction of the city's tallest office buildings. Most retail development has remained east of City Hall, where a new retail complex, The Gallery, has been constructed adjacent to the Reading Terminal.

The tour begins with a magnificent view of the city from the top of City Hall. The tour proceeds east, through the Grand Court of Wanamaker's store, then south along Broad Street past many of the city's cultural institutions. This portion of Broad Street is the Avenue of the Arts cultural district.

The tour returns north, past each of the major new office buildings, to the Benjamin Franklin Parkway, one of the finest examples of Beaux-Arts urban design in the country. Within this area are four of the most important architectural monuments in the city: City Hall, the Pennsylvania Academy of Fine Arts, the PSFS Building and One Liberty Place. Each is as spectacular on the interior as it is on the exterior.

Most of the buildings in the area are open to the public. The most exceptional interiors, in addition to the first three noted above, are: the Masonic Temple, the Cathedral of Saints Peter and Paul, the Arch Street Presbyterian Church, the Academy of Music, Wanamaker's Department Store, the Hotel Atop the Bellevue and the Shops at Liberty Place.

P Parking

1 **City Hall**
Broad & Market Sts.
242 *OP*

2 **Municipal Services Building**
1500 John F. Kennedy Blvd.
350 *OP*

3 **Masonic Temple**
Broad & Filbert Sts.
236 *OP*

4 **One East Penn Square**
1–21 N. Juniper St. **328**

5 **John Wanamaker**
1300–24 Market St. **296** *OP*

6 **Keystone National Bank**
Juniper & Chestnut Sts. **268**

7 **Girard Trust Company**
34–46 S. Broad St. **301** *OP*

8 **Land Title Building**
100–18 S. Broad St. **290**

9 **Union League**
140 S. Broad St. **234**

10 **Bellevue Stratford**
Broad & Walnut Sts.
294 *OP*

11 **Clarence Moore House**
1321 Locust St. **274**

12 **Joseph Leidy House**
1319 Locust St. **282**

13 **Academy of Music**
232–46 S. Broad St. **220** *OP*

14 **Philadelphia College of Art**
320 S. Broad St. **148**

15 **Philadelphia College of Art Addition**
320 S. Broad St. **248**

16 **The Drake**
1512–14 Spruce St. **326** *PR*

17 **1500 Walnut Street Addition**
(On 15th St.) **352**

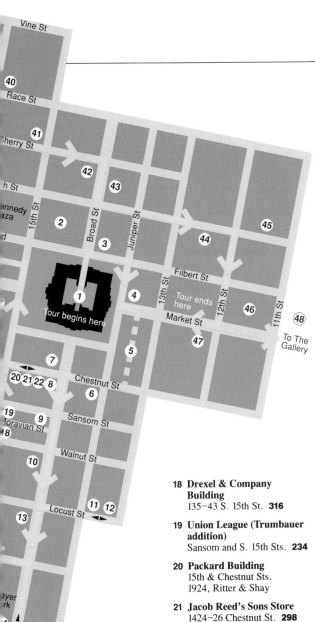

30 INA Building Addition
1600 Arch St. **370**

31 Robert Morris Hotel
1705 Arch St. **307**

32 Bell Atlantic Tower
17th and Arch Sts. **392**

33 Arch Street Presbyterian Church
1724 Arch St. **213**

34 Two Logan Square
100 N. 18th St. **386**

35 One Logan Square & Four Seasons Hotel
Race St. between 18th & 19th Sts. **374**

36 Cathedral of SS Peter & Paul
18th & Race Sts. **206** *OP*

37 United Fund Building
Benjamin Franklin Pkwy. between 17th & 18th Sts. **358**

38 Friends Select School & Pennwalt Building
Benjamin Franklin Pkwy. between 16th & 17th Sts. 1970, Mirick, Pearson, Batcheler

39 Franklin Plaza Hotel & SmithKline Beckman Office Building
Race St. between 16th & 17th Sts. **371**

40 Magee Hospital Addition
1513 Race St. **373**

41 Friends Meeting Center
15th & Cherry Sts. 1974, Cope & Lippincott

42 Pennsylvania Academy of The Fine Arts
Broad & Cherry Sts. **241** *OP*

43 Philadelphia Life Insurance Company
125 N. Broad St. 1963, Mitchell/Giurgola Assocs.

44 A. J. Holman Factory
1222–26 Arch St. **254**

45 Pennsylvania Convention Center
Arch St. between 11th and 13th Sts. **400**

46 Reading Terminal & Shed
Market St. between 11th & 12th Sts. **278** *OP*

47 Philadelphia Saving Fund Society
12 S. 12th St. **330**

48 The Gallery
Market St. between 9th & 11th Sts. **366** *OP*

18 Drexel & Company Building
135–43 S. 15th St. **316**

19 Union League (Trumbauer addition)
Sansom and S. 15th Sts. **234**

20 Packard Building
15th & Chestnut Sts. 1924, Ritter & Shay

21 Jacob Reed's Sons Store
1424–26 Chestnut St. **298**

22 Crozer Building
1420–22 Chestnut St. **287**

23 One Penn Square West
30 S. 15th St. **381**

24 Centre Square
Market St. between 15th & 16th Sts. 1973, The Kling Partnership

25 Penn Center Complex
Market St. from 15th to 20th Sts. **341**

26 WCAU Building
1620 Chestnut St. **323**

27 Liberty Place
16th to 17th Sts., Chestnut to Market Sts. **383, 388, 389**

28 Mellon Center
1735 Market St. **390**

29 Commonwealth Land Title Building
17th & John F. Kennedy Blvd. 1982, Kohn Pederson & Fox

Fairmount Park

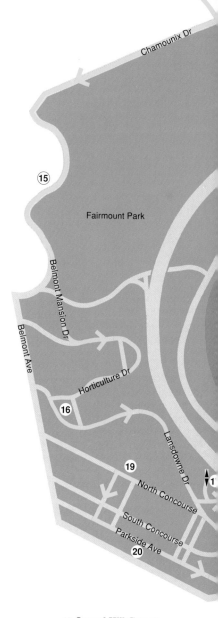

Fairmount Park is the largest park within city limits and one of the oldest in the country. Much of the area was originally occupied by the country homes and estates of colonial families. One of these, Lemon Hill, was acquired in 1844 to protect the city's water supply. In the years that followed, other estates were purchased, as well as additional land on both sides of the Schuylkill River, to create the 3,000-acre park. In 1876 the park was the site of the Centennial Exposition. Most of the Exposition buildings were demolished, but Memorial Hall and several smaller buildings still remain. The Exposition encouraged the development of large houses on the edge of the park. Parkside Avenue became a fashionable address after the Exposition, and traces of its former elegance may still be seen.

Because Fairmount Park is so large, it must be seen on a driving tour. The tour starts at the Art Museum and proceeds along the beautiful Kelly Drive, past Boat House Row, a delightful collection of Victorian buildings housing the area's rowing associations. The tour through the east park passes the major colonial mansions, all of which are open to the public. In the west park are the Exposition buildings as well as a beautiful Japanese tea house. The park also contains an unusually fine collection of sculpture. The Philadelphia Zoo, oldest in the country, is adjacent to the park and contains many fine buildings. The tour returns to the Art Museum along the West River Drive, with its magnificent view of the Philadelphia skyline.

P Parking

1 **Philadelphia Museum of Art**
26th St. & Benjamin Franklin Pkwy. **309** *OP*

2 **Fidelity Mutual Life Insurance**
2501 Benjamin Franklin Pkwy. **319**

3 **Fairmount Waterworks**
Schuylkill River behind Art Museum **144**

4 **Boat House Row**
E. River Dr.

5 **Undine Barge Club**
13 Boat House Row
1882, Furness & Evans

6 **Lemon Hill**
Lemon Hill Dr. **138** *OP*

7 **Mt. Pleasant**
Mt. Pleasant Dr. **119** *OP*

8 **Rockland**
Mt. Pleasant Drive
1800

9 **Ormiston**
Reservoir Rd. 1798 *OP*

10 **Laurel Hill (Randolph House)**
Edgely Dr. 1748; 1760 *OP*

11 **Woodford**
Strawberry Drive
1756; 1772 *OP*

12 **Strawberry Mansion**
Strawberry Drive
1797, possibly by Summerville; 1825; 1870 *OP*

13 **Laurel Hill Cemetery**
3822 Ridge Ave. **202** *OP*

14 **Philadelphia Psychiatric Center**
Ford Rd. & Monument Ave. **339**

15 **Belmont Mansion**
Belmont Mansion Dr.
1755 *OP*

16 **Japanese House**
Lansdowne Dr. east of Belmont Ave.
1953, Junzo Yoshimura *OP*

17 **Cedar Grove**
Lansdowne Dr. near Black Rd. 1748; 1752 *OP*

18 **Sweetbrier**
Lansdowne Dr. 1797 *OP*

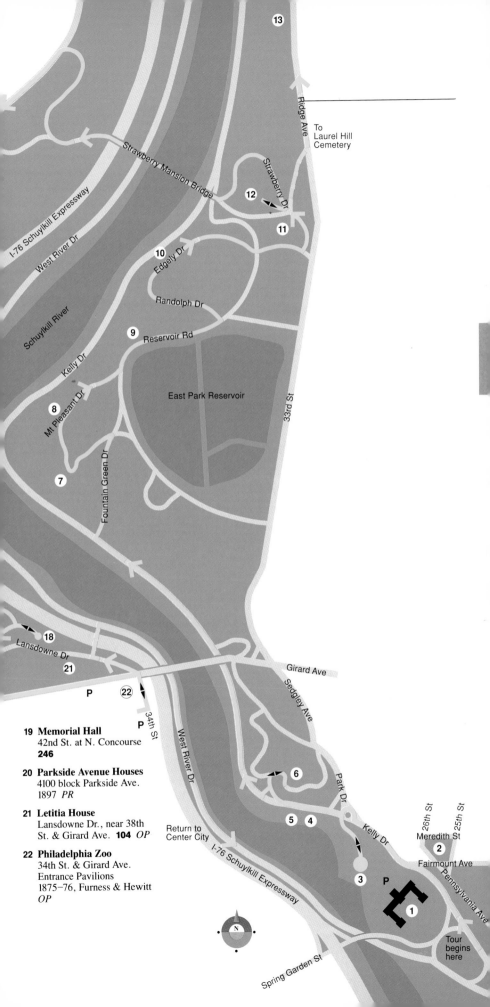

13

Ridge Ave

To
Laurel Hill
Cemetery

Strawberry Mansion Bridge

I-76 Schuylkill Expressway

West River Dr

12

Strawberry Dr

11

10

Edgely Dr

Randolph Dr

Schuylkill River

9

Reservoir Rd

Kelly Dr

East Park Reservoir

33rd St

8

Mt Pleasant Dr

7

Fountain Green Dr

18

Lansdowne Dr

21

Girard Ave

Sedgley Ave

P

22

34th St

P

6

19 Memorial Hall
42nd St. at N. Concourse
246

20 Parkside Avenue Houses
4100 block Parkside Ave.
1897 *PR*

21 Letitia House
Lansdowne Dr., near 38th
St. & Girard Ave. **104** *OP*

22 Philadelphia Zoo
34th St. & Girard Ave.
Entrance Pavilions
1875–76, Furness & Hewitt
OP

West River Dr

5 **4**

Park Dr

Kelly Dr

26th St

25th St

Meredith St

2

Fairmount Ave

Pennsylvania Ave

Return to
Center City

I-76 Schuylkill Expressway

3

P

1

Tour
begins
here

N

Spring Garden St

University City

The University of Pennsylvania and Drexel University are located in the eastern portion of West Philadelphia. The University of Pennsylvania campus contains an impressive collection of outstanding buildings by local and nationally prominent architects. The university was founded in 1751. It was originally located at 4th and Arch streets and then moved to 9th and Market. When the campus was moved to West Philadelphia in 1871, the area was still rural countryside with some scattered houses north and west of the campus.

The Penn campus has grown from its original setting around College Hall to a large urban complex covering many city blocks. Its buildings are representative of virtually every architectural style of the past 100 years and include examples of the work of Frank Furness, Louis I. Kahn, Mitchell/Giurgola, Richard Neutra and Eero Saarinen. Under the direction of Paul Philippe Cret, the Graduate School of Fine Arts, one of the finest architectural schools in the country, was an early advocate of the École des Beaux-Arts philosophy. In the 1960s, the school's faculty included many of America's leading architects. Penn's Architectural Archives, located in the Fisher Fine Arts Building, has an extensive collection of architectural documents including papers, drawings and models of Louis I. Kahn.

The easiest way to reach the University City tour is to take the Market-Frankford subway to 30th Street and exit onto 31st Street. The tour starts at Furness's Centennial Bank and proceeds through the Drexel University campus. The tour enters the Penn campus at 33rd Street and proceeds from the center of the campus past the University Museum and hospital complex to Louis Kahn's Richards Medical Building, one of the most influential buildings of modern times. The tour concludes at the 34th Street subway station.

Among the most interesting buildings open to the public are the Drexel Main Building with its wonderful interior court, the University Museum and the Fisher Fine Arts Building.

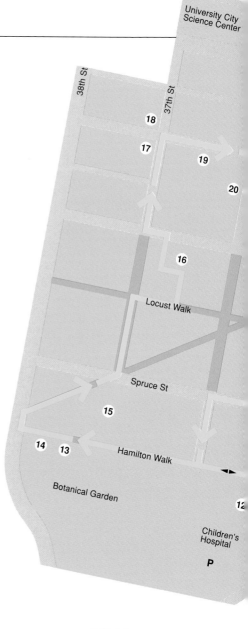

P Parking

1 **Centennial Bank**
3142 Market St. **250**

2 **LeBow Engineering Center and Center for Automation Technology**
Market St. between 31st & 32nd Sts. **394**

3 **Drexel Institute of Technology, Main Building**
32nd & Chestnut Sts.
273 *OP*

4 **University of Pennsylvania Garage**
32nd & Walnut Sts. **354**

5 **Hill Hall**
Walnut St. between 33rd & 34th Sts. **345**

6 **College Hall**
Locust Walk between 34th & 35th Sts. **239** *OP*

7 **Anne and Jerome Fisher Fine Arts Building**
34th St. between Walnut & Spruce Sts. **269** *OP*

8 **Franklin Field**
33rd & South Sts. **295**

9 **University Museum**
South & 33rd Sts. **285** *OP*

10 **Parking Garage 2**
South St. & Convention Ave.
1968, Mitchell/Giurgola Assocs.

11 **Irvine Auditorium**
34th & Spruce Sts.
1929, Horace Trumbauer

12 **Clinical Research Building**
35th St. south of Hamilton Walk **393**

13 **Richards Medical Research Building**
Hamilton Walk between 37th & 38th Sts. **343**

14 **Therapeutic Laboratories Addition**
Hamilton Walk between 37th & 38th Sts.
1964, Schlesinger & Vreeland

15 **Men's Dormitories**
Spruce St. between 36th & 38th Sts. **286** *PR*

16 **Annenberg School of Communications Addition**
Locust Walk between 36th & 37th Sts.
1985, Mitchell/Giurgola Associates

17 **Tabernacle Presbyterian Church**
3700 Chestnut St. **259**

18 **International House**
3501 Chestnut St. **360** *PR*

19 **Married Student Housing**
Chestnut St. between 36th & 37th Sts.
1970, Richard Neutra with Bellante & Clauss

20 **Institute of Contemporary Art**
36th and Sansom Sts. **396**

21 **ISI Building**
3501 Market St. **368**

Powelton and Spruce Hill

F

Powelton and Spruce Hill are examples of 19th-century residential neighborhoods created for the growing middle-class population of the city. Both areas were rural countryside, with only a few scattered houses, until the introduction of horse-drawn trolleys in the 1860s made it possible to commute easily to the city. Then there was a rapid growth of suburban houses with yards and tree-lined streets, in contrast to the dense row housing of the city.

Powelton and Spruce Hill contain many houses representative of the Italianate and Victorian Gothic styles, but more importantly, each neighborhood has retained its overall 19th-century character.

Powelton Village was first settled in 1800. Most of its houses were built speculatively

in the late 19th century as twins or double houses in the Italianate style, usually of wood frame and stucco. There are a number of mansions, some built by prominent manufacturers of the period, and several blocks of distinctive and ornate Victorian row houses.

Spruce Hill was at the western edge of the horse-drawn trolley lines and thus grew more slowly. Italianate houses, many by Samuel Sloan, dominated the first phase of suburban development. As growth moved westward, speculative rows and twin houses were built in an exuberant Victorian Gothic style. Some of the most richly detailed houses in the city can be found in the area from 40th to 46th streets south of Walnut Street.

Powelton and Spruce Hill can only be seen by a driving tour. The tour proceeds

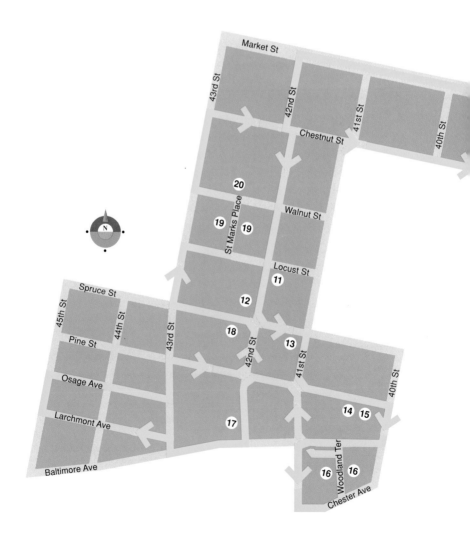

through the Drexel University campus to Powelton. Baring and Hamilton streets are most representative of the Italianate houses in the area, while the best Victorian Gothic houses are on Powelton Avenue. On the way to Spruce Hill, the route passes a new low-income housing project that has borrowed from Victorian motifs. In Spruce Hill, Italianate houses are located east of 42nd Street; west of 42nd Street are elaborate Victorian Gothic rows and twin houses, many of which show the influence of Frank Furness. All the houses on the tour are private residences.

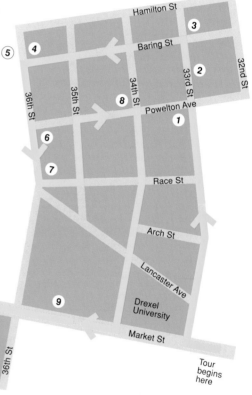

1 **Poth Mansion**
216 N. 33rd St. **266** *PR*

2 **Italianate Twin Houses**
315–17 N. 33rd St.
1860s *PR*

3 **Italianate House**
401 N. 33rd St. 1860s *PR*

4 **Cochran House**
3511 Baring St.
1891, Wilson Eyre *PR*

5 **Gaither House**
3601 Baring St. **385** *PR*

6 **3500 Powelton Avenue**
297 *PR*

7 **205 North 36th Street**
1883, F. G. Thorn *PR*

8 **George Burnham House**
3401 Powelton Ave.
1886, Theophilus Chandler

9 **ISI Building**
3501 Market St. **368**

10 **University City Family Housing**
39th to 40th Sts. on Market St. **375**

11 **Montelius House**
223 S. 42nd St. **233** *PR*

12 **Divinity School Chapel**
42nd & Spruce Sts. **315**

13 **4108–16 Spruce Street**
1869, Samuel Sloan *PR*

14 **Italianate Twin Houses**
4008–10 Pine St.
1862, John Mitchell, builder *PR*

15 **Italianate Twin Houses**
4004–6 Pine St. 1860s *PR*

16 **Woodland Terrace**
500–520 Woodland Ter.
231 *PR*

17 **420–34 S. 42nd St.**
1883, attributed to G. W. and W. D. Hewitt *PR*

18 **4206–18 Spruce Street**
265 *PR*

19 **St. Mark's Place Houses**
Between 42nd & 43rd Sts. south of Walnut St.
1890s, attributed to G. W. and W. D. Hewitt *PR*

20 **Allison House**
4207 Walnut St.
1853, Samuel Sloan *PR*
Addition, 1991, Agoos/ Lovera

Germantown

G

Germantown was founded in 1683, when Penn gave a large tract of land to Daniel Pastorius and a group of German-speaking Quakers. It was the largest early settlement outside the city having its own stores, businesses and even its own German newspaper. Most early buildings were located on Germantown Avenue, the original colonial road connecting to the city. After the yellow fever epidemics in the city in 1793 and 1796, Germantown became a popular location for summer homes. During the 19th century, Germantown grew rapidly after the commuter railroad was extended from the city in the 1840s. Many picturesque villas and Victorian mansions were built during this era for middle-class families eager to escape the noise and congestion of the city.

Germantown can best be seen by a driving tour, although it is possible to take the Chestnut Hill West train line to the Tulpehocken Station for a walking tour of the area. The driving tour reaches Germantown via the beautiful Lincoln Drive, along a natural wilderness area within the city. Germantown Avenue is the location of many of the oldest buildings and is an interesting driving tour in itself. Several blocks away, in the Walnut Lane area, is a fine collection of Victorian suburban houses. Most houses on the tour are private homes, and not open to the public. However, Cliveden, the Deshler-Morris House, Wyck and the Maxwell Mansion are open and provide excellent examples of both colonial and Victorian design.

The Germantown tour easily connects to the Chestnut Hill tour which begins on W. Allens Lane.

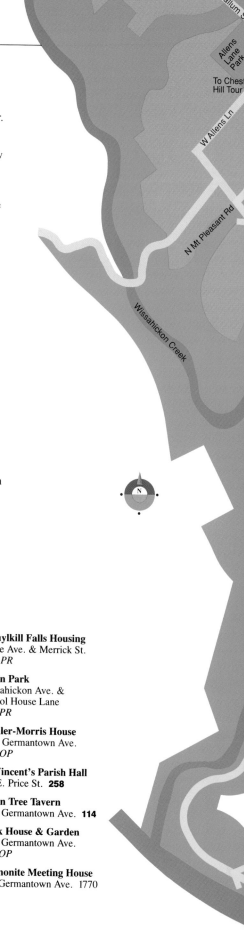

1 **Schuylkill Falls Housing**
Ridge Ave. & Merrick St.
342 *PR*

2 **Alden Park**
Wissahickon Ave. &
School House Lane
317 *PR*

3 **Deshler-Morris House**
5442 Germantown Ave.
126 *OP*

4 **St. Vincent's Parish Hall**
109 E. Price St. **258**

5 **Green Tree Tavern**
6023 Germantown Ave. **114**

6 **Wyck House & Garden**
6026 Germantown Ave.
102 *OP*

7 **Mennonite Meeting House**
6119 Germantown Ave. 1770

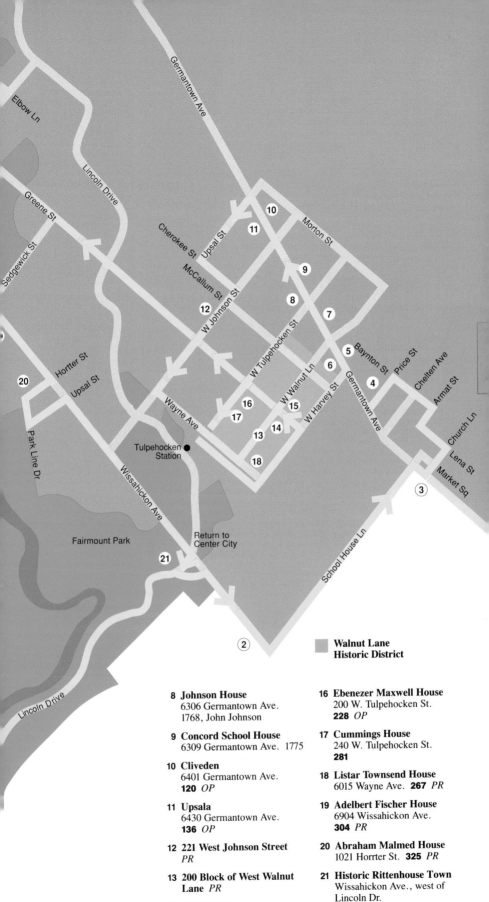

Walnut Lane Historic District

8 Johnson House
6306 Germantown Ave.
1768, John Johnson

9 Concord School House
6309 Germantown Ave. 1775

10 Cliveden
6401 Germantown Ave.
120 *OP*

11 Upsala
6430 Germantown Ave.
136 *OP*

12 221 West Johnson Street
PR

13 200 Block of West Walnut Lane *PR*

14 Mitchell House
200 W. Walnut Lane **223** *PR*

15 150 W. Walnut Lane
1860s, John Riddell *PR*

16 Ebenezer Maxwell House
200 W. Tulpehocken St.
228 *OP*

17 Cummings House
240 W. Tulpehocken St.
281

18 Listar Townsend House
6015 Wayne Ave. **267** *PR*

19 Adelbert Fischer House
6904 Wissahickon Ave.
304 *PR*

20 Abraham Malmed House
1021 Horrter St. **325** *PR*

21 Historic Rittenhouse Town
Wissahickon Ave., west of
Lincoln Dr.
1690–1810 *OP*

Chestnut Hill

Chestnut Hill originally developed along Germantown Avenue. Early commercial and residential buildings were similar to those in Germantown. But Chestnut Hill's real growth and prosperity did not occur until the 19th century, with the extension of the commuter railroad. At that time, Henry Houston, a director of the Pennsylvania Railroad, undertook a number of real estate ventures designed to attract wealthy families to the area. He built an elaborate inn and church, gave land for a cricket club and constructed nearly 100 houses. Other residents built grand Italianate villas. The area contains a fascinating mix of elaborate mansions for the wealthy and small row houses originally built for their predominantly Irish servants. Houston's efforts were followed by his son-in-law, Dr. George Woodward, who developed many outstanding housing complexes in the early 20th century, most of which are still owned and rented by the Woodward family. These included some important early examples of grouped houses. Among the architects represented in the area are Mellor and Meigs, George Howe, Robert Venturi, Mitchell/Giurgola and Louis Kahn.

Chestnut Hill can best be seen by a driving tour, although it is possible to take the Chestnut Hill West train line to the Chestnut Hill station for a walking tour of the area. The driving tour reaches Chestnut Hill via Kelly Drive and the beautiful Lincoln Drive.

In Chestnut Hill the tour winds through residential streets containing some of the best examples of Victorian, early 20th century and contemporary houses in Philadelphia. Of particular interest are the early 20th century experiments in grouped housing, such as the Benezet Street houses, Winston Court, and the Lincoln Drive complex. Most of the buildings on the tour are private residences and not open to the public.

1 **Todd House**
7321 McCallum St.
1966, Wallace McHarg
Roberts Todd *PR*

2 **French Village**
Elbow Lane & Gate Lane off
McCallum St. **318** *PR*

3 **Krisheim**
McCallum St. &
Mermaid Lane
1910, Peabody & Stearns

4 **Druim Moir and Brinkwood**
W. Willow Grove Ave. &
Cherokee St. **262** *PR*

5 **Wissahickon Inn**
500 W. Willow Grove Ave.
257

6 **St. Martins in the Fields**
W. Willow Grove Ave. &
St. Martins Lane
1888, G. W. & W. D. Hewitt

7 **Dorothy Shipley White House**
717 Glen Gary Dr. **351** *PR*

8 **Houston Sauveur House**
8205 Seminole St. **261** *PR*

9 **Charles Woodward House**
8220 Millman St. **337** *PR*

10 **Vanna Venturi House**
8330 Millman St. **349** *PR*

11 **Margaret Esherick House**
204 Sunrise Lane **346** *PR*

12 **Gravers Lane Station**
Gravers Lane & Anderson St.
255

13 **Angelcot**
Evergreen Ave. & Prospect
St. **256** *PR*

14 **Watson House**
100 Summit St. **222** *PR*

15 **Piper-Price House**
129 Bethlehem Pike **215** *PR*

16 **Woodmere Art Gallery**
9201 Germantown Ave.
1867 *OP*

17 **High Hollow**
101 W. Hampton Rd.
308 *PR*

18 **Pepper House**
9120 Crefeld St. **312** *PR*

19 **Schofield Andrews House**
9002 Crefeld St. **329**

20 **Howe-Fraley House**
10 W. Chestnut Hill Ave.
1921, George Howe *PR*

21 **Winston Court**
7821–7909 Winston Rd.
1925, H. Louis Duhring *PR*

22 **Benezet Street Houses**
24–32 Benezet St. **306** *PR*

23 **Lincoln Drive Development**
Lincoln Dr. & W. Willow
Grove Ave. **310** *PR*

a. Half Moon Houses
7919–25 Lincoln Dr.

b. Sulgrave Manor
200 W. Willow Grove Ave.

c. Linden Court
103–113 W. Willow Grove
Ave.

d. Three Houses
8008–12 Crefeld Ave.

24 **100–102 West Mermaid Lane 303** *PR*

25 **French Village**
Emlen St. & W. Allens Lane
318 *PR*

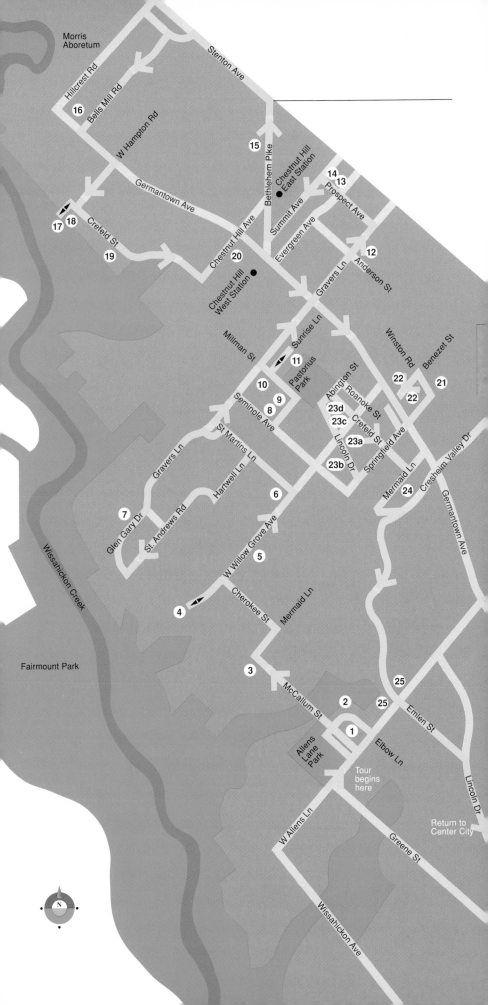

Highlights Driving Tour

J

The Highlights driving tour is designed for those who want to see some of the city's most important buildings and interesting areas in a limited amount of time. The tour takes approximately two hours. It begins at Independence Hall, proceeds through most areas covered by individual walking or driving tours as well as portions of North Philadelphia, and concludes at City Hall. The buildings listed below are the most important landmarks; other buildings along this route can be identified by consulting the tours of individual areas.

1 Independence Hall (State House) **109**

2 Second Bank of the U.S. **145**

3 Carpenters' Hall **125**

4 St. Peter's Church **116**

5 Head House & Market Shed **113**

6 Powel House **122**

7 Society Hill Towers **356**

8 Merchant's Exchange **154**

Buildings Not on Tours

Philadelphia Museum of Art

I-76 Schuylkill Expwy

Schuylkill River

Pennsylvania Ave

Benjamin Franklin Pkwy

Hamilton St

322

314

Callowhill St

311

391

Logan Circle

224

327

John F. Kennedy Blvd

City Hall

260

270

288

238 225

249

Rittenhouse Sq

208
209

237

276

211 214

32nd St

31st St

30th St

29th St

24th St

23rd St

22nd St

21st St

20th St

19th St

18th St

17th St

16th St

15th St

Broad St

Juniper St

13th St

Numbers on maps refer to
building catalog numbers.

376
379
Ridge Ave
110
Stenton Ave
253
227
Cottman Ave
369
Germantown Ave
112
Roosevelt Blvd
336
381
108
135
277 263
Hunting Park Ave
334
384
279
L-95
Schuylkill River
232
331
243
202 205
Allegheny Ave
155
City Line Ave
101
339
395
Belmont Ave
Schuylkill Expy
Lehigh Ave
Frankford Ave
Lancaster Ave
283
289
22nd St
280
272
377
Front St
Girard Ave
212
275
251
338
397
324 355
320 347
Market St
221
34th St
131
Delaware Ave
Benjamin Franklin Bridge
398
302
150
Washington Ave
111
245 115
141 103
124
Woodland Ave
Broad St
Moyamensing Ave
335
105 Pattison Ave
Penrose Ave
Walt Whitman Bridge
Delaware River
127

N

Franklin
Sq
207 123
Benjamin Franklin Bridge approach
Vine St
Cherry St
353
Filbert St
363
Race St
Arch St
146
244 332
Sansom St
Market St
137
Independence
National Historical
Park
Chestnut St
151
140 • • 235
• 321
367 129 Washington
142 Sq
Locust St
Penn's
Landing
Walnut St
153
133
Dock St
Dock St
Spruce St
Delaware River
271
Pine St
Lombard St

11th St
10th St
9th St
8th St
7th St
6th St
5th St
4th St
3rd St
2nd St
Front St

Places of Interest

Penn's Landing

Mummers Museum

Philadelphia and the eight surrounding counties contain many special attractions that are of interest not only for their activities or historic significance but also because they have distinctive physical environments or architectural features. The following are a few of the more notable places of interest:

In the City

Penn's Landing, Delaware River from Lombard to Market Sts.

In the early 1960s, the city removed some of the old piers along the Delaware River to create a 37-acre waterfront site for recreational and commercial use. Penn's Landing contains several interesting attractions and provides a dramatic view of the river and the city. Many public festivals and concerts are held in the Great Plaza, a tiered amphitheater designed by Cope Linder Associates. Historic ships permanently docked here include Admiral Dewey's flagship the USS Olympia, the submarine USS Becuna and the square-rigged sailing ship Gazela. Others visit on special occasions. The Maritime Museum operates a floating exhibit and is renovating the Port of History Museum for its new headquarters.

The international sculpture garden is a pleasant place to sit and watch the passing ships. It contains a steel obelisk by Venturi Scott Brown and Associates commemorating Christopher Columbus.

The Riverbus, departing from Walnut St., connects to the Camden, N.J., waterfront and the New Jersey State Aquarium.

The Italian Market, 9th St. between Catharine St. and Washington Ave.

South Philadelphia was the principal place of arrival for immigrants in the 19th century. Most moved to other sections of the city, but the Italians remained; now, second- and third-generation families live in the area, often in the same house in which they were born. The Italian market is a major shopping area for them as well as for people from all over the city. It is a typical outdoor European market with small stores and covered sheds spilling over into the street—a noisy, colorful, bustling place with stores that sell everything from meat, poultry, produce and pasta, to exotic spices, housewares and even clothing. There are several restaurants and bakeries filled with fresh breads and marvelous pastries. The market is a wonderful place to shop or simply to visit.

Mummers Museum, 2nd St. and Washington Ave.

The Mummers' string bands and fancy clubs are a Philadelphia institution. Their annual "strut" up Broad Street welcomes in the New Year with a flourish of fancy costumes elaborately decorated with feathers. The Mummers Museum, not far from the Italian market, pays tribute to their history and tradition. The building, designed by Ueland and Junker in 1976, is as fanciful as the organizations it represents. It contains wonderful displays of typical costumes and an audiovisual presentation that gives a fine introduction to this unique Philadelphia tradition.

Mercer Museum

Mercer Museum, interior

The Zoological Gardens, 34th St. and Girard Ave.

The Philadelphia Zoo, opened in 1874, is the oldest in the country. It is located on 42 acres within Fairmount Park. The zoo has a fine collection of animals and such special attractions as the Rare Mammal House, Hummingbird House, Bear Country, the five-acre African Plains, tropical gardens and the Children's Zoo, where the animals are free to be touched and fed. Many of the buildings at the zoo were designed by prominent architects and are interesting in their own right. The gatehouses are by Furness and Hewitt. Recent buildings include Venturi Scott Brown and Assoc.'s Widener Memorial Tree House and World of Primates; Ueland & Junker's Impala Fountain Cafe and Bohlin Cywinski Jackson's Carnivore Kingdom. Also on the grounds is the house of John Penn, William Penn's grandson, which was built from 1784–85.

Rittenhouse Square, 19th and Walnut Sts.

Rittenhouse Square was one of the four eight-acre public parks set aside in Penn's plan for the city. In the 19th century it was named after David Rittenhouse, the colonial astronomer. Public funds were collected to improve the square, which is now one of the most enjoyable and heavily used open spaces in center city. Many events are held in the square, including a flower show and a clothesline art exhibition.

The Rittenhouse Square area was a fashionable residential neighborhood in the 19th century. Several mansions remain on the square, typical of the many that once surrounded it. To the south are fine blocks of 19th-century brownstones and Victorian row houses, which can be enjoyed by walking along Spruce and Pine streets and the many streets and alleys between 17th and 25th streets.

Wissahickon Creek

The Wissahickon valley is located in the northwest section of the city, near Germantown and Chestnut Hill. It is a 1300-acre section of Fairmount Park that has been left in its natural state. The meandering creek is bordered by steep hills and rock outcroppings; paths for running, biking and horseback riding parallel the creek. Along the creek are the Thomas Mill Road Bridge, the only remaining covered bridge in a major city, and the Valley Green Inn, a late 19th-century roadhouse that is still operating as a restaurant.

In the Region

Andalusia, Bensalem, PA

Bucks County, just north of Philadelphia, contains many handsome historic buildings and historic sites. One of the most distinctive is Andalusia. Andalusia was a simple 18th-century country house until Nicholas Biddle commissioned Thomas U. Walter to add two parlors in a Doric colonnade. This transformed the house into one of the country's finest examples of domestic Greek Revival architecture. The house remains in the Biddle family, but is overseen by the National Trust for Historic Preservation. It is open to the public; information about visiting Andalusia can be obtained from the Bucks County Historical Society.

Longwood Gardens

Longwood Gardens, interior

Mercer Museum, Doylestown, PA

Dr. Henry C. Mercer was a renowned traveler, explorer, anthropologist and archaeologist. He devoted his life to the study of civilization. In 1897, he began to collect preindustrial tools and artifacts. His collection, "Tools of the Nation Maker," is the most comprehensive of its type in the world.

To display the collection, Mercer built a museum, which was designed from the inside out. There were no plans or drawings; workmen simply followed his directions. The result is an unusual and striking building in which windows, doors and even rooms appear in no particular order. It is one of the first buildings totally constructed of reinforced concrete. Both for its architecture and its extraordinary collection, the Mercer Museum is one of the most fascinating places in the region.

Longwood Gardens, Kennett Square, PA

Longwood Gardens is the former estate of Pierre S. Du Pont. Its 350 acres are magnificently landscaped in a variety of styles, including a beautiful Italian water garden. Among the most outstanding features are the huge glass conservatories, open year round. They contain 20 indoor gardens and seasonal displays. The conservatories overlook a large formal garden filled with spectacular fountains. The Peirce-Du Pont Mansion is also on the site and open to the public.

Winterthur Museum, Winterthur, DE

The Henry Francis Du Pont Winterthur Museum houses the world's greatest collection of 18th-century American antiques and artifacts. The collection was begun by Du Pont in the 1920s with the purchase of a 1737 Pennsylvania chest. Since 1951, the Winterthur Corporation has operated the museum, which now contains more than 71,000 objects. The museum consists of well over 100 authentic rooms that have been removed from early houses, restored and furnished in a historically complete manner. There is also a beautiful garden, which was landscaped under Du Pont's personal direction.

Bryn Mawr College, Bryn Mawr, PA

Within the Philadelphia area are a number of outstanding colleges and universities with handsome campuses and fine period architecture. Haverford, Swarthmore, and Bryn Mawr are among the best known.

Bryn Mawr is one of the country's finest educational institutions for women. One of the most notable buildings on its campus is the Erdman Hall dormitory, designed by Louis I. Kahn from 1960−65. The dormitory consists of three diamond-shaped units, each of which focuses around an inner court illuminated by natural light, in Kahn's distinctive manner. Although the exterior is exposed concrete and slate, its scale and siting make it part of the more traditional campus.

Bibliography and Photo Credits

American Philosophic Society.
Historic Philadelphia from the Founding until the Nineteenth Century.
Philadelphia, 1953.

Brownlee, David B., and David G. Delong.
Louis I. Kahn: In the Realm of Architecture
New York: Rizzoli International Publications, 1991.

Brownlee, David B.
Building the City Beautiful
Philadelphia, 1989.

Greiff, Constance M.
John Notman, Architect: 1810–1865.
Philadelphia: Athenaeum of Philadelphia, 1979.

Maas, John.
The Glorious Enterprise: The Centennial Exhibition of 1876 and H. J. Schwarzmann, Architect-in-Chief.
Watkins Glen, N.Y.: American Life Foundation, 1973.

Mellor Meigs and Howe.
Boulder, Colo.: Graybooks, 1991.

Miller, Fredric M., Morris J. Vogel, and Allen F. Davis.
Still Philadelphia: A Photographic History, 1890–1940.
Philadelphia: Temple University Press, 1983.

Mitchell, Ehrman and Romaldo Giurgola.
Mitchell/Giurgola.
New York: Rizzoli International Publications, 1983.

O'Gorman, James F.
The Architecture of Frank Furness.
Philadelphia: Philadelphia Museum of Art, 1973.

Philadelphia Museum of Art.
Philadelphia: Three Centuries of American Art.
Philadelphia: Philadelphia Museum of Art, 1976.

Schwartz, Frederic, ed.
Mother's House.
New York: Rizzoli International Publications, 1992.

Stern, Robert A. M.
George Howe: Toward a Modern American Architecture.
New Haven: Yale University Press, 1975.

Tatum, George B.
Penn's Great Town: 250 Years of Philadelphia Architecture.
New Haven: Yale University Press, 1975.

———.
Philadelphia Georgian: The City House of Samuel Powel and Some of Its 18th-Century Neighbors.
Middletown, Conn.: Wesleyan University Press, 1976.

Teitelman, Edward and Richard W. Longstreth.
Architecture in Philadelphia: A Guide.
Cambridge, Mass.: MIT Press, 1974.

Tinkcom, Harry M., Margaret B. Tinkcom, and Grant Miles Simon.
Historic Germantown.
Philadelphia: American Philosophical Society, 1955.

Venturi, Robert.
Complexity and Contradiction in Architecture.
Cambridge, Mass.: MIT Press, 1967.

Warner, Sam Bass, Jr.
The Private City: Philadelphia in Three Periods of Its Growth.
Philadelphia: University of Pennsylvania Press, 1968.

Webster, Richard J.
Philadelphia Preserved: Catalog of the Historic American Buildings Survey.
Philadelphia: Temple University Press, 1976.

Weigley, Russell F., ed.
Philadelphia: A 300-Year History.
New York: W. W. Norton and Company, 1982.

White, Theo B.
Paul Philippe Cret.
Philadelphia: The Art Alliance Press, 1973.

———.
Philadelphia Architecture in the 19th Century.
Philadelphia: University of Pennsylvania Press, 1953.

Wolf, Edwin 2nd, ed.
Philadelphia: Portrait of an American City.
Harrisburg: Stackpole Books, 1975.

Wurman, Richard Saul and John Andrew Gallery.
Man-Made Philadelphia: A Guide to the Physical and Cultural Environment.
Cambridge, Mass.: MIT Press, 1972.

Catalog 1
10 Historical Society of Pennsylvania. *11* The Library Company of Philadelphia. *12* The Library Company of Philadelphia. *13* The Philadelphia Museum of Art (PMA); PMA, Given by Titus C. Geesey. *14* PMA, Given by Mrs. Rodolphe Meyer de Schauensee and Mrs. James M. R. Sinkler in memory of Mrs. Lewis Audenreid. *15* PMA, Thomas Skelton Harrison Fund; Richard Saul Wurman/ GEE, Inc. *16* PMA, Thomas Skelton Harrison Fund; PMA: Bequest of Elizabeth Gratz. *17* PMA, Given by Mrs. Francis B. Gummere and Mrs. Thomas F. Branson. *20* Wyck Association. *23* Historical American Buildings Survey (HABS), Library of Congress. *29* HABS/Jack E. Boucher. *32* HABS.

Catalog 2
42 PMA, Given by Mr. and Mrs. John Mulford. *43* PMA, Given by Agnes Davisson Loughran/Will Brown; Richard Saul Wurman/GEE, Inc. *44* PMA, Given by Mrs. Walter S. Detwiler; PMA, Given by the heirs of Mr. and Mrs. James Dobson. *45* PMA, Given by George Wood Furness. *46* PMA, Given by Charles T. Shenkle in memory of his mother, Edna H. Shenkle. *47* PMA, Given by the executors of the estate of Mary T. W. Strawbridge/Will Brown; PMA, From the Edgar V. Seeler and Marie Josephine Rozet Fund. *52* HABS. *54* HABS. *55* Bower Lewis Thrower. *63* HABS/Jack E. Boucher. *75* Matt Wargo. *82* HABS/Jack E. Boucher.

Catalog 3
88 PMA, Gift of COLLAB: The Contemporary Design Group for the Philadelphia Museum of Art (COLLAB) in honor of Elisabeth L. Fraser. *89* PMA, Gift of Mr. Bayard H. Roberts and Mrs. John Wintersteen; Richard Saul Wurman/GEE, Inc. *90* PMA, Gift of COLLAB/Eric Mitchell; PMA, Gift of Adeline Edmunds/Will Brown. *91* PMA, Gift of Atelier International Ltd. *92* PMA, Given by Dr. Morton Beiler; PMA, Given by Knoll International. *93* PMA, Given by Habitat, Inc.; PMA, Gift of COLLAB. *96* HABS. *97* Paul Warchol. *107* HABS/Jack E. Boucher. *117* Venturi Rauch and Scott Brown/George Pohl. *119* Rollin R. La France. *121* Mark Cohen. *124* Tom Bernard. *127* Otto Baitz Inc. *128* Matt Wargo; Tom Bernard. *129* James Oesch; Paul Warchol. *130* Nathaniel Lieberman courtesy of Pei Cobb Freed & Partners. *131* Tom Bernard; GBQC. *133* Matt Wargo. *134* H. Durston Saylor. *135* Matt Wargo; C. Geoffrey Berken. *136* Matt Wargo; Barry Halkin. *138* Matt Wargo. *139* Brian Gassel/TVS & Assoc.

Philadelphia Architects
140 The Athenaeum of Philadelphia. *142* Princeton University. *143* Free Library of Philadelphia; Tennessee Tourist Development Office. *144* The Athenaeum of Philadelphia. *145* The Athenaeum of Philadelphia; Otto Baitz. *146* From Moses King, "Philadelphia and Notable Philadelphians," Philadelphia Historical Commission. *147* Collection of Hyman Myers; Historical Society of Pennsylvania. *148* E. Teitelman, Photography. *149* Blank and Stoller; Rittase. *150* Howe Archives, Columbia University. *151* Louis I. Kahn Collection, University of Pennsylvania and Pennsylvania Historical and Museum Commission/Lautman Photography; Kimbell Art Museum, Fort Worth, Texas/Bob Wharton; John Ebstel/Louis I. Kahn Collection, University of Pennsylvania and Pennsylvania Historical and Museum Commission. *152* Copyright © by Wendy Reid; Engineering News-Record photo; John Pottle; John Gollings. *153* Venturi Scott Brown and Associates; Tom Bernard.

Places of Interest
180 Philadelphia City Planning Commission/Skyphotos; Ueland and Junker/Lawrence Williams of Upper Darby, Pa. *181* Mercer Museum of the Bucks County Historical Society. *182* Longwood Gardens Photograph.

Index